Qualitative Research in Journalism

Taking It to the Streets

LEA'S COMMUNICATION SERIES
Jennings Bryant/Dolf Zillmann, General Editors

For a complete list of titles in LEA's Communication Series, please contact Lawrence Erlbaum Associates, Publishers, at www.erlbaum.com

Qualitative Research in Journalism

Taking It to the Streets

Edited by

Sharon Hartin Iorio
Wichita State University

LAWRENCE ERLBAUM ASSOCIATES, PUBLISHERS
2004   Mahwah, New Jersey   London

Lawrence Erlbaum Associates, Inc., Publishers
10 Industrial Avenue
Mahwah, NJ 07430

Cover design by Kathryn Houghtaling Lacey

Library of Congress Cataloging-in-Publication Data

Qualitative research in journalism : taking it to the streets / edited by Sharon
Hartin Iorio.
p. cm.
Includes bibliographical references and index.
ISBN 0-8058-4398-1 (cloth : alk. Paper)
ISBN 0-8058-4399-X (pbk. : alk. paper)

PN4784.R38T35 2003
070.407'2—dc21   2003046235
                                                              CIP

Books published by Lawrence Erlbaum Associates are printed on acid-free
paper, and their bindings are chosen for strength and durability.

Printed in the United States of America
10 9 8 7 6 5 4 3 2 1

*The editor dedicates this volume
to the journalists who provided interviews,
gave their time to this project in countless ways,
and work daily to provide accurate information
to the general public*

Contents

Foreword

When I look over the landscape of journalism today, I see changes that are almost geological in kind—the plates are shifting, the continent grinds in motion. Familiar features are still there, but from basin to range there are strange formations, and new aspects appear. Below the surface much goes on. The ground rises where before there was nothing to build on. Old ground cracks and sinks.

The hardest problem in journalism today may be to map it, to draw borders around the practice and define what's within or beyond. *Is there an audience for serious news?* One of the ways we struggle is to map the space available for journalism. The imagined line between "news" and "entertainment" is another. Does the border separating journalism from other creative treatments of reality by the media complex run through counties, or through companies, or sections of the newspaper, portions of the broadcast schedule, segments in the *Today Show?* Probably it runs through individuals—journalists—producers of news who sway one way, then another; feel commercial pressure, resist it, make space for themselves and for journalism, then lose it, regain it here, give it up over there. Where is journalism in a company like the American newspaper giant, Gannet, which is sometimes devoted to the practice with, let us say, half a heart? Where is "journalism" in that screaming empire known as Fox? Somewhere in the mix.

Difficulties in saying who is a journalist make for unstable ground in the practice. When did former political operative Tim Russert become one, and why is Net gossip Matt Drudge not one? We may be used to questions like that. But now with the Internet the possibility of opening a solo practice in journalism has returned, and we are little used to that. Put up a website with good reporting and commentary and you may be successfully practicing journalism, even though no one said you could. In March of 2003, former New York *Daily News* reporter Chris Allbritton, operating on his own, snuck over the Turkish border into Iraq and filed reports about the war to his website for readers anywhere in the world. Matt Drudge is easy to recognize as a type from the past, Allbritton is not. Who funded him? Readers did—remarkable people who contributed over $10,000 to his plan of work. Who edited and published him? He himself did. Who distributed his reports? The Internet did. Why did he do it? He wanted to report independently on the war and proved himself up to it. Which executive in the media complex said, "Go be a journalist for us?" No one. Who set up the laws of a free press under which he operated? There were none; it was a state of war. Who is more independent than Chris Allbritton? Certainly no one working for *Time* magazine or CNN.

Journalism: It's getting harder to map it, to fix it in the frame for scrutiny and analysis. Around the year 2000, where on the globe was there a free press, and therefore the possibility of real journalism (the kind a democracy starves without), and where was there not? That continent started tipping in 1989 and drifts more every day. We know that in a given nation, the press is not necessarily free or not free, and a phrase like semi-free does not help. When there is journalism only because some have the courage to report and publish in a situation of high danger and murderous threat, the practice is indistinguishable from rebellion and underground politics.

On the other hand, when a free and responsible press in an open society is forced to report news of a terror strike, and of a possible terror strike, and of the state of alert when someone in the government thinks there might be a terror strike, thus bringing on some of the psychic disruption for which terrorist acts are undertaken in the first place; when this happens to us via news reports from our own professionals, doing their job ... the practice of journalism by some is indistinguishable from the practice of violence by others, even though journalists do no violence themselves and obey all their ethical codes. Below the surface much goes on. I doubt that American journalism, if it has a soul (and what serious professional thinks it has not?), has the same soul from before September 11, 2001.

Journalism: The thing is in flux, in a degree greater than usual. In order for people to have journalism, care about it, attend to it, and benefit from it, they first have to think of themselves as a public with both the right and the need to know what's going on in the world. The person who has need for news reporting (and all the features, analysis, and commentary that surrounds it) lives for some portion of the day in historical time, one premise of which is the possibility of affecting history through individual and democratic choice. Where that possibility spreads, journalism can always find new ground; where the possibility of democratic choice dies, journalism too goes dead. But the public can go dead just by ceasing to care about the world outside; and it might if journalists are not smart, sensitive, and attuned to the problems of real people.

*   *   *   *

Why should we assume, as *Qualitative Research In Journalism* does, that social science and the tools of academic research have anything to teach journalism? The basic reason, I think, is that these people are in the same business. Scholars try to understand the world and the people in it. Journalists try to do the same thing. It's a hard problem, so they both need all the help they can get.

Two professionals alive to the same question (What's really going on out there?) can obviously instruct each other. Thus, social science, if it's any good, must have smart things to teach journalism about how better to understand people and the larger public world. One premise of this book is that. Among the many smart things discussed are focus groups turned not to selling but to grasping things like the lives of citizens or the health of the community; interviewing layered and cut for civic context, not just quotes; questionnaires with ideas inside them; disciplined observation not only of the exceptional but of the typical; community mapping showing assets as well as problems; ethnography in the service of better and more diverse reporting; oral history as cousin to the news; interpretation as the inevitable, not the occasional thing in journalism; the virtues of the case study in social science for the related practice of explanatory journalism. The authors represented here, many of whom have worked in newsrooms, set out to prove that academic research can indeed teach journalism about how to understand what's going on out there. They succeed marvelously in that.

But is the reverse proposition equally true? I think it is. Journalists have very good lessons to offer academics, those of us who study news production. The most important thing journalists can teach scholars, researchers, academic critics (and even public philosophers) is how to be useful—useful to journalism, but also to communities, publics, and nations.

I never knew if my own ideas about "public journalism" were cracked, professionally speaking, until I tried to make them useful to busy people who had newspapers to put out and broadcasts to assemble ... by deadline that day. Similarly, I found it impossible to know which of the many potent constructs and research streams in modern social science had the potential actually to improve journalism until the editors and I tried to make such literature useful at, say, a staff retreat for the *Virginian-Pilot*, a daily in Norfolk, VA (Rosen, 1999, chap.

4). I learned a lot when I discovered that news reporters and desk editors found the academic notion of "framing" a useful idea when they were trying to change the way they reported on routine public controversy (Iyenger, 1991; Neuman, Just, & Crigler, 1992). They could ask novel questions like, "How do we usually frame this story?" or, "Wait a minute, can we re-frame this story?" In fact, they did ask those questions, and started changing their work with the answers. (Framing ... who would have known?)

To try to be useful when the plates are shifting, the ground is cracking, and the global fight is on for the freedom to remain a journalist—this is a discipline worth having. The essays reported here stay within that discipline, sometimes called pragmatism, and this is what makes them different and valuable. "This line of work is being transformed," writes Sharon Iorio in her compelling over-view. I could not agree more.

—*Jay Rosen*
New York University

REFERENCES

Iyengar, S. (1991). *Is anyone responsible? How television frames political issues.* Chicago: University of Chicago.

Neuman, W. R., Just, M. R., & Crigler, A. N., (1992) *Common knowledge: News and the construction of political meaning.* Chicago: University of Chicago.

Rosen, J. (1999). *What are journalists for?* New Haven, CT: Yale University Press.

Preface

The idea for this project emerged from a discussion among professors and professional journalists who assembled in the year 2001. The setting was the national meeting of the Association for Education in Journalism and Mass Communication in Washington, D.C. In one of the discussions held at the meeting, both the professional journalists and the professors in attendance found themselves in agreement. They recognized a pressing and increasing need, whether driven by technology or other change, for techniques to help journalists better connect with the daily lives of individuals. Both groups were interested in ways to improve reporting, particularly political and social-issues coverage. Many of them shared another common bond, their interest in news that links people's personal concerns and stimulates public understanding—in other words, the practices of civic–public journalism.

As the discussion developed, the professional journalists who described new reporting techniques being implemented in their newsrooms were struck by the professors' responses. The professors perceived the work of the professionals not so much as new techniques but ones directly related to research methodologies in existence for decades. Both groups were intrigued. In academic circles, the contributions of journalism to qualitative research methodologies in the social sciences were widely known. On the other hand, the journalists knew little about this relationship, and neither group appeared to understand the results of applying and adapting qualitative (interpretative) methods to current newsroom practices.

Both groups wanted to know more. They began to ask questions. How closely did the reporting methods described by the journalists compare to specific qualitative methodologies used by social scientists? How do these qualitative methods differ from quantitative or statistical methods that journalists use daily in their work? How extensively are qualitative methods being used in newsrooms? What makes these techniques valid as reporting tools? Reliable? Sufficient to meet the requirements of objective news reporting? Are there precedents for this kind of reporting? Overall, what exactly do reporters need to know about using qualitative research in journalism?

Responses to the questions raised form the basis of this multiauthored volume and the reason for its publication. The aim of the volume is to show ways that news coverage is expanded and enhanced through the use of qualitative methods developed in the social sciences. Chapters 1 through 3 provide background for an understanding of qualitative research methods, their historical bond to news reporting and writing, and their relationship to the traditions of objectivity in media. Chapters 4 through 10 each describe a particular qualitative methodology—oral and life histories, textual analysis, focused interviews, ethnography, focus groups, civic mapping, and case studies—and show how each is being used in newsrooms. Chapter 11 demonstrates the results of pairing qualitative and quantitative methods, and Chapter 12 explains ways academics and professional journalists can form partnerships for newsroom research and street reporting.

While this volume is written for a general audience of those interested in the craft of journalism, it is important, at the outset, to make a brief statement about the volume's intellectual orientation. First, the work presented here develops from the premise that the major forms of empirical research in the social sciences are related and benefit each other. Rather than holding either qualitative (interpretative) methods or quantitative (statistical) methods to be superior to the other, the approach here is that for some projects qualitative research is best, for others quantitative research works better, for still others multiple qualitative and quantitative methods are needed. Moreover, explanatory power is strongest when a full range of appropriate methods is employed. While this conceptualization is growing in adherents, it is far from universal among social scientists, most of whom work within and advocate the sufficiency of either qualitative or quantitative research.

Understanding the standpoint from which the co-authors' view research is important because it informs another perspective of the chapter authors, most of whom are affiliated with civic-public journalism. This viewpoint is that the role of media in society is not and cannot be truly objective. The conceptualization here is that, like the most useful research projects, the best journalism employs an array of reporting techniques. Traditional reporting, however, cannot suffice for the full range of skills necessary for complete news coverage in today's interactive and global media environment. The individual journalist's personal perspective, the culture of his or her newsroom, and the mission of the media organization as an employer—all influence the choice of reporting methods. The goal of the authors of this volume is not to advocate any one method overall but to present a range of strategies for valid and reliable coverage.

This volume is written for journalists and those who hope to become journalists. Step-by-step instructions are provided to readers interested in using one or more of the qualitative methodologies presented here in their own work. Extensive examples from published news stories are embedded throughout the chapters, as well as information gathered from interviewing journalists who use qualitative journalism in their own reporting. The authors provide a full and detailed discussion of qualitative methods in journalism with specific illustrations drawn from contemporary newsrooms.

ACKNOWLEDGMENTS

This volume is made possible by the authors whose work it includes. The 12 friends and colleagues who prepared the chapters that follow worked ably and quickly to meet the rapid deadlines and respond to requests for revisions. Due to the expertise of the contributors, this was an easy volume to edit in many ways.

Many people made this volume possible. Carrie Wyatt, my assistant, helped the project in immeasurable ways, and I want to thank Shannon Littlejohn who edited the early drafts. I owe special gratitude to Dr. William Bischoff, dean of Fairmount College of Liberal Arts and Sciences at Wichita State University for his support of this research and to the colleagues who work in his office for their patience and assistance with the project. The Pew Center for Civic Journalism provided some of the graphics that enhance this work and is thanked for that contribution. The reviewers provided useful comments and suggestions. Linda Bathgate, communications editor at Lawrence Erlbaum Associates, graciously guided this book through the publication process. Editorial Assistant Karin Wittig Bates was especially helpful, and Book Production Editor Marianna Vertullo faithfully oversaw every production detail. This acknowledgment would not be complete without mentioning the members of the Civic Journalism Interest Group of the Association for Education in Journalism and Mass Communication. The inspiration for this volume sprang from the group's activities. Their continued commitment to teaching professional skills and disciplinary knowledge within the context of democratic service to society is exemplary.

—Sharon Hartin Iorio
Wichita State University

About
the Contributors

Mike Allen (PhD, Michigan State University) is a professor and the director of forensics in the Department of Communication at the University of Wisconsin-Milwaukee. His publications address issues of social influence in the context of interpersonal, organizational, and mass mediated communication. He has published three books and more than 80 articles in journals such as *Communication Monographs, Law and Human Behavior, Communication Theory, Criminal Justice and Behavior, Evaluation & the Health Professions*, and *Argumentation and Advocacy*.

Kathryn B. Campbell (PhD, University of Wisconsin–Madison) is a visiting assistant professor at the University of Oregon, where she teaches in the news-editorial sequence, coordinates an endowed internship program, and directs a summer journalism workshop for minority high school students. For nearly a decade, she has been actively involved in the research and practice of civic journalism with a special interest in cross-disciplinary community studies.

Clifford Christians (PhD, University of Illinois) is a research professor of communications in the Institute of Communications Research at the University of Illinois-Urbana. He is the author or co-author of six books, among them *Media Ethics: Cases and Moral Reasoning* (with Mark Fackler, Kim Rotzoll, and Kathy McKee, 6th ed. 2001), *Good News: Social Ethics and the Press* (with John Ferre and Mark Fackler, 1993), *Communication Ethics and Universal Values* (with Michael Traber, 1997), and *Moral Engagement in Public Life: Theorists for Contemporary Ethics* (with Sharon Bracci, 2002). His teaching and research interests include the philosophy of technology, dialogic communication theory, and professional ethics.

Janet M. Cramer (PhD, University of Minnesota) is an assistant professor in the Department of Communication and Journalism at the University of New Mexico. Her research is developed from a historical perspective and focuses on the issues of gender, race, and class in media. Cramer is a former broadcast journalist who also has worked in public relations and advertising. She has written several book chapters and has published in *Journalism & Mass Communication Monographs*.

Renita Coleman (PhD, University of Missouri) is an assistant professor at the Manship School of Mass Communication at Louisiana State University. She worked as a reporter, editor, and designer for 15 years at newspapers including the *Raleigh* (North Carolina) *News & Observer* and the *Sarasota* (Florida) *Herald-Tribune*. Among her publications are articles in *Newspaper Research Journal, Journalism & Mass Communication Educator, Journal of Health Communication,* and *Journal of Communication Inquiry.*

Lewis A. Friedland (PhD, Brandeis University) holds the rank of professor in the School of Journalism and Mass Communication at the University of Wisconsin–Madison, where he directs the Center for Communication and Democracy. A former broadcast journalist, Friedland is the co-author with Carmen Sirianni of *Civic Innovation in America* (2001) and co-edits the *Civic Practices Network*. He has published articles on the subject of media and community life in a variety of journals including *Communication Research* and *Media, Culture & Society.* He contributed to the book, *Mass Media, Social Control and Social Change.*

Tanni Haas (PhD, Rutgers University) is an assistant professor in the Department of Speech Communication Arts & Sciences at Brooklyn College. His research on the theory and practice of public journalism, journalism codes of ethics, organizational communication ethics, and qualitative research methods has appeared in *Communication Theory, Harvard International Journal of Press/Politics, Journalism: Theory, Practice & Criticism, Journalism Studies, Journalism & Mass Communication Educator, Journalism & Mass Communication Quarterly, Management Communication Quarterly,* and *Newspaper Research Journal* as well as more than half a dozen edited books. He currently serves on the editorial board of *Journalism & Mass Communication Educator* and *Newspaper Research Journal.*

Susan Schultz Huxman (PhD, University of Kansas) is an associate professor in the Elliott School of Communication at Wichita State University. Among her publications are a co-authored media literacy book, *The Rhetorical Act: Thinking, Speaking, and Writing Critically* (2003), referred articles in *Journal of Communication, Communication Studies,* and *Communication Quarterly,* and chapters in *Communication in Crisis* and *Oratorical Encounters: Selected Studies* *and Sources of Twentieth-century Political Accusations and Apologies*. She was recognized as the 1998 Kansas Speech Communication Association College Instructor of the Year. She has conducted research for Knight-Ridder, Inc. and served as a consultant to *The Wichita* (Kansas) *Eagle.*

Sharon Hartin Iorio (PhD, Oklahoma State University) is an associate professor in the Elliott School of Communication and associate dean of Fairmount College of Liberal Arts and Sciences at Wichita State University. She has worked as a newspaper reporter and in public relations. Her book, *Faith's Harvest: Mennonite Identity in Northwest Oklahoma*, received an award from the National Federation of Press Women. Among her journal publications are articles in *Journal of Communication, Journalism & Mass Communication Educator, Journalism Quarterly*, and *Journal of Media and Religion*. She has conducted research for Knight-Ridder, Inc. and *The Wichita* (Kansas) *Eagle.*

Michael McDevitt (PhD, Stanford University) is an assistant professor in the School of Journalism and Mass Communication at the University of Colorado–Boulder. He worked in the San Francisco Bay area as a reporter and editorial writer. His research explores how communication-based campaigns can stimulate citizenship among people who are otherwise disengaged from the political process. He has published in *Journalism and Communication Monographs, Communication Research, Political Communication, Journalism and Mass Communication Quarterly, Mass Comm Review*, and *Journalism & Mass Communication Educator.*

John L. "Jack" Morris (PhD, University of Missouri) is an assistant professor of journalism in the Department of Communications at Loyola University of New Orleans, Louisiana. He worked as a newspaper reporter and editor in Kansas and Colorado for nine years and taught print journalism at Adams State College in Alamosa, Colorado from 1988–2003. His research focuses on interactive communication between writers and readers to improve the quality of news writing. His book, *A Study of Audience Interaction in Journalism: Citizen-Based Reporting*, was published in 2002. He has published other articles on this topic in *Newspaper Research Journal* and *Studies in Communication Sciences.*

Jay Rosen (PhD, New York University) is an associate professor of journalism at New York University and currently is chair of the Department of Journalism there. From 1993 to 1997, he was the director of the Project on Public Life and the Press, a joint project of the Knight and Kettering Foundations designed to further public journalism. He has written in both scholarly and popular journals on the press, politics, and public life. *What Are Journalists For?* is the title of his 1999 book. Rosen's work has appeared in the *Columbia Journalism Review, Harpers, The Nation, The New York Times*, and the on-line journal *Salon*, among other venues.

Jan Schaffer (M.S.J., Northwestern University) served as executive director of the Pew Center for Civic Journalism in Washington, D.C., which was created in 1993 to help print and electronic journalists develop new models of news coverage that reconnect citizens to civic life. She shared the Pulitzer Gold Medal for Public Service for a news series that appeared in *The Philadelphia Inquirer*, where she was an editor and reporter for 22 years. She recently launched a successor project to the Pew Center, J-Lab: The Institute for Interactive Journalism at the University of Maryland that will develop interactive ways for citizens to participate in public issues.

Susan Willey (PhD, University of Missouri) is an assistant professor of journalism at Florida Atlantic University's Northern campus in Jupiter, Florida, where she is establishing a journalism program. Willey has 17 years experience as a journalist, reporter, and assignment editor. She was both the religion reporter at the *St. Petersburg Times* and a Poynter Fellow from 1993 to 1995. Her publications include articles in *Newspaper Research Journal, Journalism & Mass Communication Educator,* and *The Quill*. She edited a book on community development for the Kettering Foundation Press. Willey serves on the editorial board of the *Journal of Media & Religion*.

Part
I

1

Qualitative Method Journalism

Sharon Hartin Iorio
Wichita State University

For journalists and those who hope to be journalists in the 21st century, one thing is abundantly clear—this line of work is being transformed. Technological change has created a 24-hour news cycle where breaking news is reported around the clock, and shocking world events can be viewed almost at the instant they happen—then observed as they continue to develop. Myriad international sources disseminate social and political opinion to individuals who choose not only their mode of information delivery but the very nature of the information they receive. Yet, the most remarkable shift is not the astonishing pace of delivery or the capability of individuals to select the news they receive; the most significant development is the network of technologies that let individuals interact with people worldwide, more specifically, to interact with those who provide their news. Everyday people use newspaper call-in columns, Web sites, list serves, talk-radio, talk-television, and a host of other tools to connect with news media, and they do it every day.

The increasing accessibility to information, the speed of its delivery, and the individual's more active role in information exchange create a new dimension for journalism. Information is now so abundant and the world so interconnected that journalists must not only find new ways to provide analytical context for the growing onrush of information, they must learn to present the information in a mode that is not generalized or passive but is individualized and dynamic. Some of the ways journalism is practiced are in transition. This should not be surprising, but it is challenging.

The challenge is to fill the gaps for people that mere access to, and mediated interaction with, information cannot. To bridge that gap and survive in the current media environment, journalists will need to link individuals' personal interests and common concerns and the larger issues that touch people's daily lives. For this work, journalists are going to need specific training beyond traditional reporting skills.

Helping journalists meet these new challenges also may resolve some of the complaints directed toward journalism over time. News media, both historically and recently, have been accused of ignoring the interests of the public by allowing manipulation by politicians, special interest groups, and their own business interests (Bagdikian, 2000). One explanation for this situation is that the agenda of mainstream journalism is shaped to highlight events over issues then sensationalize those events, thereby missing stories important to individuals' common concerns. The intense focus on strong-impact news does create a uniform news product (Graber, 2001), and this, in turn, offers another focal point for public skepticism.

While the complaints appear to ring true, they emanate not from low commitment on the part of news organizations but develop from numerous, diverse, and complex causes. Nonetheless, journalists trained to know effective methods to expand reporting of grassroots problems overlooked in a media-rich atmosphere and how to apply the methods in an interactive media environment surely would not hurt the situation and likely would help it. While challenging in many respects, the milieu of abundant information and direct feedback has potential to open opportunities and correct some of the problems of the past.

THE INTERACTIVE MEDIA ENVIRONMENT

The ability of the public to have direct, ongoing interaction with mediated information is a decided advantage, but not one that substitutes for the work of journalists. According to Thompson (1995), communication technologies foster new forms of action and social relationships, but often technology use is not reciprocal. For example, talk-radio and call-in television shows, Thompson (1995) argues, are merely one-shot opportunities for individuals to broadcast an opinion. Similarly, other writers (Bennett & Entman, 2001; Poster, 1999) note that the Internet does not always encourage a public sphere for rational debate.

Rather than being diminished, the role and training of journalists become more crucial in the new media environment. New technologies open points of entry for people to exchange ideas, but interactive technology alone cannot help individuals bring their common concerns to news media attention or project a representative picture of the constituent groups in society. Those needs, however, become primary obligations of those who conceive a democratic role for the press. Following the traditional routines of journalism, however, may not always move 21st-century journalists forward. To communicate in their new environment, journalists need training greater than before.

While contemporary journalism training incorporates a range of reporting methods, the rapid changes that now impact journalism create a demand for journalists with specialized skills. The chapters included here focus on methods for journalists rather than the impact of technology or its use in the newsroom, even though some productive discussion along those lines is included. The purpose of this book is to provide journalists with the professional, empirical news-gathering tools they need to operate in the current media environment. The authors of the chapters to follow demonstrate how valid, reliable procedures developed in a particular field of the social sciences—qualitative study—can be used to increase coverage. The authors present tangible, qualitative social-science practices as a guide for:

1. Finding newsworthy but overlooked or underreported concerns;
2. Organizing that information within broader contexts; and
3. Providing a conduit for people's interaction along the way.

This kind of reporting increases traditional news coverage. The chapters that follow show how qualitative methods can be and are being used to enhance journalism.

JOURNALISM EDUCATION

University programs and professional development training for journalists teach traditional skills for reporting and writing news, but, at present, journalists do not learn a great deal about using additional methods to find and analyze information. The traditional journalism skills taught in American universities, for much of the past century, were mostly procedural (Meyer, 2001). Techniques for constructing a news story "lede," rules for editing copy, interpretation of libel and privacy laws, and other reporting conventions were the mainstays of the curriculum. Little attention was given to the development of journalism or the basis of its methods.

In 1973, Philip Meyer sought to increase professionalism in journalism by enlarging the concept of journalistic training and practice. His book *Precision Journalism* explained how the tools of quantitative social science research could and should be applied to the practice of journalism. The book focused on methods of data processing and statistical analysis. It showed journalists ways to conduct and interpret surveys and public opinion polls, and it emphasized the importance of social scientific research for high-quality journalism.

Meyer thought his work might not be accepted by journalists because, in asking journalists to apply the techniques of social science to their reporting, Meyer perceived a move away from the journalistic code of strict objectivity (1991, p. 4), but Meyer's book was received well in newsrooms and academe. Neither academics nor professional journalists viewed precision journalism as a major threat to objectivity. Perhaps this is because the epistemology on which Meyer's training rests is embedded within a positivist theoretical framework. This tradition is based on the belief that the social, like the natural, world is an orderly system. Within this framework, the role of the scientist is that of a deductive, detached observer who uses explicit procedures for the purpose of observing and measuring.

In short, precision journalism, though a new concept, was based on an established model of scientific research developed from the natural sciences, one that holds as its primary purpose the search for objective reality. This model of scientific research parallels many of the standard practices of "objective" reporting in journalism. Expanded and retitled *The New Precision Journalism*, several updated editions of Meyer's work were released, as recently as 2001. University professors welcomed the books as helping advance journalism as a discipline. Journalists appreciated Meyer's work because it helped them and did not threaten the traditional norms of objective reporting (e.g., finding facts and reporting them without wasting time).

QUALITATIVE RESEARCH AND JOURNALISM

In social science there are two overarching methodological perspectives. Meyer introduced one of them, quantitative research methods, into the nomenclature of journalism. Qualitative research emerges from a different worldview. Qualitative researchers seek to explain the world rather than measure it. The world of qualitative social science is explanatory. Dealing primarily with words, qualitative research is holistic and blatantly interpretative. Qualitative researchers go "into the field" to gather data by observation and interaction with people from whom they hope to learn. Qualitative researchers also examine extant texts or artifacts in their work. They record what they find in writing or on videotape, then analyze and interpret it to show how the world makes sense to those they study. To ensure reliable and valid findings, qualitative researchers set up strict protocols to search for answers to their research questions. The findings of qualitative research develop from "the ground (field) up" and within the context of a larger social world.

Even though qualitative research and quantitative research emerge from different epistemological orientations and the distinction between them is obvious, the two forms of research are not mutually exclusive. The past 20 years have witnessed a growing dialogue between qualitative and quantitative researchers (Jensen, 2002). Exciting work is now being conducted to specify how the two methodologies together build knowledge, as Susan Huxman and Mark Allen will explain in a subsequent chapter.

It is obvious that, from the basic approach of knowing reality to the way journalists practice their craft, qualitative research shares much in common with journalism. The emphasis on observation and in-depth interviewing to gather information, the skeptic's approach to interpretation, and the importance of perspective in explanation—all are principal foundations of traditional journalism as well as qualitative methods. Common to both the journalist and the qualitative researcher is the concern with current phenomena and the action of individuals.

In academic circles, the relationship of the journalist and the qualitative researcher has never been incompatible. As Kathryn Campbell and Lewis Friedland describe in their chapter, early qualitative researchers drew heavily on journalistic practices. In fact, at the turn of the last century, sociologist Robert Park literally took his students into the streets to discover common concerns that were shared by the general public and report a representative picture of the groups they studied based on the researchers' interaction with group members (Park & Burgess, 1925). Park, who transformed the University of Chicago into a center for participant-observer-based fieldwork and helped originate qualitative methodology, was himself a former journalist.

Theory that is associated with the social reality being observed by Park and his students developed from the thinking of Thomas & Znaniecki (1927), George Herbert Mead (Miller, 1982), and others. Working on the premise that society was formed from the micro-interaction of individuals, a theoretical orientation emerged called symbolic interaction. Another University of Chicago scholar of the period was John Dewey (1927), the leading American pragmatist of the era, whose thinking provided a philosophical base for this work. Overall, the scholarship was associated with interpretative orientations to research. The Chicago scholars were familiar with the journalistic model of investigation.

In the press, however, parallels between qualitative social scientists and journalists are virtually nonexistent. There is not much journalism training that connects the two, and some of the traditions of journalists can exacerbate the differences. For example, both qualitative researchers and journalists go into

the field as open-minded observers, but journalism traditions require an interpretation of open-mindedness that can position the journalist as "a passive and
innocent witness" (Meyer, 2001, p. 3). Likewise in-depth interviewing, which in
qualitative research results in categorizing and analyzing a wide range of different opinions, can become in the journalist's work a vehicle for framing opposing
or conflicting views in order to produce "balanced" news stories. Perhaps because a critical factor in the practice of modern journalism has been the search
for objective facts, the similarities of journalism and qualitative research for the
most part have gone unrecognized in journalism education.

THE ROAD TO THE 21st CENTURY

The sociologists, anthropologists, social psychologists, and philosophers at
the University of Chicago in the first two decades of the 20th century formed a
nucleus of intellectual thought that ignited American social science research.
As the years passed, however, the initial influence of Park and other researchers associated with the University of Chicago began to wane. Eventually, the
center of sociological study broke ties with pragmatism and the model of the
journalist-scholar as researcher, shifted its interactive orientation, and de-
parted the University of Chicago. Leadership in the study and practice of sociology moved toward positivism and embraced the quantitative methods
practiced by U.S. East Coast academics. Over the ensuing years, sociological
study developed into at least three major theoretical paradigms and several
schools of thought, among which both quantitative and qualitative methodologies are practiced. Meanwhile, the training of journalists, also fed initially by
the emergent positivist paradigm, moved toward an increasingly reified interpretation of objectivity.

The training of modern journalists can be traced as a gradual evolution that
corresponds with the development of news media technologies from the introduction of newspapers to the present. During the 1920s university programs in
journalism education began to grow in number and, eventually, became the established path to a career in the field. The curriculum developed as general education in the liberal arts and sciences. University education in journalism
included the concepts of inverted pyramid writing, and personal detachment of
the reporter from the news event. The establishment of professional training for
journalists coincided roughly with the emergence of a code of objectivity as a fully
nuanced standard by which the profession of journalism could be measured.

Although there was widespread agreement that true objectivity was impossible given human frailty, balanced reporting based on the ideal of objectivity,
it was thought, could be achieved. The theory that a code of objectivity would

provide the most effective guideline for the profession draws from a book newspaper columnist Walter Lippmann wrote as a young man in 1922. Lippmann recognized the subjective nature of public opinion and feared its effect on democratic processes. He wrote that the usefulness of journalists rested on the ability to objectify facts. As an overarching framework, the code of objectivity and the traditions for reporting and training journalists that supported it developed into a mighty, rhetorical bulwark. However, limitations could be noted as early as 1947, when a report from the Commission on Freedom of the Press (Hutchins Commission Report) pointed out considerable weaknesses in American journalism.

As corporate news systems grew and technology advanced, by the 1970s the perception was increasing that relationships between public and press were diminishing. Concerns were raised about the unintended effects of the journalistic norms. It was thought the way journalism was being practiced might be creating reactive journalists whose reporting, in a latent rather than overt manner, could be managed (Bagdikian, 1972; Tuchman, 1978). By the 1990s, with former complaints still unresolved, a new generation of critics pointed to the news media's possible connection to a different kind of problem, a decline in civic participation and increasing fragmentation of community life. These objections seemed to resonate across professional constituencies and the public both inside the United States and in other countries. The critics spanned a range of media professionals (Yankelovich, 1991; Merritt, 1995; Fallows, 1996; Dionne, 1998) and academics (Entman, 1998; Pool, 1990; Putnam, 1993, 1995; Schudson, 1995).

In examining the roots of these issues, Jay Rosen (1999a) revisited the pragmatism philosopher John Dewey developed in the early 1900s at the University of Chicago and found Dewey's work a suitable structure for contemporary journalists because it grounded the role of the journalist in the "useful" and experiential rather than the authoritative model (Dewey, 1927). Other critics pointed out that reporting practices, including the code of objectivity, once thought to benefit democracy, because they allowed news media to be watchdogs of government action, could, in current circumstances, be conceived as disserving democracy (Black, 1997; Carey, 1992, 1997). With public access to worldwide media systems, some of it interactive access, the 21st-century problem has become not whether reporting of real-world happenings can be balanced through the use of a code; they can be. The more important question is how the deeper belief systems (national, religious, or group ideologies) inextricably ingrained in all communication (Foucault, 1969/1982; Habermas, 1991; Mannheim, 1929/1986) can be accounted for in the reporting of current events. The chapter included here that is authored by Clifford Christians looks at journalism education and the traditions of objectivity in journalism and provides an ethic for journalists of today.

The influence of Dewey lay dormant in the lexicon of journalism until rediscovered by Rosen (1997; 1999a; 1999b; 1999a) and others (Carey, 1987; Peters, 1995; Glasser & Salmon, 1995; Rosen, Merritt, & Austin 1997). Similarly, the early 20th century work of sociologist and journalist Robert Park, Dewey's colleague at the University of Chicago, is now being revisited, like the work of Dewey, by 21st century scholars and journalists. The work of Dewey and others frame a philosophy for change. The work of Park and others establish a method for it. Both the criticism leveled at journalists during the last half of the 20th century and the context surrounding suggestions for remedy clearly bear on the development of current reporting practices.

FINDING COMFORT IN A NEW ZONE

By the mid-1990s newspapers and broadcast news operations across the United States were searching for ways to improve coverage, engage individuals and wide-ranging groups, and encourage participation in public life. Newspapers in Wichita, Kansas; Charlotte, North Carolina; Norfolk, Virginia; and other cities began to launch experiments in election and social issues coverage (Charity, 1996). Whether this shift was a conscious effort of news organizations to reevaluate reporting methods or not, the gauging of open dialogue with individuals and communities of people as news, nevertheless, reflects the reality of doing democratic journalism in the age of global Internet communication. The innovative techniques appealed to the Kettering Foundation, The Pew Charitable Trusts, and other private foundations. Programs were funded to reexamine the relationship of media and democratic practices and to educate students and practicing journalists to implement change in newsrooms. At the end of the decade, about half the newspapers in the United States and many radio and television stations had conducted some sort of public-civic journalism initiative (Sirianni & Friedland, 2001, p. 186). Former director of the Pew Center for Civic Journalism Jan Schaffer is author of a chapter to follow that reviews civic journalism projects to show ways academics and professionals can partner in research and reporting projects.

By and large, a noticeable shift in mainstream media news reporting to incorporate individual-level concerns actively in news coverage has occurred over the past decade. The change can be illustrated by the 2000 U.S. presidential elections where regular coverage included specific input from the general public through focus groups, collected comments of private citizens, interviews, interactive Web sites and the like. The broadening definition of news and increased interaction of journalists with widening sectors of the public beg reexamination of journalism training and the root ethic of the profession. *Portland* (Maine) *Press Herald* Editor Lou Ureneck wrote in *Nieman Reports:*

> What the press needs today is more context and insight, not less, and that context and insight inevitably bring with them the exercise of subjectivity ... The challenge to the public-minded press today is to find ways to accommodate the ever present need for fair and dispassionate inquiry and the new and growing need to generate energy, meaning and solutions ... The likelihood (is) that the press more often fails readers through timidity than bias. (1999, 2000)

In 2002, The Freedom Forum Foundation compiled insights from the careers of news executives and published them under the title *Best Practices: The Art of Leadership in News Organizations* (Coffey, 2002). Among those commenting about bringing different perspectives into the newsroom was Alberto Ibarguen, publisher of *The Miami Herald* and Nancy Maynard, a previous editor and co-owner of *The Oakland* (California) *Tribune*. The comments of Maynard reinforced Ibarguen's point. Maynard offered, in brief, that "News people generally do not spend nearly enough time talking to the people ... that they cover" (p. 41). The executives' commentary reveals the extent of assimilation into mainstream journalism made by the ideas brought forward in the 1990s.

The importance of active dialogue definitely has moved up the skill-ladder of journalism and the charge of the journalist to be indifferent and withdrawn in order to achieve fairness in reporting has moved somewhat lower on the ladder. How will journalists go about their work in the midst of this major shift? The correct routines will develop over time. At present, the threads of interpretative social science that weave through the ideas of the scholars and professional journalists past and present, the experiments of the public journalists, and the interactivity offered by the new media technologies suggest the possibilities of revisiting the connection of journalism with qualitative methodologies.

WHERE QUALITATIVE METHODS
MEET JOURNALISM

With each passing decade, journalism training has become more professional to meet whatever challenges are posed by the media environment of the era. Currently, the need exists for specialized skills to discover unreported common problems and context of issues and report them in a way that will help individuals interact with larger networks. Some journalists are applying the knowledge of qualitative social science research methods to produce verifiable and accurate reports that advance this endeavor.

There is no general epistemology that organizes qualitative methodology, but all qualitative research is based on inductive examination of collected data. To ensure that the research is fair, balanced, accurate, and truthful and to enable the reader or public to evaluate the study, qualitative researchers:

1. Conduct their studies in a natural setting,
2. Follow strict, multiple protocols for valid and reliable research design and execution,
3. Consider the background and perspective of the researcher(s) and the possible effect this might have on the research when designing the research, and
4. Include in the written report enough information on the researcher(s), the plan, and the conduct of the study to allow the readers/viewers to decide for themselves the truthfulness and accuracy of the account.

A wide range of qualitative methods exist. Like the many strands of a rope, those methods more often employed make up the wider pieces, and, entwined, the strands together produce a unified and strong methodology. One of the thicker, more prominent strands within qualitative methodology is participant observation. It is the practice that deals with going into the field, observing or interacting with a group, and then analyzing the situation in order to record commonalities and develop a written report.

To provide some organization for understanding how qualitative research works, the participant observation method can be broken down into three main categories that can then be used as a metaphor to illustrate three elemental processes within qualitative methodology. The categories are not discrete but form a continuum with the prominent reference points providing a vision of what qualitative methodology is (the range of methods involved) and how it is conducted (the protocol and level of involvement of the researcher(s)). The categories are:

Observation: What sets observational studies apart is that the researcher does not make contact with the subject(s) of the research. These researchers investigate artifacts such as pottery, fashion, or popular culture icons. They use unobtrusive measures to collect data, for example; these researchers may observe the actions of individuals, but at a distance. Investigative reporters use this technique to monitor and study the coming and going of people and their associations without disturbing the behavior of those observed. One of the largest areas of observational study is the examination of texts or written works. Textual, or rhetorical, analysis examines books, movies, and other media. To analyze a text, the researcher "reads between the lines" to interpret underlying meaning. Morris's chapter explains textual analysis and shows how reporters at *The Washington Post* use it in their work.

Participant Observation: This research happens in the social world. The researcher collects data while observing people interact and by interacting with them. Then the researcher analyzes and writes about themes found in the setting. In order to analyze the setting, the researcher maintains some level of independence in the situation. That level is dependent on the subjects studied and the purpose of the research. For example, in the focused interview study described by this author in a subsequent chapter, the researchers who conducted a one-time interview with each respondent were more marginal than connected to their subjects. The reporter who interviewed a young woman to tell the story of her life, entered her world to a limited degree. His work is discussed in the chapter on oral history by Renita Coleman. The community mapping project introduced in Kathryn Campbell's chapter placed the journalists doing the mapping in direct and, in some instances, repeated contact with the individuals and groups from which they wanted to learn. The case study described in the chapter by Tanni Haas was based largely on participation as well as observation. In that study, journalists at the *Akron Beacon Journal* spent a lengthy time period on the project and worked in partnership with a number of civic groups. In short, participant observers, within predefined limits, engage the daily life of those they study. They do so not just to have an understanding of what is going on, but to provide a systematic report. This is why the researcher must always maintain some distance in his relationship with those he is studying.

Participation: This level of research is marked by complete immersion into a culture. The researcher who takes this approach may live for extended periods in the same community with those she is studying. The danger, or, to some researchers, the benefit, is that the researcher becomes engulfed in the setting. In those cases, whether by design or chance, the researcher becomes the subjects' advocate. Since ethnography requires the researcher to enter fully into the life world of the subjects, it is the qualitative technique in which the researcher may be most susceptible to "going native." Not all ethnography is marked by complete assimilation. The student journalists in the chapter by Michael McDevitt and Janet Cramer produced their research and published their stories while retaining an analytic perspective regarding the world of the street people they studied.

On the other hand, Susan Willey's chapter advocates social action theory and shows how news organizations can become directly involved with the public in coming to judgment about an issue. Willey's chapter is devoted to focus group research, a process often associated with quantitative research and, on the qualitative technique continuum, usually found toward the more detached side of the scale.

Willey gives directions for using focus groups in participatory, action-oriented journalism. Willey's chapter clearly illustrates that in qualitative research, the research design and objectives establish the level of involvement of the researcher more than the choice of qualitative technique itself. In journalism, the extent of involvement of the journalist who uses qualitative methods for developing a project is, as in all reporting, set by the news organization and the individual reporter assigned to the story.

DOING QUALITATIVE METHOD JOURNALISM

Using qualitative methods in journalism is not difficult. Methods used range from large-scale case studies conducted by multiple teams in converged newsrooms to an oral history interview story conducted by a single reporter for a small town newspaper. The projects can extend over a period of time (creating ethnography, for example) or be done in a series of focus groups conducted in one evening.

Qualitative methods can be used by news organizations as a prereporting tool to identify networks of credible, but nonelite, sources and their relationship to political processes (mapping); or they can be used to identify grassroots issues and inform election coverage (as in the focused interview example) or in many other ways that enhance news coverage. The advantage of qualitative methodology is that it brings the reader and viewer into the story. Knowing how to get in-depth data and first-person insights and what to do with them is the essence of qualitative reporting.

Guidelines for reliable information gathering and valid documentation are detailed for each method in the chapters to follow. The following are general guidelines for applying a qualitative method in a newsroom setting.

1. Choose the right story: Not every story is right for qualitative reporting. Enterprise stories are one example of a good fit. Many stories reported with qualitative methods are "bubble up" political issues not found on political party platforms. Some develop from social problems that are being addressed outside governmental processes or are feature stories that exemplify individuals and groups. Part of choosing the right story is creating a "space" for the story—deciding its scope and parameters. It is important to choose the qualitative resources—the method—that will deliver the story best.

2. Take it outside: To make the story interactive, go into the "field" with personal/micro-level qualitative techniques. Plan ways to get input from individuals at more than one point during the story-building process. When useful, offer ways people can connect with the story through Web site, list serve, and other interactive technology. Look for themes that resonate—overlooked or under-

reported issues common across the general public or those that reflect the concerns of distinct groups of people.

3. Bring it home: Above all, build the story from the "ground up." Keep the focus on an inductive rather than deductive approach. Let the reporting be defined [framed] in the context and perspective of the participants or subjects of the reporting. To guarantee the way that information is collected and reported develops from data that is verifiable and accurate, follow the protocol of the particular method in use and utilize "triangulation" (e.g., more than one method of collecting information) to ensure lack of distortion and freedom from error. Finally, explain the news organization's purposes and the reporter(s) methods and level of involvement prominently in the final coverage that is published or aired.

NOTES FROM THE FIELD:
A PULITZER PRIZE-WINNING SERIES

In 1999, editors at *The New York Times* decided the time was right to explore, again, the changing nature of race relations in the United States. The editors were aware that national conversations about race are often viewed by the public as dead-end monologues—not conversations but opportunities for reaffirming previously held positions. "The traditional language of race was so entrenched that people just didn't want to go there again," it seemed to reporter Michael Winerip (personal conversation, 2002). He was part of a group of about 30 at the *Times* who were looking for a vehicle to move reporting about race beyond obvious, polarized, and familiar dialogues.

The group of reporters and editors at the *Times* asked themselves, what would engage readers? The team came up with the idea to write about race relations at the personal level "intuitively." "We wanted to find people who didn't pull their punches, and we wanted to come up with different situations—situations that readers would see as typical, but were relationships across situations that many might find too sensitive to talk about. We were looking for the opportunity to get the kind of story that people read and realize, 'Oh, my god, it's true!'" said Winerip.

"The stories, of course, were all true—believable, even mundane. In fact, that's what we were looking for—the mundane—the setting too small, too nuanced, to rise to the level of even a local issue in the community. The moments that we wanted to capture were situations that would not make news stories based on their importance, but reflected the common moments that consume people's daily lives. We met several times and came up with about 150 ideas. Then we narrowed it to 15." The 15-part series that resulted received a Pulitzer Prize and later became a book titled *How Race is Lived in America*

(Lelyveld, 2000). Winerip turned one of the 15 ideas into the story "Why Harlem Drug Cops Don't Discuss Race." He also handled the reporting team through the process of finding their interview locations and reporting the situations as they developed.

"We searched hard to find a wide range of people willing to be involved," Winerip said. "Some reporting projects err on the side of over-reporting situations involving the poor. We looked for a variety of experiences. For example, we wanted to do a story about race relations in the workplace, and we wanted to look at blue-collar workers. I had done some reporting on the steel mills, and someone suggested that we might look there for a story, but I didn't think that would work. For the most part, the men I had interviewed were all middle-aged, and they had substantial salaries. The industry was declining. They really didn't represent the type of worker we wanted to portray. We wanted something 'rawer.' We thought of doing the story from a union/non-union perspective. What were the lives of people, black and white, working across those divides? But that didn't seem to be the right vehicle either. We wanted to have a tough, blue-collar situation, but the point was to capture the workers' relationships, their attitudes and feelings toward each other. We thought of the chicken and pork factories along the Southeast Coast and ended up sending a reporter to live there and work in a pork factory."

Getting into the field was accomplished by trial and error. "When I went into the precinct to do my work, I met Maria. I knew right off that she was a first-rate police officer. I didn't know if I wanted to do a story about that kind of person or her first-rate squad. I had an opportunity to visit another squad, but they were bland. I decided to go back and stick with Maria." Getting into the field also took time. "You have to give reporters time to make mistakes. When [*Times* reporter] Amy Harmon was looking for a pair of executives to interview, she was turned down by, probably, 100 companies. After that it dawned on us that major established corporations wouldn't talk to us without adding so many restrictions, we just wouldn't be able to get the information we needed. But we found people in the dot.com world were independent entrepreneurs and willing to talk to us. That's how we settled on the pair of men to interview who had made millions."

In retrospect, the criteria for the stories that became part of the series were (a) a mundane situation was the vehicle for each story, (b) the situation provided the opportunity to get people's subjective perceptions, and (c) the people in the situation were willing to talk. "We had to find people willing let you come back again and again, willing to spend the time it takes," Winerip said.

Winerip's work, as the reporting coach for the team, called for him to apply many of the tools used in qualitative research. "Overall, we wanted the reporters to dig in deep and hang in. I coached the team not to take notes at first," he said. "That's an easy way to burn out or scare off the subjects [interviewees]. My counsel to the reporters was to be patient and wait awhile, and then begin taking notes. I also coached them not to get too personal at first. It's like any other relationship. It has to be given time to develop. You can't get too close too soon. Even though these people have committed to do the interviews, they don't know what they've committed to, so you have to ease into the relationship and the interviewing." In establishing the relationship, "you walk a fine line," Winerip said. "You end up liking the people. I always do, but it's not friendship. You've got to hold back and learn not to give in to friendship. Your job is not to force anything, just tell the story as it emerges, without drawing conclusions."

As the series went to publication, additional information on the topic, some of it in interactive form, complemented the 15-story series. Some accompanying stories told in first-person voices and question-and-answer stories produced by *Times* magazine correspondents appeared when a special edition of the *Times* magazine published part of the series. A Web site was created "not to mimic or regurgitate the print series but to be its own iteration of the project," Winerip said. It was a groundbreaking project for the *Times* Web site. An e-mail discussion board was heavily used. When published in book form, the reporters' first-person impressions of race relations in general and their personal perspectives on racial issues were included.

"Overall, the purpose of the series was to get to human beings and to learn from them. The series was a huge commitment. You can't do something like that cavalierly. It takes perseverance. That's the thing, the key to it all. The whole idea was to let the people talk for themselves and let the reader put it into the larger context," Winerip concluded.

The reporters at *The New York Times* did not set out to do qualitative method journalism. Certainly, many on the team, including Winerip, were not even aware of the term. The reporting that resulted did, however, correspond closely with the purposes and principles of qualitative research. The conceptualization of individuals' personal circumstances as newsworthy and important to the understanding of larger social issues of the day is indicative of the qualitative approach. From the initial desire to do in-depth, in-the-field reporting to the use of multiple settings and multiple opportunities to gather personal insights all the way to the presentation of the findings in stories that included the role of the reporters and the *Times*, the process was an unambiguous approximation of thorough qualitative research.

The qualitative method provides an avenue for reporting that reaches the individual and brings the common concerns of everyday people into the public sphere. Using qualitative research techniques in journalism is not a new idea. However, until recently, the qualitative method has not been given much attention by journalists. Changing conditions, both institutionally and technologically, now encourage this specialized training for journalists. The purpose of this volume is to focus on qualitative method journalism. The chapters in Part I provide background for understanding the early history of qualitative research in the United States and its relationship to journalism. The chapters in Part II each describe one or more qualitative methods and show how they are being applied in journalism today.

REFERENCES

Bagdikian, B. H. (1972). *The effete conspiracy and other crimes by the press.* New York: Harper & Row.

Bagdikian, B. H. (2000). *The media monopoly* (6th ed.). Boston: Beacon Press.

Bennett, W. L., & Entman, R. M. (Eds.). (2001). *Mediated politics.* Cambridge, UK: Cambridge University Press.

Black, J. (Ed.). (1997). *Mixed news: The public/civic/communitarian journalism debate.* Mahwah, NJ: Lawrence Erlbaum Associates.

Carey, J. W. (1987, March/April). The press and public discourse. *The Center Magazine*, 4–16.

Carey, J. W. (1992). The press and the public discourse. *Kettering Review* (Winter), 1–22.

Carey, J. W. (1997). Community, public, and journalism. In J. Black (Ed.), *Mixed news: The public/civic/communitarian journalism debate* (pp. 1–17). Mahwah, NJ: Lawrence Erlbaum Associates.

Charity, A. (1996). *Doing public journalism.* New York: Guilford Press.

Coffey, S. (2002). *Best practices: The art of leadership in news organizations.* Arlington, VA: The Freedom Forum.

Commission on Freedom of the Press. (1947). *A free and responsible press.* Chicago: University of Chicago Press.

Dewey, J. (1927). *The public and its problems.* Denver, CO: Swallow Press.

Dionne, Jr., E. J. (Ed.). (1998). *Community works.* Washington, DC: The Brookings Institution.

Entman, R. M. (1998). *Democracy without citizens.* New York: Oxford University Press.

Fallows, J. (1996). *Breaking the news.* New York: Vintage Books.

Foucault, M. (1982). *The archeology of knowledge* (A. M. Sheridan, Trans.). New York: Pantheon. (Original work published 1969)

Glasser, T. L., & Salmon, C. T. (1995). The politics of polling and the limits of consent. In T. L. Glasser & C. T. Salmon (Eds.), *Public opinion and the communication of consent* (pp. 417–436). New York: Guilford Press.

Graber, D. A. (2001). Adapting political news to the needs of twenty-first century Americans. In W. L. Bennett & R. M. Entman (Eds.), *Mediated Politics* (pp. 433–452). Cambridge, UK: Cambridge University Press.

Habermas, J. (1991). *The structural transformation of the public sphere* (T. Burger, Trans.). Cambridge, MA: MIT Press.

Jensen, K. B. (2002). The qualitative research process. In K. B. Jensen (Ed.), *A handbook of media and communication research* (pp. 235–253). New York: Routledge.

Lelyveld, J. (Ed.). (2001). *How race is lived in America.* New York: Times Books: Henry Holt & Company.

Lippmann, W. (1922). *Public opinion.* New York: Harcourt, Brace & Company.

Mannheim, K. (1986). *Ideology and utopia* (D. Kettler, V. Meja, & N. J. Stehr, Trans.). New York: Routledge & Kegan Paul. (Original work published 1929)

Merritt, D. (1995). *Public journalism and public life: Why telling the news is not enough.* Hillsdale, NJ: Lawrence Erlbaum Associates.

Meyer, P. (1973). *Precision journalism.* Bloomington, IN: Indiana University Press.

Meyer, P. (1991, 2001). *The new precision journalism.* Bloomington, IN: Indiana University Press.

Miller, D. L. (Ed.). (1982). *The individual and the social self: Unpublished work of George Herbert Mead.* Chicago: University of Chicago Press.

Park, R. E., & Burgess, E. W. (1925). *The city.* Chicago: University of Chicago Press.

Peters, J. D. (1995). Historical tensions in the concept of public opinion. In T. L. Glasser & C. T. Salmon (Eds.), *Public opinion and the communication of consent* (pp. 3–32). New York: Guilford Press.

Pool, I. S. (1990). *Technologies without boundaries: On telecommunication in a global age.* Cambridge, MA: Harvard University Press.

Poster, M. (1999). The net as a public sphere. In D. Crowley & P. Heyer (Eds.), *Communication in history* (pp. 335–337). New York: Longman.

Putnam, R. (1993). *Making democracy work.* Princeton, NJ: Princeton University Press.

Putnam, R. (1995). Bowling alone: America's declining social capital. *Journal of Democracy, 6*(1), 65–78.

Rosen, J. (1999a). Deliberation in order to write. *Kettering Review, 19*(1), 53–60.

Rosen, J. (1999b). *What are journalists for?* New Haven, CT: Yale University Press.

Rosen, J., Merritt, D., & Austin, L. (1997). *Theory and practice: Lessons from experience.* Dayton, OH: Kettering Foundation.

Schudson, M. (1995). *The power of news.* Cambridge, MA: Harvard University Press.

Sirianni, C., & Friedland, L. A. (2001). *Civic innovation in America: Community empowerment, public policy, and the movement for civic renewal.* Berkeley, CA: University of California Press.

Thomas, W. I., & Znaniecki, F. (1927). *The Polish peasant in Europe and America.* New York: Knopf.

Thompson, J. B. (1995). *The media and modernity.* Stanford, CA: Stanford University Press.

Tuchman, G. (1978). *Making news: A study in the construction of reality.* New York: Free Press.

Ureneck, L. (1999, 2000). Expert journalism. *Nieman Reports, 53*(4) & *54*(1).

Yankelovich, D. (1991). *Coming to public judgment: Making democracy work in a complex world.* Syracuse, NY: Syracuse University Press.

2

Connected Research

The Chicago School Precedent

Lewis A. Friedland
University of Wisconsin–Madison

Kathryn B. Campbell
University of Oregon

The very term "qualitative research" implies that it is something set apart, defined by certain methods or approaches—that is, by particular "qualities." By implication, "qualitative research" is done in contrast to "quantitative research," which has its own rules for summing up social, psychological, and political life in numbers and equations. These assertions are more or less true, but they are also more or less beside the main point, at least the one we want to make in this chapter. Qualitative research, as practiced in the founding traditions of sociology at the University of Chicago, is defined not so much by how it goes about knowing, but how it defines what it wants to know about. That is to say, the goal of research in the Chicago tradition is to get as complete as possible an understanding of what is being studied, and that means always trying to understand the larger picture, or context.

Research in this tradition, called the Chicago School of sociology, often tries to look at whole communities—neighborhoods, social groups, or even big cities; occasionally, it tries to look at all of these at once in relation to each other. It is a kind of research that tries to understand people, their actions, and institutions in all of their complicated interactions with each other. Qualitative research understands that this complex picture of social or community life sometimes will not show statistical relationships among "variables,"[1] such as the classifications such as gender, education, and income that are the mainstay of quantitative research. This emphasis on the whole community does not necessarily make qualitative research better than variables-based, quantitative research, but it does make it different—even when, as was often the case in the larger Chicago School studies, statistical and other data also were used to understand how the complicated parts of a large community fit together.

So, more than anything else, qualitative research as we will use the term is holistic, meaning that it tries to situate the things it studies in their broadest possible context. There are many ways to do this, and most of them rely on various forms and combinations of interviews and observation. The largest possible picture of some group of social phenomena is the goal.

THE CHICAGO SCHOOL METHOD

Qualitative research can be described in a number of ways, and each has a different shade of meaning. "Ethnography" is literally writing about people or culture. It grew from the writings of the early anthropologists who lived with tribal cultures outside of the United States and wrote up everything possible (or at least everything they could see) about the way the people lived and worked together. The hallmark of this work was the anthropologists' close contact with people—their research "subjects"—over a period of time. Their research methods included both "participant observation," meaning that they watched their research subjects while doing things with them; and "depth interviews," meaning that they participated in extended conversations over time, asking people about what they were doing and what it meant. The term "fieldwork" grew to mean just this kind of research: going out into the "field," that is, the places where people conduct their daily lives. This remains a defining element of all qualitative research.

At about the time that early anthropologists were visiting countries beyond the borders of their homelands, sociologists at the University of Chicago were asking the same kinds of questions about life in the United States. The shape and size of the city of Chicago was changing quickly in the early part of the 20th century under the pressures of urban industrialization and massive immigration. Understanding these changes—and the social problems that accompanied them—posed a huge challenge for researchers. In some ways, the communities that sociologists wanted to investigate were much more complex than the societies studied by the anthropologists. The anthropologists went to remote areas in order to grasp society and culture as a whole, in locations where things were presumed to change very slowly and societies were coterminous with small groups. In Chicago, however, waves of immigrants speaking different languages and dialects—Swedish, Yiddish and dozens of others—and African Americans moving from the South mingled in a city that could not expand quickly enough to feed, house, and offer work to all of them. They competed for housing and jobs and often clashed in village-like ghettos. Each group was a whole community, and to understand these grinding, intersecting communities in relation to one another required understanding each separately. The Chicago researchers handled that challenge by going into each of these communities, living in them, and describing the lives of the people there as a whole—much the way anthropologists approached the study of culture. The Chicago researchers used the techniques of depth interviews and participant observation (while never shying away from the tools of mapping or statistical data). The task was to get the broadest picture possible of how the city worked, to discover how such a cacophonous clash of languages, interests, and ways of life could hang together—much less integrate—to make something that could be properly called a city at all.

Howard Becker, a sociologist who was trained at the University of Chicago after World War II and is one of the leading practitioners of qualitative research in his generation, described the larger goal this way:

> The point is not to prove, beyond doubt, the existence of particular relationships so much as to describe a system of relationships, to show how things hang together in a web of mutual influence or support or interdependence or what-have-you, to describe the connections between the specifics the ethnographer knows by virtue of having been there. (1996, p. 56)

UNIQUE QUALITIES OF THE CHICAGO METHODS

"Having been there" and the focus on the interconnection of groups and relationships are, more than anything else, what distinguishes qualitative from quantitative research. A more formal way of understanding this relationship at the broadest level is that qualitative research proceeds by understanding "cases" that are, often, very dense and complex bundles of actors, actions, and meanings. From the standpoint of qualitative researchers, cases are extremely rich sources of data, and a great deal can be learned from a single, well-done case study. Another way of saying this is that a qualitative case contains many different elements, each of which is, in a way, its own case within a case.

For example, if we want to study the relationship between a civic journalism-oriented newspaper and its community, we can see this as one large case: the case of a community-newspaper relationship, and, indeed, it is. However, within this larger umbrella, there are a number of different cases. The newspaper itself is a case; the editors and the reporters are separate cases. All have different roles—institutional, interpersonal, and professional. They have a relationship: their roles mesh, meld, and sometimes clash. All of the people involved have ideas about what good journalism is, about how to do it, and about where the line should be drawn between the newsroom and the community. We can multiply this for publishers, photographers, graphic artists, and so on. Perhaps editors and reporters learned about civic journalism in a workshop given by a foundation. Then the foundation and its own set of relationships and ideas become part of the case.

All of this occurs before the researchers even begin to think about the community. We have already suggested just how internally different (or "differentiated") any one group can be. For example, most communities in the United States include a group of elites, that is, the leaders in business, political, government, and social circles. Most communities also have dozens, if not hundreds, of civic and community associations. People are often divided by class, income, or social status—and, certainly not least, they can be divided by race and ethnic background. Different cross-sections of the community might respond very differently to journalism initiatives. In North Carolina, for example, when *The Charlotte Observer* began its landmark project on race, crime, and community called "Taking Back Our Neighborhoods," wealthier white residents in one part of town saw things quite differently than African Americans in others. The people within the African American community saw things differently, depending, for example, on whether they were homeowners. Each of these issues was a case that in turn made up the case of civic journalism in Charlotte, and each had to be examined. At the newspaper, researchers interviewed editors, reporters of all sorts, graphic designers, editorial writers, and many others. The researchers walked the streets, not only in the Charlotte neighborhoods covered by the series but also in neighborhoods that were not. They talked to African Americans in poor neighborhoods and to African American homeowners; to working-class White citizens; to downtown businessmen; to the chief of police and to officers on the beat (for this case and others of public journalism, see Sirianni & Friedland, 2001). Each told a different story, and each account went into making up the case.

The richness of a single case allows for qualitative researchers to describe an extraordinary amount of complexity and, at the same time, to achieve the primary goal of any good social science: reducing the complexity of any social phenomenon so that we can understand it better and compare it to similar cases. Case-based research can describe how groups are organized, internally and in relation to each other; the histories of events, that is, how things happened; the meanings of events, both to the actors themselves, in their own words, and to outside observers, either other interview subjects or the researchers themselves. One hallmark of this work then is its "thickness" or rich detail. Contemporary anthropologist Clifford Geertz (1973) describes the goal of his research as "thick description." Again, Howard Becker (1996):

> A few basic questions seem to lie at the heart of the debates about these methods: Must we take account of the viewpoint of the social actor and, if we must, how do we do it? And: how do we deal with the embeddedness of all social action in the world of everyday life? And: how thick can we and should we make our descriptions? (p. xiv)

These questions lie at the intersection of the main perceived differences between qualitative and quantitative research. A quantitative researcher might say that the case that we just described is only one case, or has "an N [number] of one." To say anything meaningful, the quantitative researcher might add, many cases of the same thing are needed, and the only way to make sure that they are the same thing is to ask the same question in the same way of many different subjects at about the same time (put differently, to make sure that the questions are "valid."). This is done to make sure that the researcher(s) can generalize from all of these variables through the use of statistics that allow measurement of both how the variables relate to each other ("correlate") and the amount of error in the measurement ("reliability"). This kind of research has a large N, often in the hundreds or higher for each variable, sometimes also called (confusingly) cases.

This is an old argument. Sometimes it is framed as the conflict between "inductive" research, in which social scientists look at many individual things (cases) in order to build up generalizations about them that can then be "tested" through "deductive" research. Deductive researchers propose hypotheses and then test them (using experiments, surveys, or other quantitative techniques). Qualitative researchers do not like this description, because it appears to reduce what they do—the generation of complex studies involving many different variables in relationship—to "one" thing, that is, one variable, which is then seen to be insufficient for genuine hypothesis testing. However, most serious social scientists recognize this story as tired at best, describing a certain kind of division of labor, and silly and misleading at worst. The ultimate goal of social science is the explanation of complex social phenomena, and both quantitative and qualitative methods are needed to do this. Indeed, when we turn to the classical origins of American sociology, the Chicago School, we find that this is precisely what happened.

WHY DID THE CHICAGO SCHOOL EMERGE?

One of the most important problems that the early sociologists at the University of Chicago wanted to address was that of social integration. From the late 19th century and into the 1930s, the United States was under extraordinary pressure. Up to that time, there had been something like a consensus (certainly among political and intellectual elites but one also shared by many Americans) that the United States was a white, Protestant nation, built on rural values of hard work and self-sufficiency. Torrents of new immigrants—mostly from southern and eastern Europe but also from Asia, Latin America, and elsewhere—began to undermine this consensus. To put it differently, this older vision of American democracy and community no longer worked. Democracy and community life came to be seen as problems to be solved rather than ideals that could be taken for granted.

Some of the most important thinking about the problems of democracy and community was also taking place at the University of Chicago during this period. In particular, the philosopher John Dewey and George Herbert Mead began to rethink traditional ideas. They saw that a democracy that depended on unchanging, fixed ways of life might not survive. Dewey addressed this question directly through his writings on democracy and through his influential works on the philosophy of education. Mead sought to understand how perceptions of self are formed in relation to others. Each opened new perspectives on social-psychological change and integrating new experiences.

The Chicago researchers built on this foundation. They developed new techniques of investigation that were fitted to the problems at hand: rapid urbanization under the pressure of immigration; the strains in social integration, and the challenge to democracy. They tried to develop new theory to help guide their study of the social world. The techniques included ethnography, of course, but the researchers also embraced mapping and use of statistical data. The goal was to understand the city (and, by implication, the nation) in its complexity, and every research technique that could be borrowed, refined, or invented was needed.

What does this have to do with journalism research and practice today? Everything. The problems of understanding and integrating diversity in a globalizing age pose incredible new challenges to both social science and journalism. The holistic approach of the Chicago School is more, not less, necessary today. It gives journalists both inspiration and license to engage fully in the process of discovery. The world is not simply out there, fixed, waiting to be turned into variables and measured. It is changing shape before our eyes, and only an ensemble of methods that is adequate to capturing that change is adequate to journalism or social science in the 21st century.

FOUNDING SCHOLARS

As we have suggested, journalists in search of theoretical, empirical, or polemical inspiration would be hard-pressed to exhaust the potential of the work produced in the first third of the 20th century in the developing discipline of sociology at the University of Chicago—a body of research, theory, and research methods known as the Chicago School. Robert E. Park, a journalist who had not earned his PhD in philosophy until he was 48, and his colleagues at the University of Chicago helped invent the academic discipline of sociology, creating the methods they needed to develop and test theory in the real world and insisting that sociology be of some practical use.

Founded in 1892 as part of a well-funded private university, the Department of Social Science and Anthropology was headed by Albion Small, a theorist who promoted empiricism and saw the study of sociology primarily as preparation for citizenship and a way to improve society. One of Small's faculty appointments was W. I. Thomas, whose theories attempted to explain social change and motivation and who espoused systematic, multifaceted research culminating in comparative analyses. His major work, coauthored with Florian Znaniecki, was the five-volume study, *The Polish Peasant in Europe and America* (1918). Thomas in turn recruited Park, the former newspaper reporter. Park, along with his research partner, Professor Ernest W. Burgess, developed theories of human ecology and urban change, including the natural history of the city. Together, they supervised a generation of graduate researchers who studied various aspects of city life, using Chicago as their laboratory.

Park and Burgess encouraged their students to test their developing theories of urban change using data they collected firsthand and data gathered by others for other purposes. This type of fieldwork has since been refined into methodologies such as case studies and participant observation. The use of statistical data was central to their work; the researchers collected some data themselves, but Burgess also worked creatively with census data. Students learned statistical methods from the pioneers in that field: L. L. Thurstone, Emory Bogardus, and William F. Ogburn. Some scholars have attempted to pin the subsequent divide in sociology over quantitative versus qualitative methods on the Chicago School, or to label the Chicago School as atheoretical, but those approaches are pure mythmaking. The theory-guided, multimethod approach is the true Chicago tradition, well illustrated in a series of monographs such as *The Hobo* (Anderson, 1923), *The Ghetto* (Wirth, 1928), *The Taxi-Dance Hall* (Cressey, 1925), and *The Gang* (Thrasher, 1927).

In sociology, debate over the Chicago School legacy begins with the question of whether it can properly be called a "school" and ranges widely, touching on the extent to which the Chicago School sociologists were social reformers, were influenced by pragmatist philosophy, and were deliberately or just misguidedly reconstructed by succeeding generations in order to justify new theories or to legitimate new methodologies. Critics charge that the Chicago sociologists were conservative apologists for the status quo who failed to recognize the implicit norms of their own work. Others dispute the strength of the link from the Chicago School to Mead's symbolic interactionism, and Herbert Blumer's version of it. What has rarely been appreciated, even in sociology, is the vitality and excitement that permeated the interdisciplinary work of the Chicago sociologists and the passion connecting their academic and personal lives. It is this interdisciplinary, interconnected, multimethod approach to understanding the complexities of community life that offers journalists a critically needed historical and theoretical grounding for their contemporary work.

IMPLICATIONS FOR JOURNALISM

A thorough grounding in the exploratory theory and methods found in the work of the Chicago School has several implications for journalism and journalism research. First, the Chicago School sociologists began with the idea that social relationships were not static, nor could they be captured by single and discrete approaches to understanding them. These innovative thinkers used every bit of information available to them: firsthand data they collected; secondhand statistical data from social service agencies; newspaper accounts; and myriad personal documents such as letters and diaries.

The Chicago School's multimethod approach appears to be regaining some favor today as sociologists try to apprehend the incredible complexity of contemporary communities and are urged by their colleagues to forgo the variables paradigm as the sole method of understanding social interaction (Abbott, 1997). That is, the collection and analysis of statistics is deemed important and necessary, but not sufficient. This acknowledgment clearly has implications for journalists and journalism researchers who are teaching themselves the kind of sociological research envisioned by the Chicago School. The journalistic connection to Park is especially strong:

> Dr. Park had been a newspaperman before he turned to sociology. He had been fascinated by the city. The problems which the city presented interested him greatly. He was interested in the newspaper, its power of exposing conditions and arousing public sentiment, and in taking the lead in crusades against slums, exploitation of immigrants, or corruption in municipal affairs. The exposés by Lincoln Steffens, and the whole tradition in journalism which he stimulated, was the point of departure in this thinking. But Dr. Park found that, while newspaper publicity aroused a great deal of interest and stirred the emotions of the public, it did not lead to constructive action. He

decided that something more than news was needed, that you had to get beneath the surface of things. So he returned to the university. (Burgess & Bogue, 1964, p. 3)

A second implication for contemporary journalism research is that it need not be presented in the jargon of expertise or in obfuscated, pedantic prose; one of the strengths of the Chicago School is the accessible nature of its published work. The clearly explicated ideas and research published in Chicago generated an entire discipline. Part of that explication is the presentation of information in a graphically meaningful way. Both characteristics of Chicago research are exhibited in the eminently readable books it produced in the 1920s and 1930s, such as *The Hobo* (Anderson, 1923), *The City* (Park, 1925a), *The Gang* (Thrasher, 1927), *The Ghetto* (Wirth, 1928), and *The Jack-Roller* (Shaw, 1930/1966).

A third implication for journalism is the discovery of a tradition of acknowledged community connections. Park (1939, p. vi) wrote that sociology is important as a community resource of information, and he spelled out the dual role of the sociologist: sociologist as scientist and sociologist as member of the human community whose expectation is that his research will be applied beneficially.

A final implication for journalism research is simply the sense of excitement that the Chicago School sociologists can inspire. As Abbott (1997) exhorted his colleagues in sociology:

> Sociology stands before a great new flowering. New methods are available for borrowing. Problems for analysis are more pressing and more exciting than ever. Above all, we possess a goodly heritage of both theoretical and empirical work in the contextualist, interactionist tradition, bequeathed us by the Chicago School. That work provides a foundation and an example for where sociology ought to go. (p. 1182)

Abbott's words are equally applicable to the practice and study of journalism today.

HISTORICAL CONTEXT FOR CHICAGO SCHOOL RESEARCH

Qualitative methods did not, of course, spring forth fully formed from the Chicago School. Research ideas were borrowed, revised, tested, revised again, codified in a graduate student handbook (Palmer, 1928), and field tested again. The sociologists' work drew from and complemented practical social research in three other areas: the massive study of poverty conducted by Charles Booth in London, the urban research done by Jane Addams and the settlement house pioneers in Chicago, and the community studies undertaken by the tireless activists who sustained the social survey movement in the United States for more than 30 years.

Charles Booth

Booth's *Labour and Life of the People in London* series was published in multiple volumes between 1889 and 1902, reflecting more than a decade of careful and detailed research. Booth (1889, 1891) began his mammoth study of urban poverty and associated factors such as employment and religious life by surveying and then mapping London neighborhoods—house by house, street by street, block by block. He demonstrated conclusively that individual behavior, social structure, and social welfare (and, it might be argued, civic life) were inextricably interconnected (Booth, 1902). He created what might now be called a database of statistics on wages and households that informed debate over British social policy for decades following the completion of his 17-volume study.[2] His analyses were accompanied by thick descriptive material that brought the streets of London to life amid the pages and pages of tables and charts. Booth directly and indirectly provided the model for the type of research encouraged by the Chicago School sociologists. As Booth had done, the Chicago School researchers found ways to combine qualitative and quantitative research, tacking back and forth between theory-driven deductive reasoning and inductive theory building.

Jane Addams and Hull-House

Charles Booth and the Chicago School academics were not the only researchers to use maps, surveys, interviews, census data, and the like as they tried to understand the complexity of urban life. Burgess and Bogue (1964), in their "long view" of urban sociology, readily acknowledge the work of Booth's contemporaries at Hull-House:

> It is important to make clear that the Department of Sociology studies were not the first field studies in Chicago. If you go back as far as 1895 in the Hull House Papers, you will find urban studies. It would be correct to say that systematic urban studies in Chicago began with these Hull-House studies. Edith Abbott and Sophonisba Breckenridge, in what was then the Chicago School of Civics and Philanthropy (later the School of Social Service Administration of this university), had carried on a series of studies of the immigrant and of the operation of Hull-House. They began these studies as early as 1908. And of course there were other isolated studies of Chicago during the early decades of the twentieth century. Similar work had been going on in New York City and in other cities where there had been social surveys or investigations of slums. (p. 4)

Hull-House, founded by Addams, was the second settlement house in the United States[3] and arguably the most influential. Its founding ideal was the "conviction that social intercourse could best express the growing sense of the economic unity of society" with the wish that "the social spirit" would be the "undercurrent of the life of Hull-House, whatever direction the stream might take" (Residents, 1895, p. 207). Hull-House had living space for up to 20 permanent residents, a library branch, art gallery, clubs and class space, coffee houses, gymnasium, a kindergarten, a music school, a co-op women's apartment, a men's club, a theater, and the first public playground in Chicago. Hundreds of visitors, including immigrant residents of the neighborhood, streamed into Hull-House weekly to talk and learn about everything from philosophy and politics to finding a job and raising a family.

The founding Hull-House residents, comprising for the most part a group of educated, middle-class social reformers, set out immediately to survey their neighborhood with the intention of providing statistics upon which plans for social improvements could be based (Residents, 1895). Led by Florence Kelley, the survey work was modeled on the Booth studies. The painstaking house-by-house survey of income, household size, and ethnicity included personal interviews with residents and provided the data for *Hull-House Maps and Papers*, first published in 1895.

The Social Survey Movement

As the settlement house activists pursued their studies, another strand of research developed into what came to be known as the social survey movement, sustained in great measure by the Russell Sage Foundation. The social survey movement comprised nearly 3,000 studies undertaken by large and small cities across the United States between the turn of the century and the early 1930s. The leaders of the social survey movement were, in general, associated with the Russell Sage Foundation[4] and explicitly committed to social reform. They also were well acquainted with the Booth studies, the work of Addams and Kelley at Hull-House, and with the academic investigations of the Chicago School. The Russell Sage Foundation's financial support was critical to the social survey movement, which was rooted in the ideals of the charity organizations of the period. The social survey movement arose, in no small part, because the charity organizations decided that direct giving would not provide a long-term solution for poverty and its associated social ills, including the truly grim working conditions found in newly industrialized cities. The Russell Sage Foundation cataloged, published, and distributed a large library of reports and instructional pamphlets for citizens in communities wishing to survey themselves; it encouraged the use of maps and other graphic devices to illustrate survey findings; and it helped finance many of the social survey studies.

The benchmark survey was undertaken in Pittsburgh in 1906. The architects of the study, led by journalist Paul U. Kellogg, eschewed the muckraking approach popular in the same period. When Kellogg was asked to investigate and report on living and working conditions in Pittsburgh, he put together a research team and sought sponsorship from the Charity Organization Society of New York, for whom he worked as managing editor of a leading philanthropic journal of the period, *Charities and The Commons*. He also asked for and received funding from the newly formed Russell Sage Foundation. In 1907, Kellogg and a team of researchers began to investigate and document the working and living conditions in Pittsburgh, a heavily industrialized city whose name was already synonymous with iron and steel.

The survey results were published in six volumes between 1909 and 1914, but the books were only part of the story of this innovative research. The findings were presented in speeches, magazine articles, photographs, and a traveling exhibition; thus the Pittsburgh Survey was notable for its organized attempt to publicize its findings among the people who had been surveyed. In keeping with the researchers' goals of empowering residents through information, dissemination of the survey results to the people of the city was an integral part of the enterprise. The Pittsburgh Civic Exhibit of November and December 1908 displayed maps, photographs, drawings, and inventive graphic displays (Kellogg, 1909, p. 519), such as a 250-foot-long frieze of human silhouettes representing the number of deaths from typhoid fever in 1907. The 622 silhouettes of men, women, and children were placed 3 inches apart along the walls of an exhibit room in Carnegie Hall; large signs over the doors compared Pittsburgh's death rate from typhoid to the lower rate of other large cities and demanded: "Who is responsible for this sacrifice?" (Wing, 1909, p. 923).

The Civic Exhibit also included an opening session on the "civic bearings" of the survey (Kellogg, 1909, p. 519). As Koven (1992) noted:

> The Pittsburgh survey can be viewed as a tentative initiative to make the survey the basis for dialogue across class lines between the surveyors and the community. At the very least, it defined the community not only as objects but as consumers of the survey. (p. 370)

On April 18, 1912—shortly after the survey itself was completed, but before all of the six volumes had been published—Kellogg addressed the Academy of Political Science on "The Spread of the Survey Idea." He noted that the survey movement had captured the imagination of the citizenry, with more communities asking for surveys than there were people to conduct them. Surveys, he said, were wanted in cities such as Buffalo, Sag Harbor, Syracuse, and Springfield; in the states of Kentucky, Rhode Island, New Jersey, Pennsylvania, Illinois, Missouri, Minnesota, Texas, and Kansas; and even as far away as British Columbia and India.

DEVELOPING THEORY AND METHODS TOGETHER

At the settlement houses and throughout the social survey movement, the researchers' goal was to grasp the complexities of modern urban life for the explicit purpose of civic improvement and reform. At the University of Chicago, academic research in sociology took a short step in a slightly different direction. The goal of understanding urban life was accompanied by a more explicit desire to develop theory that could explain it—theory that would be used, of course, by social planners, rather than the academics themselves, for the betterment of society.

The Natural Areas of the City

One of Park and Burgess' most tested theories was that of the "natural areas" of the city. Park contended that cities tend to "conform to the same pattern, and this pattern invariably turns out to be a constellation of typical urban areas, all of which can be geographically located and spacially defined" (1925b, p. 11). Cities, these urban ecologists believed, are made up of interrelated parts. The Chicago sociologists saw the city as a natural area—one that grows in relatively predictable ways that could only be modified by the landscape and might be affected a bit by human intervention, but nevertheless one whose character was shaped by natural processes of selection and differentiation.

Park and Burgess theorized that cities also undergo a natural process of concentration and decentralization, with business, culture, and politics concentrating in the center at the points where transportation systems intersect (Park, 1925a). Decentralization, their theory suggested, occurred in the push for residential areas away from the center. These natural processes, they believed, also sifted and winnowed the population. The Chicago School sociologists tended to talk about the growth of cities as a succession of invasions, comparable to the introduction of a new plant species into an area. The "invasions" often started in the center, where it was easier for newcomers to get a foothold—a place where they could find other immigrants, good transportation, and cheap housing—but then moved successively out through a series of concentric zones. The Chicagoists expected social disorganization as a result, but they also expected reorganization as a natural accommodation to the change. They expected immigrants of all ethnic, racial, and religious backgrounds to follow this pattern, describing communities such as the "Little Sicilys," the "Chinatowns," and the Jewish ghettos as transition zones.

To test their theories of social organization and disorganization, the Chicago sociologists, using a cadre of graduate students, poked and probed the various neighborhoods and socioeconomic aspects of their own city—always with the idea that their research was intended to inform the future study of all cities. Thomas, one of the earliest members of the Chicago school faculty, pioneered the methods that were subsequently adapted by Park, Burgess, and their students as they immersed themselves in the everyday life of Chicago. Together, they produced a remarkable series of sociological studies published between 1923 and the mid-1930s. This chapter concludes with a brief review of Thomas and Znaniecki's study of Polish immigrants and Anderson's study of hobos, illustrating how the Chicago researchers employed various methods to make sense of what they were finding and to relate each of the parts to the others.

The Polish Peasant in Europe and America

Thomas and Znaniecki noted in this classic work, first published in 1918, that people live their lives neither scientifically nor statistically. "We live by inference," Thomas and Znaniecki stated flatly, and what is needed are continuing life history studies "along with the available statistical studies to be used as a basis for the inferences drawn" (1918, p. 301). Statistics, he said, must be put in the context of life histories and constantly checked for validity. In other words, Thomas was arguing for an iterative, complementary, and interactive methodology upon which to base the emerging discipline of sociology.

Thomas and Znaniecki (1918) theorized that the behavior of Polish immigrants had social causes, not racial or ethnic origins (p. 58). In their research, Thomas and Znaniecki used various kinds of documents in various parts of their study. For example, letters from Poland were sources for their description of the immigrants' lives before they came to the United States. Newspapers and other archives provided information they used to describe the changes in Polish politics, economics, and families; parish albums were used for similar purposes in the United States; and a detailed life history of one man, Wladek Wisznienski, was used to support the authors' social theories. Doctors, social workers, editors, and teachers were interviewed for the study, but the Polish people themselves were not. Thomas, it seems, did not approve of personal interviews with his subjects, which he felt "manipulated the respondent excessively" (Bulmer, 1984, p. 54).

The Hobo

The multimethod approach to research employed by the Chicago sociologists is also well illustrated by a series of monographs, most based on doctoral dissertations completed under the direction of Park and Burgess. The first was Anderson's *The Hobo,* published in 1923. (Another of these monographs, *The Taxi-Dance Hall,* is discussed extensively in chap. 8.)

Park wrote introductions for many of these books, and in *The Hobo's* preface, he promptly declared the intended generalizability of the studies:

> It is, in fact, the purpose of these studies to emphasize not so much the particular and local as the generic and universal aspects of the city and its life, and so make these studies not merely a contribution to our information but to our permanent scientific knowledge of the city as a communal type. (1923, p. xxvi)

Man, Park added, has made the city, but the city has also made the man; and in this case, the city has turned a particular type of man—the pioneer—into the hobo (1923, p. xxiii).

Anderson's own preface to his book offered a similar assessment. He had become interested in the life of the wanderer, he acknowledged, mainly because he had been one, both during his upbringing as one of 12 children of Swedish immigrant farmers and as a young man skinning mules, laying railroad track, and working in lumber camps and mines across the United States. After finally finishing high school and college in Utah, he hopped his last freight to the University of Chicago for graduate school, arriving in 1920.

The Hobo is a classic example of the integrated methodology that the Chicago sociologists used to investigate urban life. The monograph brims with rich descriptive prose as Anderson revealed to his readers the intricacies of "Hobohemia," its Main Stem (the central area), as well as its inhabitants, their lifestyles, and their ways of thinking. Along the way, his anecdotal and statistical evidence accumulated for the argument he made about the causes of this "vagabondage": "(a) unemployment and seasonal work, (b) industrial inadequacy, (c) defects of personality, (d) crises in the life of the person, (e) racial or national discrimination, [and] (f) wanderlust." Any solution to the problem of homeless men that does not address these fundamental structural problems at the "core of our American life," he concluded, is simply insufficient (Anderson, 1923, p. 86).

Anderson's (1923) study also included a look at the complicated role of elites, whom he called "influentials," in Hobohemia. For example, he found that Dr. Ben Reitman, "King of the Hobos," was disdained by the hobos, dismissed as an aristocrat because he owned a Ford (p. 173). The hobos, Anderson reported, were great and voracious readers; to some extent, they were writers as well, publishing in hobo newsletters and progressive publications. Public speaking was a form of neighborhood entertainment; the Hobo College even provided a public sphere of sorts and training in public speaking—plus lunch (pp. 226–227). Anderson's detailed and yet holistic approach to the study of Hobohemia captured the complex web of relationships and activities in a community of people masked by stereotypical depictions of the nation's vagabonds.

In *The Hobo*, Anderson organized his evidence empirically as well. He offered a typology of homeless men (1923, pp. 87–88) that defined hobos as migratory workers. He classified nonworkers as tramps and bums, distinguishing between those who traveled and those who did not. He estimated the numbers of homeless at "probably" more than a million (p. 105) and provided a classification of the kinds of work hobos did (p. 107). His search for documents turned up few employment records, prompting him to comment: "Their records are not merely inadequate; they are a joke" (p. 111). Clearly, such records and documents were important to his research and their absence was felt.

Drawing on his research as well as his personal experience, Anderson speculated about the factors that defined the relationship among hobos, other citizens, and the police. He suggested that the more hobos who congregated in a given area, the more an individual hobo was seen as a problem despite the fact, he noted, that the average hobo hasn't the courage to be a first-class crook (pp. 163–165). Anderson also suggested that the hobos' longings for a classless society drew them to socialist labor movements (p. 167) even though, ironically, they were basically unfit for group life (p. 247). Although one of the study's sponsors, the Committee on Homeless Men of the Chicago Council of Social Agencies, pinpointed unemployment as the underlying problem of Hobohemia, Anderson's consistent message, derived from his intimate knowledge of his subject, was that hobos desired their way of life and would return to it—despite the best efforts of reformists, missions, homeless agencies, and educators.

THE AUTHORITY OF MULTIPLE RESEARCH METHODS

The inclusive research of the Chicago sociologists and their contemporaries demonstrates that qualitative and quantitative methods have a shared history. Booth pioneered mapping and data collection in whole communities; settlement house activists and the social survey advocates drew upon Booth's work and championed civic participation as the path to social reform. At the University of Chicago, Thomas and Znaniecki provided a working model for collecting and analyzing life histories; subsequent research refined and improved on their methods while inventing others. The data classification, depth interviews, and participant observation techniques explored in *The Hobo* and other Chicago School studies demonstrate research whose goal was understanding the city and its residents in the largest possible social context.

We want to reemphasize that the reconstruction of context in the Chicago model demanded that statistical data be used whenever it was available, and often, that it be collected when it was not. The interplay of observation, interview, research, and classification, however, always flowed into the larger theoretical and empirical task of understanding the city, and, through the lens of the city, the larger social forces reshaping the nation.

We have looked at the Chicago School for several reasons. The first is the enormity of the task that they undertook. To seek to understand the city as an organic whole is an extraordinary undertaking and rarely attempted. In the field of mass communication, a few remarkable research projects have tried, however, to begin to build a larger contextual understanding of whole cities, making use of both qualitative and quantitative data. Professor Sharon Iorio (1998) of Wichita State University directed a 1992 qualitative study in Wichita, Kansas, that is one of the earliest examples of research using multiple depth interviews in a single city to guide a civic journalism project. Professor Sandra J. Ball-Rokeach (2001) of the Annenberg School for Communication at the University of Southern California is currently attempting to reconstruct social and communication patterns in large parts of Los Angeles. Professor Jack McLeod of the University of Wisconsin has spent 40 years developing a complex portrait of Madison, Wisconsin, using primarily quantitative techniques (see, for example, McLeod et al., 1996). As authors of this chapter, we are also engaged in large-scale civic mapping and ethnography in Madison and plan other community-wide studies.

Some readers of this volume will themselves become researchers. Regardless of their inclinations toward qualitative or quantitative studies, we urge them to consider the larger problems of reconstructing relationships in a single community. Others will become journalists, perhaps civic journalists, and the problem of constructing the context of community will be central to all of the work that they do. Journalists who learn to look at communities as complex webs of relationships among people and institutions will find a whole series of interconnections that will deepen any story. The theory that we offer here says that a community is woven of interconnected fabric, Becker's "web of mutual influence." If we are right, then the best way to report on community fairly and accurately—or to research the effects of such reporting—is to know that web and to follow its connections using a variety of qualitative and quantitative methods. The result will be research and reporting in the authentic, authoritative voice of one who has truly "been there."

ENDNOTES

[1]Throughout this chapter, we have chosen to set apart, with quotation marks, some of the terms commonly used in quantitative and qualitative research. We have done so deliberately to try to call attention to their meaning and the role they play in determining the way we ask questions and seek answers.

[2]The publication history of the Booth studies is complex. The most readily available publications are those that collapsed the studies into four volumes, the second of which was an appendix of maps.

[3]The first was Neighborhood Guild in New York, founded in 1886. Hull-House was modeled on Toynbee Hall in London's East End; it still exists and has a lively website at www.toynbeehall.org.uk/

[4]The Russell Sage Foundation was established by Margaret Olivia Sage, who gave a goodly portion of her husband's $65 million estate to various charities in the early 1900s. Widowed at 78, she was adamant about using the money to improve social and living conditions in the United States. With an initial endowment of $10 million, the Russell Sage Foundation began its work in 1907. The new foundation's board quickly established that it would not provide aid to individuals, it would not fund university research, and it would not contribute to church-sponsored endeavors. It would and did, however, provide funding for large-scale community surveys (Glenn, Brandt, & Andrews, 1947).

REFERENCES

Abbott, A. (1997). Of time and space: The contemporary relevance of the Chicago School. *Social Forces, 75*(4), 1149–1182.

Anderson, N. (1923). *The hobo.* Chicago: University of Chicago Press.

Ball-Rokeach, S. J. (2001). Storytelling neighborhood: Paths to belonging in diverse urban environments. *Communication Research, 28*(4), 392–428.

Becker, H. (1996). The epistemology of qualitative research. In R. Jessor & A. Colby & R. A. Shweder (Eds.), *Ethnography and human development: Context and meaning in social inquiry* (pp. 53–71). Chicago: University of Chicago Press.

Booth, C. A. (1889). *Labour and life of the people: Volume I, East London* (2nd ed., Vol. I). London: Williams and Norgate.

Booth, C. A. (1891). *Labour and life of the people: Volume II, London continued* (Vol. II). London: Williams and Norgate.

Booth, C. A. (1902). *Life and labour of the people in London: Final Volume* (2nd ed. Vol. IV). London: Macmillan and Co., Limited.

Bulmer, M. (1984). *The Chicago School of Sociology.* Chicago: University of Chicago Press.

Burgess, E. W., & Bogue, D. J. (1964). Research in urban society: A long view. In E. W. Burgess & D. J. Bogue (Eds.), *Contributions to urban sociology* (pp. 1–14). Chicago: University of Chicago Press.

Cressey, P. G. (1969). *The taxi-dance hall.* Montclair, NJ: Patterson Smith. (Original work published in 1925)

Geertz, C. (1973). Thick description: Toward a interpretive theory of culture. *The interpretation of cultures* (pp. 3–30). New York: Basic Books.

Glenn, J. M., Brandt, L., & Andrews, F. E. (1947). *Russell Sage Foundation, 1907–1946* (Vol. 1). New York: Sage.

Iorio, S. H. (1998, August). *Public discourse, economic/fiscal policy issues, and civic journalism.* Paper presented at the Association for Education in Journalism and Mass Communication, Baltimore, MD.

Kellogg, P. U. (1909, January 2). *Charities and The Commons* (Vol. XXI, 14).

Koven, S. (1992). Surveying the social survey. In M. Bulmer, K. Bales & K. K. Sklar (Eds.), *The social survey in historical perspective, 1880–1940* (pp. 368–376). Cambridge, England: Cambridge University Press.

McLeod, J. M., Daily, K., Guo, Z., Eveland Jr., W. P., Bayer, J., Yang, S., & Wang, H. (1996). Community integration, local media use, and democratic processes. *Communication Research, 12*(2), 179–209.

Palmer, V. (1928). *Field studies in sociology.* Chicago: University of Chicago Press.

Park, R. E. (1923). Preface. In N. Anderson, *The hobo* (pp. 00–00). Chicago: University of Chicago Press.

Park, R. E. (1925a). The city: Suggestions for the investigation of human behavior in the urban environment. In R. E. Park, E. W. Burgess & R. McKenzie (Eds.), *The city* (pp. 1–46). Chicago: University of Chicago Press.

Park, R. E. (1925b). A spacial pattern and a moral order. In E. W. Burgess (Ed.), *The urban community: Selected papers from the proceedings of the American sociological society, 1925* (pp. 3–18). Chicago: University of Chicago Press.

Park, R. E. (1939). *An outline of the principles of sociology.* New York: Barnes & Noble, Inc.

Residents of Hull House. (1895). *Hull-House maps and papers.* Boston: Crowell & Co.

Shaw, C. R. (1966). *The Jack-Roller.* Chicago: University of Chicago Press. (Original work published in 1930)

Sirianni, C., & Friedland, L. A. (2001). *Civic innovation in America: Community empowerment, public policy, and the movement for civic renewal.* Berkeley, CA: University of California Press.

Thomas, W. I., & Znaniecki, F. (1918). *The Polish peasant in Europe and America.* New York: Alfred A. Knopf.

Thrasher, F. (1927). *The gang.* Chicago: University of Chicago Press.

Wing, F. E. (1909). Thirty-five years of typhoid. *Charities and The Commons* (Vol. XXI, 19).

Wirth, L. (1928). *The ghetto.* Chicago: University of Chicago Press.

3

The Changing
News Paradigm:
From Objectivity to Interpretive Sufficiency

Clifford G. Christians
University of Illinois at Urbana-Champaign

The contemporary version of the press traces its beginning to the 1890s. The media developed into an industrial structure, and the first forays into journalism education appeared. The press took shape as a complex and diversified social institution, with journalists an expert class pursuing specialized tasks. The North American press began understanding itself during this decade not as a political forum or socializing force, but as a corporate economic structure marketing a commodity for consumers. Structural patterns of authority and accountability were utilitarian in form, and utilitarianism characterized the press's organizational culture, which in turn was rooted in industrial production and market distribution. The industrialization and commercialization of the media displaced an earlier news culture that had used partisan advantage as its main standard. With the industrialization of the press, media occupations, especially journalism, began to redefine themselves as middle-class professions and sought a place within the rising university system.

A university education for journalists was first seriously attempted late in the 19th century. By 1910 when Flexner had written his monumental Report to the Carnegie Foundation for the Advancement of Teaching on professional training in a university context, journalism education had adopted a functional

41

model for itself compatible with the utility theory that dominated the first debates about the commercial press' character and role. The key impetus behind the creation of these early university programs in journalism was the need for the press to enhance its respectability in the face of heated public criticism. In the early and mid-19th century, journalism was a low-prestige occupation in a highly competitive market. Because journalists were perceived to have very little power, the public was not impressed by the typical newspaper or reporter, but was not especially alarmed either.

However, circumstances began to change dramatically as the 19th century neared its end. The press expanded rapidly in all the urban centers of Britain, with major national newspapers coming into existence and playing a prominent role in British journalism for most of the following century (*People*, 1881; *Daily Mail*, 1896; *Daily Express*, 1900; *Daily Mirror*, 1903). While multiple ownership of weekly newspapers started early in the 18th century, press chains created by the press barons in the late 19th and early 20th centuries began gaining a dominant market position (Curran & Seaton, 1997, pp. 28–29).

Newspapers in the United States grew in circulation, industrialized their production, and introduced economies of scale through modern distribution and through reliance on advertising that led to increasing monopolization of local markets in the later 19th and early 20th centuries. The rising power of the press made lapses that earlier had been colorful now seem to be dangerous. Newspaper owners, like railroad magnates, were seen by many as robber barons and anti-democrats. This popular perception of corruption had a significant amount of truth to it. In response, respectable elements of the press sought to develop a more polished public image.

Major new communication technologies between 1837 (telegraph) and World War I (telephone, 1876, and wireless, 1899) gave birth to the modern international communication system. These technologies spawned some of the first transnational companies: Marconi (operating in several countries with the parent company in the United Kingdom); Siemens and Slaby-Arco (Telefunken after 1903) in Germany; Thomson in France; Western Union, AT&T, and United Wireless in the United States; Philips in the Netherlands (Fortner, 1993, p. 77). The first submarine cable was laid across the straits of Dover in 1851, and the first transatlantic cable was laid in 1866. Britain completed its first direct cable to Bombay in 1870 and to Australia in 1872.

With the development of the submarine telegraph, the turn of the century marked the zenith of the monopolistic power of the great cable companies, to be overturned themselves by Marconi. Monopoly became a crucial issue for international communication henceforth, with regulation entangled by domestic and imperial interests. "The period up to World War I was one of rising nationalism, creation and consolidation of empires, and intense commercial rivalry. The tendency was to equate national interests with those of a country's major industrial concerns" (Fortner, 1993, p. 87). As long distance technologies established new centralizations of power, cooperation was necessary for technical reasons. However, in these early years of the transnational communication system, "it was nation against nation, company versus company, suspicion opposing suspicion ... [in the] competition to control the means of communication and to establish commercial hegemonies and information monopolies" (Fortner, 1993, p. 92).

OBJECTIVITY AS NORM

Concerns about media ethics followed the same trajectory. Journalistic conduct has been criticized and debated since the oldest known newspaper published in Germany in 1609. However, abuses of the press were not explicitly linked to ethical principles until the end of the 19th century. During the 1890s a transition occurred from everyday commentary in newspaper articles to a more reflective period related to ethical precepts (Dicken Garcia, 1989). A commonsense utilitarianism emerged as the overall framework. Sensationalism had been a staple of the entire century, but it took serious institutional form in the late 1890s from the Hearst and Pulitzer circulation battles during the Spanish-American War. As electronic communication systems were established, privacy became an urgent issue as sensitive diplomatic, military, and commercial information crossed multiple borders, especially in Europe (Fortner, 1993, pp. 88–89). Freebies and junkets, scourged by media critics since 1870, were treated more systematically in the context of individual accountability. A platform was laid for the free press–fair trial debate, although with virtually no progress beyond insisting on the press's rights.

The initial work of the 1890s, though rudimentary in ethics, evolved into a serious effort during the 1920s as journalism education was established within the liberal arts. Four important textbooks in journalism ethics emerged from America's heartland during this period: Crawford's *Ethics of Journalism* (1924), Flint's *The Conscience of the Newspaper* (1925), Gibbons's *Newspaper Ethics* (1926), and Henning's *Ethics and Practices of Journalism* (1932). None recognized the others in quotation or argument, yet they were similar in the topics they considered central: reporters and sources, economic temptations and conflicts of interest, national security, free press–fair trial, deception, fairness, accuracy, sensationalism, and protection of privacy.

This arousal of ethical inquiry followed a period of intense media criticism. Muckrakers such as Sinclair (1919) exposed the corruption of the money power in the wire services and in daily newspapers that were increasingly monopolistic. Thinkers such as Lippmann (1922) perceived the fundamental irrationality of public opinion and the failure of journalism to inform it properly. Some professional leaders themselves recognized the perils. Writing in 1924, Lord Reith of the BBC, for example, articulated a strong ethos of public service: "I think it will be admitted by all that to have exploited so great a scientific invention [radio] for the purpose and pursuit of entertainment alone would have been a prostitution of its powers and an insult to the character and intelligence of the people" (MacDonald & Petheram, 1998, p. 83). Moreover, the experience of propaganda in World War I and the rise of the motion picture in the 1900s and 1910s produced a palpable feeling of cultural peril among both reformers and traditional opinion leaders.

However, the flurry of activity in the 1920s, the growth of professional societies with codes of ethics, the expansion of curricula into the liberal arts—none of these could prevent the demise of ethics in the face of an antithetical worldview, scientific naturalism. Scientific naturalism aggressively ordered the structure of knowing during this period—naturalism in the sense that genuine knowledge can be identified only in the natural laws of the hard sciences (Purcell, 1973). For Quine (1953), philosophical inquiry was natural science reflecting on itself, and all meaningful knowledge was continuous with the paradigmatic disciplines—physics, chemistry, and biology. Advances in the physical sciences became the applauded ideal as academicians—including those in communication—promoted its methods and principles. One pacesetting educator, Murphy, concluded in 1924: "Journalism ... is emerging from an imaginative type of writing into one governed by scientifically sound principles. We now recognize that the scientific attitude toward news materials is the only safeguard we have against journalism graduates being capricious and emotional" (p. 31). Centered on human rationality and armed with the scientific method, the facts in news were said to mirror reality. Universities institutionalized the conventions of objective reporting in journalism curricula. The period from the 1930s is typically described as the social scientific phase of communications study, and objectivity was a quasi-scientific method appropriate to it (Emery, Emery, & Roberts, 2000).

Carey correctly attributed the emergence of objectivity in journalism to the struggle within the press for a legitimate place to stand within the complexities of rapid industrialization:

> With the end of partisan journalism, journalists were deprived of a point of view from which to describe the world they inhabited. That world was less and less governed by political parties, and journalists were set free of those parties in any event, so journal-

ists, capitalizing on the growing prestige of science, positioned themselves outside the system of politics, as observers stationed on an Archimedean point above the fray of social life. (Carey, 2000, p. 335)

Originally this form of journalism—beginning most prominently with the wire services—was rooted "in a purely commercial motive: the need of the mass newspaper to serve politically heterogeneous audiences without alienating a significant segment" of them. Subsequently this strategy of reporting "was rationalized into a canon of professional competence and ideology of professional responsibility." Journalists became "a relatively passive link in a communication chain that records the passing scene for audiences" (Carey, 2000, pp. 137–138).

Stretched across the fact-value dichotomy of scientific naturalism, journalistic morality became equivalent to unbiased reporting of neutral data. The seeds of this ethic of independence existed already in Henning (1932), though duty to the public realm dominated (as it did with Gibbons, 1926). Presenting unvarnished facts was heralded as the standard of good performance, with readers and viewers presumably deciding for themselves what the facts meant. Objective reporting was not merely a technique, but a moral imperative (Lichtenberg, 2000). Reporters considered it virtuous to bracket value judgments from the transmission of information. In C.P. Scott's famous declaration in the *Manchester Guardian* (6 May 1921): A newspaper's "primary office is the gathering of news ... The unclouded face of trust [must not] suffer wrong. Comment is free, but facts are sacred" (quoted in MacDonald and Petheram, 1998, p. 53). Patterson (1948), for example, made an impassioned plea in his Don R. Mellet Memorial Lecture that reporters demonstrate moral leadership in improving democratic life, and the cornerstone of their responsibility he considered "objective reporting and unslanted facts." News corresponds to context-free neutral algorithms, and ethics is equated with impartiality.

Concern for ethics during the 30s through 60s occurred only on isolated occasions. The Report of the Commission on Freedom of the Press in 1947 was the most famous counterstatement of this period. Occasionally there were pockets of resistance in journalism's intellectual and vocational life, but the professional statistical model prevailed nonetheless. The scientific worldview was the ruling paradigm. A preoccupation with that value-centered enterprise called ethics seemed out of place in an academic and professional environment committed to facticity.

Attacks on the objectivist worldview have multiplied through hermeneutics, critical theory in the Frankfurt School, American pragmatism, Wittgenstein's linguistic philosophy, Gramsci, and, in their own way, Lyotard's denial of master narratives and Derrida's sliding signifiers. The antifoundationalism of our own day indicates a crisis in maintaining an incontrovertible domain separate from human consciousness. Institutional structures and policies remain neutrality-driven, but in principle the tide has turned at present toward restricting objectivism to the territory of mathematics, physics, and the natural sciences. Objectivity has become increasingly controversial as the working press's professional standard, though it remains entrenched in various forms in our ordinary practices of news production and dissemination. In Carey's more dramatic terms:

> The conventions of objective reporting were developed as part of an essentially utilitarian-capitalist-scientific orientation toward events.... Yet despite their obsolescence, we continue to live with these conventions as if a silent conspiracy had been undertaken between government, the reporter, and the audience to keep the house locked up tight even though all the windows have been blown out (Carey, 2000, p. 141).

INTERPRETIVE SUFFICIENCY

This mainstream view of news as objective information is too narrow for today's social and political complexities. A more sophisticated concept is truth in journalism as authentic disclosure. The notable Hutchins Commission Report called for this alternative in 1947. It advocated a deeper definition of the press's mission as a "truthful, comprehensive and intelligent account of the day's events in a context which gives them meaning" (*Commission for Freedom of the Press*, 1947, p. 2). Bonhoeffer's *Ethics* contends correctly that a truthful account takes hold of the context, motives, and presuppositions involved (Bonhoeffer, 1995, ch. 5). In his terms, telling the truth depends on the quality of discernment so that penultimates do not gain ultimacy. Truth means, in other words, to strike gold, to get at "the core, the essence, the nub, the heart of the matter" (Pippert, 1989, p. 11).

Qualitative Methods

Once knowledge is released from epistemological objectivism, guidelines must be sought somewhere. For their orientation and specificity, media that enhance public life turn to interpretive studies or what is often called qualitative research. Forsaking the quest for precision journalism does not mean imprecision, but precision in disclosure and authenticity. To replace news gathering rooted in the methods of the natural sciences, rigorous qualitative procedures must be followed instead. Fiction and fabrication are not acceptable substitutes for fact and accuracy. Reporters aiming for critical consciousness among the public will seek what might be called interpretive sufficiency. They will polish their research and writing skills in terms of qualitative strategies. Explicit appeal to the interpretive approach will enhance the news story's completeness, rather than crudely tailoring events into a cosmetic cohesion. While interpretive sufficiency, in some form, has long served as a trademark of distinguished journalism, it is an everyday imperative for citizen-based reporting. In effect, with interpretive sufficiency we raise the ante, weaving it into our expectation of ordinary press performance.

Interpretive studies are an alternative view of human knowing. In this perspective, investigations must be grounded historically and biographically, so that they represent complex cultures adequately. The concepts of social science are not derived from a free-floating and abstruse mathematics, but resonate with the attitudes, definitions, and language of the people actually being studied. Journalists trained in qualitative research identify with social meanings in their role as participants and as observers formulate seminal conclusions about these meanings.

Through disciplined abstractions (Lofland), ethnomethodology, contextualization, thick description (Geertz), coherent frames of reference (Schutz), case studies, naturalistic observation, and other research practices, news workers can stake out a claim to interpretive sufficiency and assume responsibility for their efforts. Through an understanding of interpretive methodologies, reporters come to grips with the complex ways ethnographers insert themselves into the research process. A rich literature has been developed on constructing the life histories of ordinary people. In a fundamental sense, qualitative approaches are a temperament of mind—"the sociological imagination," Mills (1959) called it—rather than merely a series of techniques for handling the telephone, minicam, or interview pad. However, while the creative process always remains central, tough-minded standards and valid procedures can be taught and learned.

Validity

It is widely understood and accepted that research in the objectivist tradition must be externally and internally valid. Interpretive approaches need to meet these criteria as well, though in terms consistent with their own assumptions. Interpretive studies enforce the maxim that research imprisoned within itself, and therefore self-validating, is unacceptable. The principle of external validity compels naturalistic observers to be circumspect in generalizing to other situations. The cases and illustrations that have been selected must be representative of the class, social unit, tribe, or organization to which they properly belong. Interpretation arises in natural settings, not contrived ones; therefore, the more densely textured the specifics, the more external validity is maintained. This concern is particularly apropos in preparing case studies, a favorite qualitative tool because it allows in-depth and holistic probing. The goal is identifying representative cases for examination rather than spectacular ones that are anecdotal and idiosyncratic.

Regarding internal validity, interpretive accounts must reflect genuine features of the situation under study and not represent the aberrations or hurried conclusions of observer opinion. There must be sympathetic immersion in the material until the researcher or journalist establishes, in Blumer's (1954) phrase, "poetic resonance" with it. Does the investigator know enough to identify the principal aspects of the event being studied and to distinguish these main features from digressions and parentheses? Using the body as an analogy, the blood and brain must be separated from fingers and skin, all of which are parts of the whole organism but of differing significance. If true interiority has occurred—that is, if the details accurately reflect the natural circumstances—then the data are valid and reliable even though not based upon randomization, repeated and controlled observation, measurement, and statistical inference.

Interpretive sufficiency seeks to open up public life in all its dynamic dimensions. It means taking seriously lives that are loaded with multiple interpretations and grounded in cultural complexity. Ethnographic accounts have the "depth, detail, emotionality, nuance, and coherence" that permit a "critical consciousness to be formed" by readers and viewers (Denzin, 1997, p. 283). The thick notion of sufficiency supplants the thinness of the technical, exterior, and statistically precise received view. Rather than reducing social issues to the financial and administrative problems defined by politicians, the news media enable people to come to terms with their everyday experience themselves.

Triangulation

Effective use of triangulation is one way to describe interpretive sufficiency. The goal is to build up a fully rounded analysis of some phenomenon by combining all lines of attack, each probe revealing certain dimensions of the human world being investigated. The point is not to advocate eclecticism as such, but to avoid the personal bias and superficiality that stem from using only one kind of examination. Triangulation takes seriously the way humans attach meanings to social reality. The process of disentangling from within is complicated by the fact that reporters are interpreting a world that has been interpreted already. "Objective reality can never be captured. We can know a thing only through its representations" (Denzin & Lincoln, 2000, p. 5; cf. Flick, 1998). The assumption is that the different lines of interpretation each reveal different aspects of reality, "much as a kaleidoscope ... will reveal different colors and configurations of the object to its viewer" (Denzin, 1989, p. 235).

Triangulation occurs in several forms. It may refer, for example, to method—that is, combining document analysis with unstructured interviewing with unobtrusive observation, and combining this mixture in order to improve perspective. One can also take a social problem, prisons and incarceration, for instance, and triangulate it by viewing it historically (how does the contemporary situation differ from previous time periods), synchronically (what are the relevant facts about the problem today, using a variety of data sources), and theoretically (what ethical or anthropological system is relevant in gaining perspective on it). Theoretical triangulation is an obvious possibility, too, focusing several conceptual outlooks on a single object to see which one explains more. In investigator triangulation different evaluators, researchers, and experts are used.

Beyond these approaches is a kind of multiple triangulation in which all the various facets and insights generated are placed in interaction and cross-fertilization until the structural features of a setting or event are illuminated. Comprehension of actual context only accumulates gradually, so the search is always an ongoing one until we finally reveal the exact contours of the details unearthed. "The facts never 'speak for themselves.' They must be selected, marshaled, linked together, and given a voice" (Barzun & Graff, 1992, p. xxii). In this sense, the crystal is a better image of interpretive design than the fixed, two-dimensional triangle. Crystals:

> combine symmetry and substance with an infinite variety of shapes, substances, transmutations, multidimensionalities, and angles of approach. Crystals grow, change, and alter, but are not amorphous. Crystals are prisms that reflect externalities *and* refract within themselves … casting off in different directions. (Richardson, 2000, p. 934)

Also in Denzin's application of the crystalline metaphor: "Triangulation is the display of multiple, refracted realities simultaneously" (Denzin & Lincoln, 2000, p. 6). The aim is always multiple insights. The emphasis in interpretation is on discovery rather than applying routinized procedures. What we see when we view a crystal depends on how we hold it up to the light.

GENERAL MORALITY

The deficiencies in the epistemology of objective social science have become transparent. The enlightenment model placing facts and values in two separate domains has been discredited. A positivistic epistemology that insists on neutrality regarding definitions of the good and puts human freedom at odds with the moral order is now seen as fundamentally flawed. Objectivity as a unidimensional framework of rational and moral validation accounts for some of the good ends we seek, such as minimal harm, but those issues outside the objectivity calculus are excluded from the decision-making process. The way power and ideology influence social and political institutions, including the press, is largely ignored. Under a rhetorical patina of rational choice for autonomous actors, a means-ends system operates in fundamentally its own terms.

Even more unsettling has been the recognition that neutrality is not pluralistic but imperialistic. Reflecting on our past experience with it, disinterested investigation under presumed conditions of value freedom is increasingly seen as de facto reinscribing the agenda in its own terms. In the social sciences, quantitative analysis is procedurally committed to equal reckoning, regardless of how research subjects may constitute the substantive ends of life. However, experimentalism is not a neutral ground for all ideas; rather, it is a "fighting creed" that imposes its own ideas on others while uncritically assuming the "very superiority that powers this imposition" (Taylor et al., 1994, pp. 62–63). In Foucault's (1979, pp. 170–195) more decisive terms, social science is a regime of power that helps maintain social order by normalizing subjects into categories designed by political authorities (cf. Root, 1993, ch. 7). A commitment to objectivity is not neutral but represents only one range of ideals, and is itself incompatible with other good ends.

This noncontextual model that assumes "a morally neutral, objective observer will get the facts right" ignores "the situatedness of power relations associated with gender, sexual orientation, class, ethnicity, race, and nationality." It is hierarchical (scientist–subject) and biased toward patriarchy. "It glosses the ways in which the observer-ethnographer is implicated and embedded in the 'ruling apparatus' of the society and the culture." Scientists "carry the mantle" of university-based authority as they venture out into "local communities to do research" (Denzin, 1997, p. 272). There is no sustained questioning of expertise itself in democratic societies that belong in principle to citizens who do not share this specialized knowledge (cf. Euben, 1981, p. 120). Such historians of reporting as Carey lament an escalating professionalism that wrenches journalism from its civic moorings and recasts it as a scientistic-technocratic estate remote from everyday life. "The practices of writing and reporting the journalist thinks of as constituting objectivity" actually cast the citizen into the disempowered "role of student to be educated by the press rather than a participant in the process of self-government." Under the procedures of objective reporting, "journalists are reduced to brokers in the communication process ... allied structurally if not sympathetically with the persons and institutions they report" (Carey, 2000, pp. 139, 337). The genius of qualitative approaches is to confront that sequestering and insider mentality head-on; it enables us to work the backyards and sidewalks, but with *savoir faire* and competence.

Interpretive Social Science and Public Journalism

Interpretive approaches do not incline us to construct an apparatus of professional ethics. They work instead within the general morality. Rather than developing rules for experts, their preoccupation is the moral dimension of everyday life. Professionals committed to qualitative standards do not establish codes of ethics for themselves, but reflect the same social and moral space as the citizens they report. How the moral order works itself out in community formation is the issue, not, first of all, what media practitioners by their own standards consider virtuous. The moral domain is understood to be intrinsic to human beings, not a system of rules, norms, and ideals external to society and culture. Lincoln (1995) clarified the issues in these terms: Interpretive social science

> brings about the collapse of the distinctions between standards, rigor, and quality criteria and the formerly separate consideration of research ethics. In effect, many of the proposed and emerging standards for quality in interpretive social science are also standards for ethics.... This dissolution of the hard boundaries between rigor and ethics in turn signals that the new research is a relational research—research grounded in the recognition and valuing of connectedness between researcher and researched, and between knowledge elites and the societies and communities in which they live and labor. (p. 278)

Investigators are not constituted as ethical selves antecedently, but moral discernment unfolds dialectically between reporter and citizen. The dualism of means and ends is rejected, with the ends of interpretive sufficiency reconciled with the means for achieving them. "Methods vie among themselves not for experimental robustness, but for vitality and rigor in illuminating ... how we can create human flourishing" (Lincoln & Denzin, 2000, p. 1062).

Interpretive Journalism and Public Life

Rather than searching for neutral principles to which all parties can appeal, professional guidelines rooted in the general morality rest on a complex view of moral judgments. They are seen as a composite that integrates everyday experience, beliefs about the good, and feelings of approval and shame into an organic whole. This is a philosophical approach that situates the moral domain within the general purposes of life that people share contextually in their personal and social relations. Ideally, it engenders a new normative core for responsible reporting.

In an interpretive perspective, social entities are considered moral orders and not merely lingual structures. Societies are not formed by language alone. There are no selves-in-relation without moral commitments to nurture them. Our widely shared moral intuitions—respect for the dignity of others, for instance—are developed through discourse within a community. A self exists within "webs of interlocution," and all interpretation implicitly or explicitly "acknowledges the necessarily social origin of any and all of our conceptions of the good." Moral frameworks are as fundamental for orienting us in social space as the need "to establish our bearings in physical space" (Mulhall & Swift, 1996, pp. 112–113). Consequently, as journalism deals with the moral dimension in news, editorials, features, and investigative reporting, it is not in alien territory. In fact, according to Taylor (1989), "Developing, maintaining and articulating" our moral intuitions and reactions are as natural for humans as learning up and down, right and left (cf. pp. 27–29).

The sinews that hold citizens together are moral. Our communal web is not primarily political interests or economic interdependence or information technology but a commitment of conscience that preconditions the ethos of external apparatuses. This bondedness entails an ethics situated in creatureliness. Rather than privileging an individualistic, transcendental rationalism, moral commitments are inscribed in our worldviews through which we share a view of reality and perspectives on the common good. This ontological model is actually closer to the way the moral imagination operates in everyday life and refuses to separate moral agents from all that makes them unique. Instead of constructing a purely conceptual foundation for morality, the moral order is positioned fundamentally in the creaturely and corporeal. "In this way ... being ethical is a primordial movement in the beckoning force of life itself" (Olthuis, 1998, p. 141).

From this perspective, public life cannot be facilitated in functional language only, but journalists ought to speak of moral issues in appropriately moral discourse. And when they critique events that are vacuous or unjust, they must do so in terms of common values that have wide acceptance in the community as a whole. In this sense media professionals participate in their readers and viewers' ongoing process of moral articulation. In fact, culture's continued existence depends on identifying and defending its normative base. Therefore, public texts must enable us "to discover truths about ourselves"; reporting ought to "bring a moral compass into readers' lives" by accounting for things that matter to them (Denzin, 1997, p. 284). Communities are woven together by narratives that invigorate their common understanding of good and evil, happiness and reward, and the meaning of life and death. Recovering and refashioning moral discourse help to orient our citizenship. News is not the transmission of specialized data, but, in style and content, a catalyst for moral agency.

Taylor emphasized that moral judgments are capable of rational elucidation. Our moral intuitions often seem to be purely instinctual, like taste reactions to food (Taylor, 1989, pp. 27–36). However, human beings are capable of explaining what merits their obligations and they typically do so in terms of their beliefs about the nature of humanness. Agreements and disputes about values can be articulated and sifted. In fact, moral commitments cannot be intuitive only; they must be nurtured through discourse derived from and shared by a community. Agreements and disputes about values can be articulated and sifted. In these terms, qualitative researchers or journalists act morally when their accounts enable those studied to specify the character and identity of their moral instincts and to work them out in the public arena.

Moral Literacy

If our public life is not merely functional, but knit together by an admixture of social values, then moral literacy ought to be privileged in the media's mission. If societies are moral orders, and not merely lingual structures, in other words, communication in the public arena ought to stimulate the moral imagination. We have heard this language in a sanitized sense. "Do these programs have any redeeming social value?" For an interpretation to be sufficient, it ought to enable us to traverse the moral landscape. At that epiphanal moment when the principial contours of the taken-for-granted world are illuminated, news enhances the moral dimension of social dialogue. Our understanding of the self and public life increasingly exists in media texts. Therefore, in mass-mediated cultures oriented toward normlessness and illusive textuality, reporters find their appropriate role in opening windows on the moral landscape. As Glasser observed, "The hard-hitting stories, the investigative stories, lack a morally sensitive vocabulary" (cf. Glasser, 1992, p. 44; Ettema & Glasser, 1998). Journalism instead ought to appeal to listeners and readers about ordering human values. They further a community's ongoing process of moral evaluation by penetrating through the political and economic surface to the moral dynamics underneath. Rather than merely providing readers and audiences with information, the press's aim is morally literate citizens.

Wherever one observes reenactments of purposeful history and justice, there one sees the results of moral literacy. News can be considered redemptive when it serves as an instrument not of accommodation but of critique and social change. Documentaries, commentators, and public broadcasting often resonate with a redemptive accent, stir the human conscience, and liberate their viewers from the dominant text. We all know stations and reporters who have refused infotainment and sought to awaken the civic conscience. Major league awards are still won by professionals in journalism who distinguish themselves for public service. Editorials have raised our consciousness of anti-Semitism, and heightened our moral awareness of racism and gender discrimination. Over time and across the media, one observes a redemptive glow

on occasion in which the news media have facilitated moral discernment by
their insight into humankind as a distinctive species and by their affirmation
of purposeful history.

CONCLUSION

In his classic study, *The Moral Foundations of Professional Ethics,* Goldman
(1980) argued that the general morality is the ultimate framework for understanding professional norms. For him, "the most fundamental question for professional ethics is whether those in professional roles require special norms and
principles to guide their well-intentioned conduct" (p. 1). For professionals in
medicine, law, business, journalism, government, and so forth, we typically assume that their roles require unique principles or specially weighted norms. In
fact, the standard approach is to define ethical codes as sharply as possible according to the peculiar demands each field entails—aggressively defending clients in law, for instance, the physician's responsibility to clients, journalists'
obligation to sources, and the commitment of business executives to stockhold-
ers. Obviously, "special institutional obligations exist when their recognition
has better moral consequences than would refusing to recognize them"
(Goldman, 1980, p. 22). Yet Goldman concluded: "The central problem in professional ethics as actually practiced is not that professionals often fail to live up
to their unique official codes and professional principles; nor that they lack the
will to enforce them. It is rather that they often assume without question that
they ought to live up to them" (p. 33). The ultimate standard for professionals is
not role-specific ethical principles, but the general morality.

Journalism is an institution of power. Decisions and policies can be self-serving,
and practitioners defensive when criticized. Competition and careerism often
cloud the application of professional codes or ethical guidelines. Journalists may
have an understanding with sources that all information will be treated confiden-
tially, for example, and then change their mind when they come to believe the
public has a right to know this privileged material. Whereas we agree in the general morality that we ought to keep our promises, in this case canons of professional practice allow self-defined exceptions for the journalist as expert.

A preoccupation with privilege and authority cuts journalism loose from the
very public it is meant to serve. Objectivity rooted in the prestige of science has
fueled the status of specialized expertise in the mainstream press. On the other
hand, interpretive efficiency presumes that facts and values are intermixed
rather than dichotomous. Given the moral dimension intrinsic to the social order, interpreting its various configurations sufficiently means elaborating the
moral component. In addition, to resonate intelligently with peoples' values

means that journalists know the general morality, which they share with the public at large. Rather than refining professional codes of ethics, the challenge for journalists is the moral life as a whole—no harm to innocents, truth telling, reparations for wrong actions, beneficence, gratitude, honor contracts, human dignity. For taking journalism to the streets, interpretive standards understand moral behavior in interactive terms—with reporters operating in the same arena as citizens themselves.

· REFERENCES

Barzun, J., & Graff, H. F. (1992). *The modern researcher* (5th ed.). Orlando, FL: Harcourt College Publishers.

Blumer, H. (1948). What is wrong with social theory? *American Sociological Review, 19,* 3–10.

Bonhoeffer, D. (1995). *Ethics* (N. H. Smith, Trans.). New York: Macmillan.

Carey, J. W. (2000). The communications revolution and the professional communicator. Afterword: The culture in question. In E. S. Munson & C.A. Warren (Eds.), *James Carey: A critical reader* (pp. 128–143, 308–339). Minneapolis, MN: University of Minnesota Press.

Commission for Freedom of the Press (1947). *A free and responsible press.* Chicago: University of Chicago Press.

Crawford, N. (1924). *The ethics of journalism.* New York: Knopf.

Curran, J., & Seaton, J. (1997). *Power without responsibility: The press and broadcasting in Britain* (5th ed.). London: Routledge.

Denzin, N. K. (1989). *The research act: A theoretical introduction to sociological methods* (3rd ed.). Englewood Cliffs, NJ: Prentice Hall.

Denzin, N. K. (1997). *Interpretive ethnography: Ethnographic practices for the 21st century.* Thousand Oaks, CA: Sage.

Denzin, N. K., & Lincoln, Y. S. (2000). *Handbook of qualitative research* (2nd ed.). Thousand Oaks, CA: Sage.

Dicken Garcia, H. (1989). *Journalistic standards in nineteenth-century America.* Madison, WI: University of Wisconsin Press.

Emery, M., Emery, E., and Roberts, N. (2000). *The press and America: An interpretive history of the mass media* (9th ed.). Needham Heights, MA: Allyn & Bacon.

Ettema, J., & Glasser, T. (1998). *Custodians of conscience: Investigative journalism and public virtue.* New York: Columbia University Press.

Euben, P. J. (1981). Philosophy and the professions. *Democracy, 1,* 112–127.

Flick, U. (1998). *An introduction to qualitative research: Theory, method and application.* London: Sage.

Flint, L. (1925). *The conscience of the newspaper: A casebook in the principles and problems of journalism.* New York: Appleton.

Fortner, R. S. (1993). *International communication: History, conflict, and control of the global metropolis.* Belmont, CA: Wadsworth.

Foucault, M. (1979). *Discipline and punish: The birth of the prison* (A. Sheridan, Trans.). New York: Random House.

Gibbons, W. (1926). *Newspaper ethics.* Ann Arbor, MI: University of Michigan.

Glasser, T. (1992). Squaring with the reader: A seminar on journalism. *Kettering Review,* Winter, 42–46.

Goldman, A. (1980). *The moral foundations of professional ethics.* Totowa, NJ: Roman & Littlefield.

Henning, A. (1932). *Ethics and practices in journalism*. New York: R. Long & R. R. Smith.

Lichtenberg, J. (2000). In defence of objectivity revisited. In J. Curran & M. Gurevitch (Eds.), *Mass Media and Society* (3rd ed., pp. 238–254). London: Arnold Hodder.

Lincoln, Y. S. (1995). Emerging criteria for quality in qualitative and interpretive research. *Qualitative Inquiry, 1*, 275–289.

Lincoln, Y. S., & Denzin, N. K. (2000). The seventh moment: Out of the past. In N. K. Denzin & Y. S. Lincoln (Eds.), *Handbook of qualitative research* (2nd ed., pp. 1047–1065). Thousand Oaks, CA: Sage.

Lippmann, W. (1922). *Public opinion*. New York: Scribner's.

MacDonald, B., & Petheram, B. (Eds.). (1998). *Keyguide to information sources in media ethics*. London: Mansell Publishing.

Mills, C. W. (1959). *The sociological imagination*. New York: Oxford University Press.

Mulhall, S., & Swift, A. (1996). *Liberals and communitarians* (2nd ed.). Oxford, England: Blackwell.

Murphy, L. (1924). News values and analysis. *Journalism Bulletin, 2*, 29–31.

Olthuis, J. H. (Ed.). (1998). Face-to-face: Ethical symmetry or the symmetry of mutuality? In J. H. Olthuis (Ed.), *Knowing other-wise* (pp. 134–164). New York: Fordham University Press.

Patterson, G. H. (1948, March 12). *Social responsibilities of the American newspaper*. (Eighteenth address, Don R. Mellet Memorial Fund, pp. 5–14.) New York: New York University, Department of Journalism.

Pippert, W. (1989). *An ethics of news: A reporter's search for truth*. Washington, DC: Georgetown University Press.

Purcell, E. A. (1973). *The crisis of democratic theory: Scientific naturalism and the problem of value*. Lexington: University of Kentucky Press.

Quine, W. V. (1953). *From a logical point of view: Nine logico-philosophical essays*. Cambridge, MA: Harvard University Press.

Richardson, L. (2000). Writing: A method of inquiry. In N. K. Denzin & Y. S. Lincoln (Eds.), *Handbook of qualitative research* (2nd ed., pp. 923–948). Thousand Oaks, CA: Sage.

Root, M. (1993). *Philosophy of social science: The methods, ideals, and politics of social inquiry*. Oxford, England: Blackwell.

Sinclair, U. (1919). *The brass check: A study of American journalism*. Pasadena, CA: Published by author; reprinted University of Illinois Press, 2003.

Taylor, C. (1989). *Sources of the self: The making of the modern identity*. Cambridge, MA: Harvard University Press.

Taylor, C., Appiah, K. A., Habermas, J., Rockefeller, S. C., Walzer, M., & Wolf, S. (1994). *Multiculturalism: Examining the politics of recognition*. Princeton, NJ: Princeton University Press.

Part
II

4

Qualitative Case Study Methods in Newsroom Research and Reporting:

The Case of the Akron Beacon Journal

Tanni Haas
Brooklyn College

INTRODUCTION

The qualitative case study occupies a unique position in the social sciences in that it is defined more by its object of inquiry (the case) than by the particular research methods used to study it. The case study, as Stake (1994, p. 236) noted: "is not a methodological choice, but a choice of object to be studied." The object can be an individual, a group, an organization, even an entire community, among many other things. Thus, depending on the specific goals of the study and characteristics of the object of inquiry, the qualitative case-study researcher will often use different research methods simultaneously, including participant observation, in-depth interviews, focus group discussions, document analysis, and archival research. Some of the most well-known case studies have been written by journalists, have been about journalism, or both, notably Bernstein and Woodward's (1974) account of the Watergate cover-up and Cantril and Herzog's (1940) description of the panic caused by Orson Welles' 1938 Halloween radio broadcast of a fictional invasion of Martians. Nevertheless, little scholarly attention has been paid to how journalists can apply principles of qualitative case-study research for purposes of newsroom research and reporting. This is both surprising and unfortunate considering that case-study scholars have developed practical guidelines that journalists can use to plan, execute, and evaluate their research and reporting.

While no universally agreed upon definition of case-study research exists, most scholars agree that its primary goal is to obtain an in-depth understanding of a complex phenomenon, both in and of itself and in relation to its broader context (see Gillham, 2000; Merriam, 2001; Patton, 2002). Indeed, one of the most prominent case-study scholars, Yin, defined the case study as "an empirical inquiry that investigates a contemporary phenomenon within its real-life context, especially when the boundaries between phenomenon and context are not clearly evident" (Yin, 1994, p. 13). This definition also highlights how the case study differs from other widely used research strategies, notably experiments and surveys. In contrast to the experiment, where the investigator deliberately manipulates the context (or condition) within which certain predetermined variables can be studied, the case-study researcher studies the phenomenon within its naturally occurring environment. Unlike the survey, where the investigator often gathers relatively small amounts of data about a large number of cases, usually individual respondents, the case-study researcher often gathers large amounts of data about one or a few cases (see Gomm, Hammersley, & Foster, 2000, pp. 2–4 for development). Moreover, where the ethnographer typically aims at a holistic understanding of a given phenomenon, often a specific culture or subculture, the case-study researcher is particularly interested in understanding the complex interplay between a given phenomenon and its broader context.

Although many social scientists acknowledge the advantages of case-study research, notably the ability to capture the complexity of a phenomenon within its real-life context, this research strategy has not been without its critics. The most frequently voiced criticism is that the study of one or a few cases does not provide a basis for scientific generalization. Several retorts have been leveled in response to that charge. While some scholars argue that the goal of case-study research is not to generalize to a larger population of cases but to obtain an in-depth understanding of the particular case or cases (e.g., Stake, 1994), others argue that case studies, like experiments, are generalizable to theoretical propositions and not to populations. Yin (1994, p. 10), for example, argued that the case study, like the experiment, does not represent a sample, and that the investigator's goal is to generalize theories (analytic generalization) and not to enumerate frequencies (statistical generalization).

This chapter offers an overview of the qualitative case study as a research strategy and its relevance to contemporary journalistic practice. Following a description of the various steps involved in preparing the case study, different data collection and analysis techniques and the final development of the case report are discussed. The chapter concludes by examining an actual journalistic case study, the *Akron* (Ohio) *Beacon Journal*'s widely acclaimed race-relations series "A Question of Color," that illustrates many of the practical challenges of doing qualitative case-study research.

SELECTING THE CASE

The first and most important step in the qualitative case-study research process is to formulate the research questions (Yin, 1994) or issues (Stake, 1994) to be investigated. Regardless of whether the investigator aims to work deductively to test theory or inductively to generate theory, case-study scholars agree that the study should be based on one or more research questions–issues. These questions–issues, in turn, should guide both the selection of the case or cases to be investigated and research methods used (see Gall, Borg, & Gall, 1996; Gomm et al., 2000; Scholz & Tietje, 2002).

To identify the research questions–issues that are most significant for a given investigation, and to gain some precision in formulating them, reviewing the literature on the topic is useful. While a thorough review of the pertinent literature may lead to one or more research questions–issues, the investigator should not hesitate to modify, or even replace, them as the study unfolds. Since the goal of qualitative case-study research is to capture the complexity of a phenomenon within its real-life context, the investigator is expected to refine continuously the research questions–issues as new and previously unexpected aspects of the phenomenon come to light, a process that Partlett and Hamilton (1976) called progressive focusing. This process resembles that of the journalist who starts out his or her investigation of a given topic with a preliminary idea of what it entails, but upon researching it in greater detail, comes to realize that it contains other, more significant issues than originally anticipated.

When designing the study, the investigator also needs to choose between a single and a multiple case-study design (see Yin, 1994), of either holistic or embedded character (see Scholz & Tietje, 2002). The single case-study design is appropriate when the investigator is able to identify: (a) a critical case (a case that meets all the conditions for testing a theory); (b) an extreme case (a case so extraordinary that it warrants investigation in and of itself); or (c) a revelatory case (a case that offers the opportunity to study a phenomenon previously inaccessible to scientific investigation; Yin, 1994, pp. 38–40). The multiple case-study design, in contrast, is appropriate when the goal of the investigation is to replicate the results obtained from different cases. Such replication can either be aimed at producing similar results (literal replication) or at producing contrasting results for predictable reasons (theoretical replication; Yin, 1994, p. 46). Thus, while literal replication requires the investigator to select cases that replicate each other and produce corroborating evidence, theoretical replication requires the investigator to select cases that cover different theoretical conditions or produce contrasting results for predictable, theoretical reasons. For example, one may consider the proposition that an increase in computer use in newsrooms will occur when such technologies are used for both administrative and journalistic applications, but not for either alone. To pursue this proposition in a multiple case-study design, two or more cases may be selected in which both types of applications are present to determine whether, in fact, computer use did increase over a period of time (i.e., literal replication). Two or more additional cases may be selected in which only administrative applications are present, the prediction being little increase in computer use (i.e., theoretical replication). Finally, two or more additional cases may be selected in which only journalistic applications are present, with the same prediction of little increase in computer use, but for different reasons than the administrative-only cases (i.e., theoretical replication). If this entire pattern of results across the multiple cases is indeed found, the six or more cases, in the aggregate, would provide substantial support for the initial proposition.

Both single and multiple case-study designs can be holistic or embedded in character. Whereas in a holistic case-study the investigator treats the case as a single unit of analysis, in an embedded case-study the investigator focuses attention on two or more units of analysis within the case (Scholz & Tietje, 2002, pp. 9–10). Units of analysis refer to the cases being investigated and can be, depending on the particular purpose of the study, an individual, a group, a department, or even an entire organization, among many other things. Again, while the investigator may decide upon the appropriate unit(s) of analysis prior to data collection, he or she should remain open to modifications as the actual investigation unfolds.

Besides formulating relevant research questions–issues, selecting one or more cases to be investigated, and determining the appropriate unit(s) of analysis, case-study scholars recommend that two additional steps be taken before data collection begins: preparing a case-study protocol and conducting one or more pilot studies. Yin (1994, pp. 63–74) suggested that the case-study protocol, which is intended to guide the investigator in carrying out the case study, should include: (a) an overview of the case-study project (background information about project objectives, substantive issues to be investigated, relevant readings about the topic); (b) field procedures (major tasks in collecting data, potential sources of information, procedural reminders); (c) case-study questions (research questions to be investigated, table shells for the array of data collected, potential sources of information for each research question); and (d) a guide for the case report (outline of the report, format for the narrative, bibliographical information, and documentation). While it is always desirable to have a case-study protocol, it is particularly important when conducting a multiple case-study, a study comprising multiple investigators, or both. The case-study protocol may help strengthen the reliability of findings by ensuring that the investigator uses the same data collection procedures for each case, multiple investigators follow the same data collection procedures when studying one or more cases, or both. For journalists who often investigate multiple cases as part of a single investigation and frequently work in teams on large-scale, complex investigations, it is thus particularly important to prepare a comprehensive case-study protocol prior to data collection.

The final preparatory step is to conduct one or more pilot studies, which may help the investigator refine data collection plans with respect to both the content of the data to be collected (substantive issues) and the procedures to be followed in collecting the data (methodological issues; Yin, 1994, pp. 74–76). While the pilot study or studies may be selected according to different criteria, including convenience, access, and geographical proximity, the purpose remains the same: to help the investigator refine the overall research design and develop relevant lines of questions. Although potentially costly, it is useful for journalists to conduct one or more pilot studies, especially prior to embarking on a large-scale, complex investigation, because it may ultimately save resources by clarifying the overall goal of the investigation and particular data collection procedures to be followed in the field.

COLLECTING THE DATA

The qualitative case study is, as previously discussed, defined more by its object of inquiry than by the particular research methods used to study it. Thus, the defining characteristic of the data collection process is not which particular methods are used, but rather how those methods are used. While different case studies call for the application of different research methods, including participant observation, in-depth interviews, focus group discussions, document analysis, and archival research, there are at least three data collection principles that should be followed for all case studies: (a) triangulation of research findings; (b) creation of a case-study database; and (c) maintenance of a logical chain of evidence.

One of the most important principles of qualitative case-study research is the use of multiple, as opposed to single, sources of information (see Gillham, 2000; Stake, 1994; Yin, 1994). The use of multiple sources of information helps the investigator develop what Yin (1994, p. 34) calls convergent lines of inquiry. That is, any fact or conclusion pertaining to the case study is likely to be more convincing or accurate if it can be corroborated by three or more different sources of information. It also helps address potential problems of construct validity (the development of correct operational measures for the concepts being studied) insofar as multiple sources of information provide multiple measures of the same phenomenon. The use of multiple sources of information, or data source triangulation, is a common journalistic practice whereby journalists attempt to corroborate the views expressed by certain sources of information by consulting other sources.

While data source triangulation is common journalistic practice, other important kinds of triangulation are less common and more likely to be at odds with mainstream journalistic assumptions and practices. Besides data source triangulation, case-study scholars recommend methodological triangulation, theory triangulation, and investigator triangulation (see Denzin, 1989; Merriam, 2001; Patton, 2002). In contrast to data source triangulation, which merely requires the investigator to confirm given findings by consulting at least two other sources of information, methodological triangulation requires the investigator to use different research methods to confirm those findings. In practice, this implies that the journalist would need to corroborate the views expressed during in-depth interviews with study participants through other means such as participant observation and document analysis. For example, if the subject of a story claims to act in a certain way, the journalist would need to confirm the claim through actual observation of that person's behavior (i.e., participant observation) and by consulting documents that verify the claim (i.e., document analysis). Theory triangulation is possibly more challenging in that it would require the journalist to analyze the data collected from different, even contrasting theoretical perspectives rather than settle for one theoretical perspective in advance. This would require the journalist to move beyond the current practice of fitting the data collected into predetermined story formats and, instead, remain open to alternative story formats emanating from the data itself. The final and possibly most challenging means of corroborating research findings, investigator triangulation, would require the journalist to share the findings with colleagues to remain open to alternative interpretations of their significance. Investigator triangulation is at odds with mainstream journalists' self-understanding as professionals who are capable of collecting, interpreting, and verifying information without outside interference.

Besides using various means of triangulation, case-study scholars recommend that the investigator create a formal, presentable case-study database (Yin, 1994) or case record (Patton, 2002) that organizes and documents all the data collected. By separating documentation into two different collections, the database and the final case report, it becomes possible for other investigators to review the evidence directly and not be limited to the written report, thereby increasing the reliability of the entire study. In practical terms, this would require the journalist not only to keep a separate log of the data collected during the investigation, but also to organize it in such a way that other journalists, whether actively involved in the investigation or not, would be able to evaluate the evidence cited in the final case report. While the development of a case-study database would help increase the reliability of the study, the sharing of its content with other journalists may violate the widely held norm of confidentiality.

Finally, Yin (1994) suggested that to increase the reliability of the case report, the investigator should maintain a logical chain of evidence that makes explicit the links between the research questions asked, the data collected, and the conclusions drawn. The principle is to allow an external observer, the reader of the case study, to follow the derivation of any evidence from initial research questions to ultimate case-study conclusions. The external observer should be able to trace the investigator's steps in either direction, from questions to conclusions or from conclusions back to questions. Thus, the final case report should make sufficient citation to the relevant portions of the case-study database, such as by citing specific observations, interviews, and documents. The case-study database, upon inspection, should reveal the actual evidence and also indicate the circumstances under which the evidence was collected. These circumstances, in turn, should be consistent with the specific procedures outlined in the case-study protocol, and a reading of the case-study protocol should indicate the links between the content of the protocol and the initial research questions. One way of strengthening the chain of evidence is to create and publicize a Web site containing additional information that for space considerations could not be included in the story itself.

ANALYZING THE EVIDENCE

As with all qualitative research, there is no single moment at which the analysis of the data collected begins and no commonly agreed upon method of analysis for qualitative case-study research. Indeed, data analysis is an iterative process that begins when the first data is collected and continues as emergent insights and tentative hypotheses direct subsequent phases of data collection. Yet, while data analysis occurs simultaneously with data collection and depends in large part on the interpretive training and skills of the investigator, certain data analysis strategies have been developed that are particularly useful for qualitative case-study research, notably pattern-matching, explanation-building, and time-series analysis (see Yin, 1994).

The first data analysis strategy, pattern-matching, is a deductive approach that requires the investigator to compare an empirically derived pattern with one or more theoretically based ones. The investigator attempts to find empirical evidence in the case that each causal link in the theoretical model is significant and of the expected sign (i.e., a positive or negative correlation). In a multiple case-study design, replication can be claimed if two or more cases are shown to support the same theory. The empirical results may be considered even more robust if two or more cases support the same theory, but do not support one or more equally plausible, rival theories. The best rival theory is not simply the absence of the target theory or hypothesis (i.e., the null hypothesis), but a theory that attempts to explain the same outcome differently. In practical terms, pattern-matching would thus require the journalist to identify one or more theories with which to compare the empirical results of the investigation. If, for example, the goal of the investigation is to explain why white students on average receive higher grades than black students in the public schools of a given city, the journalist would not only need to find empirical evidence to substantiate that claim, but also identify one or more theories that explain those educational disparities. The results would be considered even more robust if the journalist is able to find the same educational disparities in several different cities, find empirical support for one particular theory, or both, but not one or more equally plausible, rival ones.

In contrast to pattern-matching, which essentially requires the investigator to use one or more theories as templates with which to compare the empirical results of the study, explanation-building is an inductive approach that requires the investigator to use the data collected to build up an explanation about the case or cases. Instead of starting out with one or more theories to be tested, the investigator tries to generate theory from the data collected. To explain the case is to stipulate a set of causal links about it, in which an important aspect is to entertain one or more plausible, rival explanations. The goal is to show that these rival explanations cannot be built, given the actual data collected. Explanation-building can also be used as a supplement to pattern-matching, as when used to generate a new, more plausible model after pattern-matching has disconfirmed an initial model. Returning to the previous example, explanation-building would require the journalist to attempt to build up an explanation for the observed educational disparities between white and black students rather than compare the results with one or more theories. In building up a likely explanation, the journalist would also need to consider one or more rival explanations.

The third data analysis strategy, time-series analysis, requires the investigator not only to show that the existence, sign, and magnitude of each causal link in the theoretical model is as expected, but also to confirm the temporal sequence of events relating to the variables in the model. This requires the investigator to conduct observations at three or more points in time, not merely before and after observations, in order to establish that the magnitude of a given effect is outside the range of normal fluctuations of the time-series. The essential logic of time-series analysis is thus to compare a trend of data points with: (a) a theoretically based trend specified before the onset of the investigation, versus (b) some rival trend, also specified earlier, versus (c) any trend based on some artifact or threat to internal validity. In contrast to pattern-matching and explanation-building, time-series analysis would thus require the journalist in the previous example to show not only that educational disparities exist, but also that those disparities are not based on certain regularly occurring fluctuations, such as changes in the amount of financial support offered black students from the local board of education. The journalist, in a word, would need to study educational disparities between white and black students over a sustained period of time to rule out potentially significant factors impacting the distribution of grades.

Regardless of which specific analytic strategy is selected, the investigator must do everything to ensure that the analysis is of the highest quality. Yin (1994, pp. 123–124) suggested that three principles underlie all good qualitative case-study analysis. First, the analysis must show that it relied on all the relevant evidence. The analytic strategies, including the development of rival theories, must be exhaustive. The analysis should show how it sought as much evidence as was available, and the interpretations should account for all of this evidence and leave no loose ends. Second, the analysis should include all major rival explanations. If someone else has an alternative explanation for one or more of the findings, this explanation should be included as a rival explanation. Third, the analysis should address the most significant aspects of the case study. Whether it is a single or multiple case-study, the analysis must demonstrate the best analytic skills if it is to be on target.

WRITING THE REPORT

As with data analysis, there is no particular moment at which the investigator begins writing on the final case report and no universally agreed upon way of organizing it. Indeed, as the investigator collects data, he or she is expected to create a case-study database that forms the basis for the latter development of the case report. While there is no universally agreed upon way of organizing the final case report, case-study scholars agree on the importance of certain preparatory steps, notably the need for the investigator to share his or her field notes with study participants prior to, during the writing of the case report, or both, a procedure commonly referred to as member checking (see Gillham, 2000; Merriam, 2001; Yin, 1994).

Since one of the goals of qualitative case-study research is to capture the phenomenon under investigation from the insider (or emic) perspective of study participants themselves, it is important that the investigator have participants examine drafts of writing where their actions, words are featured, or both, sometimes when first written up but usually when no further data will be collected from them. The goal of this procedure, Yin (1994, pp. 144–146) noted, is to validate the essential facts and evidence presented in the case report. Thus, from a methodological perspective, the corrections made through this process will enhance the accuracy of the case study, hence increasing its construct validity. While clearly important, the procedure of member checking is likely to be at odds with the mainstream journalistic ideal of independence, or the belief that the form and content of reporting should be determined by journalists themselves rather than their sources of information or any other nonjournalistic actors.

If member checking is at odds with prevailing journalistic assumptions and practices, the formats commonly used for organizing the final case report have parallels among contemporary reporting genres. The two most common formats for organizing the final case report are what Gall et al. (1996) called the analytic and reflective formats, a distinction that resembles Van Maanen's (1988) distinction between realist and confessional ethnographic tales. The major characteristic of the analytic case report is an objective writing style in which the investigator's voice is silent or minimized, and there is a conventional organization of topics: introduction, literature review, methodology, results, and conclusion. This is essentially the same style and organization used to report quantitative research. The reflective case report, in contrast, typically uses various narrative devices to bring the case alive, and the investigator's voice is clearly heard.

The analytic-reflective distinction mirrors the common journalistic distinction between hard news and feature writing. While the hard news story is typically told from the vantage point of a disembodied and disembedded writer, the feature story typically describes how the writer came to know the subject matter of the story and positions the writer as a central element of the story.

Regardless of whether the investigator uses an analytic or reflective format for the final case report, it is important that the report include what Erickson

(1986) called particular description, general description, and interpretive commentary. Particular description consists of quotes from interviews and field notes and narrative vignettes. General description explains to the reader whether those quotes and vignettes are typical of the data set as a whole. Interpretive commentary offers readers a framework for understanding both forms of description. While journalists typically include much particular and general description in their reporting, they often do not include enough interpretive commentary. In the scholarly literature on journalism, this neglect is commonly referred to as a lack of context. Taken together, the inclusion of particular description, general description, and interpretive commentary would allow readers to engage in what Stake (1994) called naturalistic generalization, that is, to reflect on whether the views expressed in the final case report resonate with their own experiences.

"A QUESTION OF COLOR"

The *Akron Beacon Journal* launched in late February 1993 a 10-month-long race-relations series called "A Question of Color." This series, which subsequently was awarded the 1994 Pulitzer Prize for public service journalism, comprised 30 articles that appeared in five installments. While the series was not originally planned as a qualitative case study, it adhered to many principles of this kind of research.

It is worth noting, first, that consonant with principles of qualitative case-study research, the series was based on an explicitly stated research issue. In the inaugurating article, *Beacon Journal* editors explained that the goal of the series was to examine "the impact [of race] on life in the Akron-Canton area ... [H]ow blacks and whites think and feel about themselves and one another" ("Race: The great divide," 1993, p. A1). While the editors did not, as case-study scholars recommend, ground the series in any pertinent literature on the subject, they did situate it within a broader contemporary context. They explained that the series was inspired by the racially motivated assault on Rodney King and the subsequent riots in Los Angeles a couple of years earlier.

Although the research issue underlying the series was not subsequently modified as a result of the actual investigations, important changes in the scope of the series did occur, changes that mirror Partlett and Hamilton's (1976) call for progressive focusing on the part of the investigator. Disappointed with the lack of public attention to the first installment, it was decided, as Dale Allen, one of the editors responsible for the series, recounted, to go "beyond consciousness raising to enable readers who wanted to be part of the solution to come together to set a community agenda" (quoted in Merritt, 1998, p. 99). In announcing the series' expansion (Dotson & Allen, 1993, pp.

A1, A11), the Beacon Journal promised to help involve local civic groups "in the process of improving race relations" (p. A1). Members of local civic groups were encouraged to contact the newspaper if they were interested in signing up for "multiracial partnerships that can work toward common goals" (p. A11). The Beacon Journal hired two part-time facilitators, a retired minister who was white and a retired school principal who was black. The two became responsible for matching up groups with shared interests.

To examine the impact of racism and racial inequality, the Beacon Journal used what case-study scholars call a multiple case-study design (Yin, 1994) with embedded subunits of analysis (Scholz & Tietje, 2002). Instead of treating Akron as one overarching case, Beacon Journal reporters examined each of the five counties of Akron separately and, for each county, focused attention on specific issues, notably housing, education, employment, and crime. The selection of cases (e.g., counties) and subunits of analysis (e.g., issues) resulted from the actual investigations, a practice consistent with principles of qualitative case-study research. Based on census data and a large-scale telephone survey with local residents, Beacon Journal reporters documented that the five counties of Akron were differently affected by racism and racial inequality. The specific issues under investigation were selected through focus group discussions with local white and black residents and in-depth interviews with various experts on racism and racial inequality, notably local government officials and university professors.

While Beacon Journal reporters thus used methodological triangulation to plan their investigations (e.g., telephone surveys, focus group discussions, and in-depth interviews), they did not, as case-study scholars recommend, compare the data collected with any preexisting theories of racism and racial inequality (e.g., pattern-matching) or use the data collected to generate a theory of racism and racial inequality of their own (i.e., explanation-building). Instead, they merely summarized their findings with a minimum of editorial commentary. This, in turn, may be attributed to the widely held belief that journalists should help inform, rather than form, public opinion.

While Beacon Journal reporters did not use any formal data analysis strategies, they did report the findings of their investigations in conformity with certain principles of qualitative case-study writing. Most important, the 30 articles that comprised the series included what Erickson (1986) called particular description, general description, and interpretive commentary. Taken as a whole, the series included articles that: (a) quoted at length the views and experiences of local residents and experts (particular description); (b) reported on whether those views–experiences were illustrative of the larger sample of participants (general description); and (c) placed the views–experiences expressed within a broader framework through reference to relevant census data and the results from the telephone survey (interpretive commentary).

Moreover, many of the articles framed the issues examined as open-ended questions rather than as closed-ended answers, thereby encouraging readers to reflect on whether those issues resonate with their own experiences, a practice consistent with what Stake (1994) called naturalistic generalization. For example, in an article exploring potential discriminatory practices within the school system of Akron, the reporters asked the following rhetorical questions after having discussed why white students on average receive higher grades than black students:

> When does a "C" reflect racism by the professor and when does it simply reflect "C" work? Who should decide? Who decides what role African cultures played in the evolution of Western civilization? If historians have determined the role was minimal, is it racist to portray it that way? Or is it simply good history? How much does it matter if all or most of the historians are white? (Kirksey, Jenkins, & Paynter, 1993, p. A14)

While *Beacon Journal* reporters quoted at length the views and experiences of both local residents and experts, they retained the emic perspectives of local residents while mediating the perspectives of experts. A quantitative content analysis of sourcing patterns found that not only were considerably more local residents cited than government officials and university professors combined (103 and 63, respectively), the testimony of local residents also appeared more in the form of full quotations than partial quotes–paraphrases. The ratio of this latter measure was 3.28, 0.65, and 0.90 for local residents, government officials, and university professors, respectively (see Haas, 2001 for development).

To their credit, *Beacon Journal* editors decided to corroborate further the testimony of both local residents and experts. Toward the end of the series, the editors publicly responded to the views and experiences expressed by inviting 17 of the newspaper's editors and reporters, nine white and eight black, to participate in focus group discussions about the newspaper's coverage of white and black crime. Each participant was asked to review 2 months' worth of newspapers, paying particular attention to the crime coverage. During one evening in late December 1993, three focus group discussions were held: one all white, one all black and, later that evening, one including all the participants. The article reporting on the results of those discussions (see Dyer, 1993) not only recounted the participants' views at length, but also in their own words, thereby retaining the participants' emic perspectives and allowing readers to compare the opinions expressed by the editors and reporters with those of local residents and experts.

CONCLUSION

The prior discussion suggests that qualitative case-study research is not an alien approach to newsroom research and reporting, but rather represents a description of journalism done well. Indeed, the very purpose of case-study research, to obtain an in-depth understanding of a complex phenomenon, both in and of itself and in relation to its broader context, is central to some of the best contemporary journalism, notably explanatory journalism with its focus on elucidating complex issues and their relations to wider societal developments. Case-study scholars have developed practical guidelines for case selection, data collection and analysis, and report writing that journalists can use to plan, execute, and evaluate their research and reporting. Yet, as the prior discussion and example of the *Akron Beacon Journal*'s "A Question of Color" series suggest, the conduct of qualitative case-study research poses certain challenges to the practice of journalism, some of which are at odds with mainstream journalistic assumptions and practices. These challenges include remaining open to alternative story formats emanating from the data collected itself, sharing research findings with colleagues and study participants prior to publication, and using research findings to either test preexisting theories or generate new ones.

REFERENCES

Anonymous (1993, February 28). Race: The great divide. *Akron Beacon Journal*, p. A1.

Bernstein, C., & Woodward, B. (1974). *All the president's men*. New York: Simon & Schuster.

Cantril, H., & Herzog, H. (1940). *Invasion from Mars*. Princeton, NJ: Princeton University Press.

Denzin, N. (1989). *The research act: A theoretical introduction to sociological methods*. Thousand Oaks, CA: Sage.

Dotson, J., & Allen, D. (1993, May 2). You're invited to help promote racial harmony. *Akron Beacon Journal*, pp. A1, A11.

Dyer, B. (1993, December 29). The struggle for balance. *Akron Beacon Journal*, pp. A1, A6–A7.

Erickson, F. (1986). Qualitative methods in research on teaching. In M. Whittrock (Ed.), *Handbook of research on teaching*, (pp. 119–161). New York: Macmillan.

Gall, M., Borg, W., & Gall, J. (1996). *Educational research: An introduction*. White Plains, NY: Longman.

Gillham, B. (2000). *Case study research methods*. London: Continuum.

Gomm, R., Hammersley, M., & Foster, P. (2000). *Case study method: Key issues, key texts*. Thousand Oaks, CA: Sage.

Haas, T. (2001). Public journalism project falls short of stated goals. *Newspaper Research Journal, 22*, 58–70.

Kirksey, R., Jenkins, C., & Paynter, B. (1993, August 22). Public education, win few, lose many. *Akron Beacon Journal*, pp. A1, A4–A5.

Merriam, S. (2001). *Qualitative research and case study applications in education*. San Francisco: Jossey-Bass.

Merritt, D. (1998). *Public journalism and public life: Why telling the news is not enough*. Mahwah, NJ: Lawrence Erlbaum Associates.

Partlett, M., & Hamilton, D. (1976). Evaluation as illumination: A new approach to the study of innovative programs. *Evaluation Studies Review Annual, 1*, 140–157.

Patton, M. (2002). *Qualitative research and evaluation methods*. Thousand Oaks, CA: Sage.

Scholz, R., & Tietje, O. (2002). *Embedded case study methods: Integrating quantitative and qualitative knowledge*. Thousand Oaks, CA: Sage.

Stake, R. (1994). Case studies. In N. Denzin & Y. Lincoln (Eds.), *Handbook of qualitative research*, (pp. 236–247). Thousand Oaks, CA: Sage.

Van Maanen, J. (1988). *Tales of the field: On writing ethnography*. Chicago: University of Chicago Press.

Yin, R. (1994). *Case study research: Design and methods*. Thousand Oaks, CA: Sage.

5

Focus Groups
Newsroom Style

Susan Willey
Florida Atlantic University

When staffers at the *Savannah Morning News* began their 1998 election coverage, they decided to sponsor backyard barbecues around the city. Reporters tapped their sources within a strong network of neighborhood associations and asked people to hold a barbecue for 10 to 15 of their neighbors. The newspaper provided the food. The neighbors provided the conversation.

The insights gained from listening to these conversations ultimately drove the newspaper's coverage of the campaign and changed the focus of the coverage. As reporters listened to the people talk, they realized the primary area of concern centered on the city's drainage problems. The candidates had been talking about housing, an issue that had much less salience with the citizens. The backyard barbecue conversations were a reality check on what earlier polls revealed and what candidates were saying, said *Morning News* Managing Editor Daniel Suwyn. "We have a mantra in our newsroom," Suwyn said. "We are only as good as the quality of our conversations" (personal communication, March 6, 2002).

Journalists are discovering that by listening to citizen conversations they can enrich their news reports, and that realization is changing newsgathering methods. The Savannah newspaper is one of a growing number of news media organizations that are tapping creative research methods in their efforts to understand their communities and citizens' views better. From backyard barbecues and advisory panels to town meetings and newly defined focus groups, the news media are taking an increasingly active role in promoting citizen participation and community action. Bloor, Frankland, Thomas, and Robson (2001) called this kind of group methodology "a potential tool of a new citizen science" (p. 98).

Yet the decades-old focus group methodology of the social sciences does not always fit well with newsroom needs. Instead, editors, and reporters are transforming the old models into what is becoming a new form of journalism research, a crossbreed of several group methodologies specifically designed for newsrooms' research requirements. Journalists are concerned less about the science of research than about the information they obtain through the methods. In a speech to the Newspaper Association of America Research Conference, Knight-Ridder executive Virginia Dodge Fielder argued that it is not the "wonderfully creative, groundbreaking research" that matters in news reports. It's whether journalists are able to move beyond the structured research project and connect with their community, encourage public deliberation on important issues, and obtain sufficient information to inform readers and encourage citizen action (Fielder, 1995).

The newsroom venture into group conversations leads reporters onto the streets and into the neighborhoods. Focus group techniques made inroads into newsrooms during the early 1990s, about the time journalism practitioners and academicians started their own conversations about journalism's purpose and role in a democratic society. As the journalism reform movement—known as public or civic journalism—gained momentum, focus groups and community conversations became definitive elements in newsgathering (Merritt, 1998; Rosen, 1999). More than a decade later, newsroom focus group methods have been refined and redefined, moving beyond listening techniques and interviews into community partnerships and citizen action. The key focus was, and still is, on citizen conversations, which not only reconnect journalists to their communities, but also help involve citizens in the democratic process. From its inception, civic or public journalism encouraged experimentation and group methods became part of the newsgathering efforts (Merritt, 1998).

This chapter looks at several reporting projects and group research methods used by editors and reporters in their newsgathering processes. These include: the *Savannah Morning News* and its "Vision 2010" project; *The Lawrence Journal-World* and its "Finding Common Ground" series; and *The Cincinnati Enquirer's* massive reporting project on race relations, "Neighbor to Neighbor."

As these examples illustrate, the term focus group has many meanings in the newsroom. The newspapers in the forthcoming examples used a mixture of methodologies, some that closely followed focus group procedures and others that deviated from the traditional structured form. The research purpose was to give journalists what they needed, insight and information to enhance their news coverage. Previous research shows that journalists tend toward a combination of group interview techniques to get information. Although the groups fall under the general categories of group interviews or focus groups, the designs of the groups themselves are often distinct, according to the newsroom's research purpose (Willey, 1997). The same holds true for the newsroom methods in the examples discussed in this chapter.

Newsroom research follows patterns similar to standard qualitative methodology, including defining the research questions, determining the best methods by which to obtain the answers to the questions, and participating in detailed planning as well as comprehensive data gathering. There is also some form of triangulation in the research process. Reporters use variants of qualitative methodology such as focus groups, community conversations, and town meetings. They also rely on more traditional methods such as information gained from polls and surveys, documents, and individual interviews to verify their findings.

Unlike the social scientist, newsrooms do not claim to create a scientific study. Instead, they analyze the data gathered in a journalistic fashion for use in their stories. As in scientific research, often the information gleaned at the beginning of the project spawns more questions and, in some cases, changes the research question itself.

To understand the evolution in these newsgathering methods, it is necessary to clarify the term focus groups and look at its roots and uses in the social sciences. Because newsrooms are experimenting beyond group newsgathering efforts into community partnerships and action, it is important to consider also the philosophical underpinnings of the qualitative methodology of action research, which is seeing renewed interest among several academic disciplines (Coghlan & Brannick, 2001; Stringer, 1999).

ACADEMIC FOCUS GROUPS

Focus groups have been used in marketing research since the 1920s and utilized for decades in a variety of social science research (Frey & Fontana, 1991; Krueger, 1988; Morgan, 1993). However, Fern (2001) wrote that, even into the late 1970s, there were few disciplines other than marketing using focus group methodology. He distinguished between theory and applied focus group research. Theory-based research falls more within the academic realm and is created for the purpose of generating or affirming theory. Applied research is done primarily for decision-making purposes. Researchers conducting applied research are only concerned about information relating to their specific needs.

The journalist's use of focus groups falls within the applied area and has a different purpose from that of academic studies or media marketing research. Early researchers of the focused interview technique had predicted that its use could easily be expanded into a variety of social science investigation. Merton (1987) suggested in the 1950s that the focused interview is a "generic research technique" that could be "applied in every sphere of human behavior and experience" (p. 562).

Instead of seeking response about a product's appeal or studying media message reception, journalists seek insight into citizens' attitudes, beliefs, and community concerns—their "views of reality" (Frey & Fontana, 1991). The data obtained are used to develop news reports. However, the social science definition of focus group is more precise than the way most journalists use the term. A focus group is a specific type of group in terms of its "purpose, size, composition, and procedures" (Krueger, 1988, p. 18). Social scientists say the focus group is "a nondirective technique that results in the controlled production of a discussion within a group of people who do not know one another, but who share similar characteristics" (Flores & Alonso, 1995, pp. 84–113). The focus group is designed for discovery and to answer the how and why questions. Focus groups not only help answer research questions but also generate new questions (Morgan, 1993).

Once academic researchers decide to use focus group methodology, a target population is determined and a participant profile developed. Random telephone surveys help locate potential group members, who are sometimes offered small monetary incentives to participate. Because the idea is to validate the information collected by comparing the findings from one group to the others, no legitimate study can be conducted with only one focus group. Four or five groups, each with about 8–10 participants, are usually sufficient to obtain the data necessary for the research (Flores & Alonso, 1995; Frey & Fontana, 1993). Focus groups work best with participants from homogeneous populations. The small number of people participating and the groups' homogeneity help create a comfortable and nonthreatening atmosphere that encourages discussion (Knodel, 1993).

It is important that focus group members perceive researchers as unbiased to enable the free flow of conversation, which strengthens validity. The group meets at a neutral location, and the moderator is someone who is not connected to the research endeavor. Participants are asked to sign a consent form that may include permission to videotape the discussion, to allow people to observe the interaction behind a one-way mirror, or to publish the conversations (Flores & Alonso, 1995). Researchers must decide how to address confidentiality, an important issue in focus group research. Usually, participants are assured their names will not be revealed in the research report.

The qualitative data obtained through focus group research may be analyzed manually or through computerized textual analysis programs. However, focus group researchers remind us that the purpose is not to quantify the data, rather to understand the why of what was said (Morgan, 1993). By cross-checking notes and referring to tape recordings, researchers identify patterns or themes in the conversations. To enhance validity, the moderator may verify key points made in the discussion or ask group members to make a final statement. The moderator and research team meet immediately after the focus group session to discuss the findings. This debriefing is sometimes tape-recorded for future reference. In addition, focus group data are often used in triangulation with other methods such as surveys (Krueger, 1993).

JOURNALISM FOCUS GROUPS

The qualitative methodology of the focus group seems particularly well suited for journalism, but reporters do not necessarily follow the stringent academic guidelines for focus groups. Instead they use hybrid group methodology that fits their needs. For example, the aspect of confidentiality, in journalistic endeavors, may mean that reporters decide, with the participants' permission, to use quotes from group members' discussions. Reporters may decide to listen only to the discussion, take notes, and then contact individual participants at a later date for an on-the-record interview. Sometimes journalists serve as moderators, but in other instances outside moderators are used. The group conversations may be recorded, but it is unlikely that devices such as a one-way mirror would be used in journalistic group methods.

Some newsrooms use group conversations to define the research questions themselves while others use the conversations to refine the question already being investigated. For example, in 1998, when *The Savannah Morning News* decided to do a series called "Aging Matters," that examined various issues facing the city's older population, the editors and staff realized they had little knowledge about the topic. They had to educate themselves first before they could even begin the series so they arranged a series of group meetings, by calling together people from various social service agencies, caregivers, and senior citizens. Reporters asked a general question then took notes as they listened to the conversations.

The University of Missouri School of Journalism did the same thing in 1996 when students embarked on their annual reporting project for *The Missourian*, the university newspaper. That year the project focused on religion in the community, but editors soon discovered that neither students nor faculty had sufficient knowledge about the topic to begin the project. They held a series of meetings with members of various faith groups and asked them to talk about their beliefs, as reporters listened. Faculty and students also convened panel discussions with clergy and academic religious experts. These resource panels allowed the student reporters to ask questions about the complexities of different faiths, which provided them with new information and introduced them to new contacts in the community (Willey, 1997, pp. 21–23).

These kinds of group listening processes not only help educate reporters, but also bring heightened awareness into the kind of values that are operating within targeted groups. Bloor et al. (2001) argued that focus groups are able to shed light on normative understandings and meanings. They provide insights that can be used to interpret survey or polling data, or even to contest the quantitative findings as happened in the Savannah backyard barbecue conversations where group discussions honed in on drainage problems, an issue that was not high on the polling radar screen.

For journalists, focus group methodology has another benefit in that it allows citizens to be participants in the research, or the news report, itself. This helps establish a better rapport between the media and their readers or viewers (Willey, 1997). Focus groups also provide a diversity of new sources for journalists to tap. As Bloor et al. (2001) wrote: "Focus groups have been portrayed as a medium for democratic participation in scientific research" (p. 93). From the beginning, focus groups have generated information on how the public understands or views the world, that can serve as a balance to expert opinion (Bloor et al. 2001). This helps balance journalists' reports. Yankelovich (1991) argued that journalists tend to dismiss citizen insights and instead use expert sources.

In his book *Coming to Public Judgment: Making Democracy Work in a Complex World*, Yankelovich (1991) wrote that journalists traditionally cover news from the top down. This expert focus, part of what he calls the "Culture of Technical Control," devalues citizen-based knowledge and understanding, contributes to the disconnect among citizens, media and public institutions, and encourages citizen withdrawal from public life (pp. 8–10). This, then, affects our national conversation on how to address issues of critical importance to our common life (pp. 91–98). For journalists, tapping citizens' knowledge helps bridge this gap and, at the same time, encourages talk among participants. Focus groups can help facilitate citizen participation during the news media's newsgathering process and, as can be seen in the project examples here, they may also encourage citizen action.

Focus group adherents say that the first thing to do is determine the purpose of the group. Once that is defined, several other elements come into play to create a successful group methodology. Krueger (1988) cited several factors that can influence the quality of focus group research: clarity of purpose, appropriate environment, sufficient resources, appropriate participants, skillful moderator, effective questions, careful data handling, systematic and verifiable analysis, appropriate presentation, and finally, "honoring the participant, the client and the method" (p. 67). In general, newsrooms appear to adhere to nearly all of these criteria in planning and creating their reporting projects, except for journalists the data analysis is less focused on scientific rigor to generate theory than on the information needed for the news stories.

There are several advantages to using group methodology. By bringing together groups of people who share their views, beliefs, and feelings about specific issues, participants begin interacting with one another. This is part of the focusing element in focus group methodology. The objective is to encourage discussion (Bloor, et al., 2001). During group conversations, one person's comment may spark other comments and participants become fully involved in the discussion. It is this interaction that results in rich and detailed information about the specific topic, which is considered the primary advantage of focus groups. The insights gained from focus groups also provide important information for reporters and may even affect the framing of the story. As Morgan (1993) wrote:

> Focus groups are not just a different way of doing things we have been doing all along. They may also lead us to change the very way that we are thinking about the problems that interest us. (p. 10)

In general, researchers choose focus groups when there is a power gap between decision makers, experts, or professionals, and the desired target group. For journalists, this can translate into a diversity of voices for their reports. Focus groups also are an excellent tool to use when investigating behavior or issues and when it is difficult for people to find ways to come together to talk. This was the case when *The Cincinnati Enquirer* wanted to begin community conversations about race. Focus groups also serve as a good source of information when researchers are seeking explanations and opinions (Morgan & Krueger, 1993).

Often, the participants' interactive conversation reveals information and issues that had never occurred to the journalist or researcher (Agar & MacDonald, 1995). For the media then, focus groups can be an excellent exploratory technique to seek citizens' opinions on issues that will be part of a proposed news report. The information received from these structured groups helps reporters focus on the topic issues and helps generate story ideas and sources, as well as provide new perspectives.

Because focus group data is qualitative rather than quantitative and because group size is usually limited to encourage conversation, the results cannot be generalized, or applied, to broader populations as survey data are. Unlike public forums or working groups, focus groups are not convened to seek recommendations or solutions. Instead, researchers and reporters use focus groups to listen to opinions and concerns of citizens and to gain new perspectives on problems or issues confronting the targeted group. The conversations are analyzed and the information used to recommend new areas of study or research, or to shed light on the specific issue being investigated. Focus groups also may require a significant investment of time and money, especially if numerous groups are convened. Reporting projects using group methodology involve detailed planning and a strong commitment to allocate sufficient staff time and organizational funds to organize the groups, select and train moderators, and to analyze the data. Sometimes, focus groups and conversations only whet the appetite of participants for future endeavors. They can energize participants to form new groups on their own that may decide to focus on action.

ACTION RESEARCH

One of the criticisms voiced about academic research is that it seems too distanced from people's lives. Action research attempts to bridge this gap. It broadens the research agenda from creating and sharing knowledge to putting that knowledge to work within communities (Coghlan & Brannick, 2001, p. xi). Researchers argue that "action research can help us build a better, freer society" (Greenwood & Levin, 1998, p. 3). Many scholars credit Lewin's work as a social scientist during the 1940s as the origins of action research. His innovative research for the U.S. government during World War II used new methods, now known as natural experiments, which provided study participants with real-life and familiar settings. From the beginning, action research was grounded in societal concerns with the purpose of social change. Lewin saw action research as a way to encourage citizen participation in democracy and to change society for the better (Greenwood & Levin, 1998).

Action research's philosophical roots may be traced to Dewey and his belief in participatory democracy and pragmatic research philosophy (Greenwood & Levin, 1998, p. 72). Public journalism advocates also cite Dewey as the philosophical foundation for their views on journalism's mission in a democratic society (Rosen, 1999). In the 1980s, social scientists Argyris, Putnam, and Smith (1990) examined the concept of "action science," which, they said, "seeks knowledge that serves action" (p. 36). The purpose of such research is to generate practical knowledge that extends into the realm of responsible action, action that serves societal needs (pp. 43, 75). In some cases, focus group participants decide to act on their discussions. This was seen in a health needs-assessment project undertaken in Madison County, North Carolina in 1989 (Plaut, Landis, & Trevor, 1993). Researchers there studied how focus groups not only helped define health care needs, but also helped mobilize the community to make sure those needs were addressed. In this example, focus group methods encouraged community involvement (p. 217).

The examples in this chapter show that media outlets often try to create a knowledge base via their news reports so citizens can be informed when they gather together in group discussions. Yankelovich (1991) said this shifts the focus of news reports from the hierarchical structure of experts to citizen-based knowledge. Greenwood and Levin (1998) saw action research as a way not only to involve citizens in democratic decision-making processes, but also to create an "arena for lively debate ... that respects and enhances the diversity of groups" (p. 11).

Action research is grounded in the idea that new knowledge can be generated from citizens in conversation with one another. This creates a symbiotic relationship among researchers, ordinary citizens, and experts so that a more egalitarian approach to problem solving occurs. Scholars engaged in action research say that, when this happens, the results can be liberating (Greenwood & Levin, 1998, p. 77). Because action research moves beyond conversations into action, the entire process is grounded in participatory democracy. As Greenwood and Levin (1998) wrote: "We argue that AR, in addition to generating valid knowledge and effective social action, embodies democratic ideals in its core practices. This democracy is involved in both the research process and the outcomes of the research" (p. 113).

In the following examples, newsrooms borrow elements from both action research and focus group methodologies to create hybrids of group newsgathering techniques. In some instances, newsrooms foster partnerships with other media or civic organizations to help with the research and, in some situations, to encourage action. The newsroom style of qualitative methodology is clearly operating within each of the examples in this chapter. Reporters and editors decide on the research questions or story project; they identify the best methods to use to obtain the information they are seeking; they identify the population needed for participation; and they create the group and proceed with the research, data analysis and the writing of the news story or series. Throughout the projects, however, reporters and editors maintain control of the reporting endeavor.

THE *SAVANNAH MORNING NEWS*: "VISION 2010"

Group Conversations and Community Action

When the *Savannah Morning News* editors and reporters decided to focus on the area's school system for their "Vision 2010" project, they had difficulty deciding how to approach the series. As Managing Editor Daniel Suwyn said: "We were tired of writing stories that highlighted the failure of schools, so we took what we had learned from our election stories and the 'Aging Matters' stories and decided to turn this over to our community and make them assignment editors" (personal communication, March 6, 2002).

The staff first defined the population needed to participate in the discussion. This included nonprofit and social service sources, parents, educators, and business leaders. Five leaders from these groups were selected and asked to provide the paper with a list of 10 people that fit into these categories. The editors and reporters filled in the gaps and included additional citizens from the city and county governments and the older population. Eventually, they created a diverse group of more than 60 people. This group was then broken down into smaller discussion groups. Identifying sources was a critical step in the reporting process.

The newspaper staff developed what Suwyn calls "relationship trees" to further expand the groups. To do this, reporters identified leaders such as the mayor, and then asked the large group to name three people who had the mayor's ear. "These were the people who we wanted to have the conversations with," Suwyn said (personal communication, March 6, 2002). Once the smaller groups were formed, moderators led the participants in discussion. Reporters listened and took notes. "We wanted to know what the school system looked like from the different perspectives, and what the ideal school system might look like," Suwyn said. "We found what the themes were, and people were surprised to see a lot of common threads. People had gotten caught up in the language, and they didn't see all the common threads" (personal communication, March 6, 2002).

New ideas were generated, and the group members felt empowered to act. Participants visited from 13 to 30 area schools and, with a grant from the Pew Center for Civic Journalism, the newspaper was able to pay the expenses for 15 group members to visit schools in Macon, Houston, Charlotte, Jacksonville, and Washington, DC. These members then reported their findings to the group. The Pew Center for Civic Journalism, established by the Pew Charitable Trusts to encourage experimentation in news reporting and citizen participation in public life, provided grant monies for these civic reporting projects.

The newspaper wrote about all the visits and group activities, spawning more community interest in the endeavor, Suwyn said. "Even then, we had a good dialogue going" (personal communication, March 6, 2002). The early discussions, on the other hand, were difficult. People disagreed and school board officials resisted efforts to change. The commitment of the group members and the newspaper, however, helped turn skepticism into cooperation. Suwyn said that "Vision 2010" is now "so deep in the community" that it has grown measurably beyond the original 60 or so group members (personal communication, March 6, 2002).

The community reporting project also helped trigger citizen action. The Junior League voted to devote its funds and energy to the "Vision 2010" project through 2005. Business leaders in Savannah started a venture capital trust fund and hired a professional fund-raiser to raise $5 million to enable schools to experiment with new approaches that are outside the regular budget capabilities. Schools can apply for money, volunteers, and other resources for specific projects. A portion of the monies will be used to fund programs such as a $10,000 annual award to the most innovative teacher. The project's successes brought more support, and, eventually, even the critics became convinced that it was a worthwhile effort, Suywn said.

Ever since the public, or civic, journalism movement began, scholars have struggled with ways to assess the success of civic journalism projects (Lambeth, Meyer, & Thorson, 1998). Fielder (1995) asserted that reporting projects work when journalists connect with their community, encourage public deliberation and provide sufficient information to inform readers, and encourage citizen action. With the *Savannah Morning News's* project, there was measurable evidence of increased civic participation, Suwyn said. The Pew Center for Civic Journalism agreed and awarded the *News's* "Vision 2010" project the 2002 James K. Batten Award for excellence.

THE *LAWRENCE JOURNAL-WORLD*: "LAWRENCE IS GROWING: FINDING COMMON GROUND"

Neighborhood Discussions and a Town Meeting in a Converged Media Project

When Richard Brack, managing editor of the *Lawrence Journal-World*, looked at his Midwestern town of Lawrence, Kansas, population 80,000, he knew the overriding issue of concern was growth. During the past 10 years, the city had expanded rapidly, and people appeared to be sharply divided into two groups—for or against continued growth. Many people liked the small-town atmosphere of the area and were distressed to see any growth that threatened that way of life. Others were equally adamant that without growth the city would wither away, and its best and brightest students would leave for better jobs elsewhere, as had happened in other similar cities.

Lawrence is a little different from other Kansas farming communities, Brack said (personal communication, March 8, 2002). The University of Kansas is located there, and the city sits in a county that was one of only two in the state that were won by Al Gore during the 2000 presidential election. Brack knew his first step would be to challenge the dualistic framing that existed in the citizens' minds. "I wanted to find out what some of those 'in-the-middle' perspectives were. Who were the stakeholders here?" (personal communication, August 17, 2002).

The goal was simple. The newspaper wanted to talk with various segments of the population and to also find new voices, the so-called middle ground that reporters knew was out there but so far had remained silent. In spring 2002, the newspaper, its online division, and sister cable news operation launched what would be a 6-month project, "Lawrence is Growing: Finding Common Ground." The newspaper chose focus groups as an initial step in the research process. The newspaper staff selected a cross-section of people from the community, including business people, university faculty, students, farmers, and newcomers to the area. Brack described the selection process as "brainstorming" rather than methodological. "We weren't trying to be scientific," Brack said. "We just wanted to get an idea of how people were feeling about growth. And it wasn't just the focus groups. The reporters were going out and walking the neighborhoods to just talk with people to see what was on their minds. We were in the process of gathering information" (personal communication, August 17, 2002). Two focus group meetings were held, each with about 15 participants. The university's counselor to the chancellor moderated the discussions. Reporters listened.

Once the newspaper and television staffs better understood the concerns, they did a 4-week series that introduced the idea of stakeholders in the community, provided a history of growth in the area, and then offered a comparison of other similar communities and discussed how they handled growth. The purpose was to stimulate community conversation. The articles provided a common knowledge base from which to begin. Brack said, "We wanted our readers to know that we wanted to know what they thought. We created bulletin boards and encouraged people to e-mail us" (personal communication, March 8, 2002).

Although the electronic messages did not constitute virtual focus groups, the use of computer correspondence illustrates the potential of using e-mail communication in newsroom newsgathering and research efforts. Social scientists, too, are exploring cyberspace meetings as a way to generate discussion. Although computer-mediated discussion groups have existed in some form for more than 20 years, the academic use of these forums has been limited (Bloor et al., 2001). For the *Journal-World*, the computer conversations served as an additional tool to promote community discussion and illustrated how the convergence of print, broadcast, and online media can contribute to reporting projects. The paper supplemented the data obtained in this forum with online polls, as well as a scientific poll of the population in Douglas County, where Lawrence is situated.

At the end of the 4-week reporting project, the newspaper sponsored a community meeting that was billed as an interactive community forum. More than 200 people attended. Dozens more called in or e-mailed questions or comments. The meeting also was broadcast live in the Lawrence area and replayed several times. The initial 6-week series provided a knowledge base so citizens could be on the "same page" for the ensuing discussion, Brack said (personal communication, March 8, 2002). The series generated interest, as did the online conversations. By the time the town meeting was held, citizens were able to clarify the issues and identify the following areas of concern: schools, traffic, open space, transportation, business and economic development, and social capital, a term used to describe a system of strong links among citizens and associations in the community (Putnam, 2001).

The newspaper then organized a series of neighborhood meetings, located the meeting sites, and found a moderator. The goal was to have each group of about 30–50 people focus on the identified topics and to try to devise a plan to handle growth. At the same time, the local television station, 6News, began broadcasting stories on the specific issues to be addressed at the next meeting. There were companion pieces in print, and discussion was encouraged online. The neighborhood meetings drew good crowds, but people tended to attend only the meetings that were scheduled to address the particular issue in which they were interested, Brack said.

The discussions at each meeting were then reported to the community via the newspaper and the television station. "We wanted to get as many people involved as we could," Brack said. "We wanted to hear from everyone" (personal communication, March 8, 2002). The final town meeting was held in a downtown theater where the findings were presented to citizens and community leaders. The plan, Brack said, represented "the voice of the people" on growth issues. By taking an active role in encouraging community discussion, the newspaper learned that citizens saw the preservation of open space and farmland as the most important issues, but neighbors talking with neighbors had another benefit—growing social capital.

"New relationships formed," Brack said. "There were whole diverse groups of people who were willing to come together and talk about this, and they were surprised at how much common ground there was among them" (personal communication, March 8, 2002). Six months later, Brack said he sees the changes that the reporting project created in the community. "The discourse is a lot more civil now that it was before. People here are still opinionated, but these discussions went a long way to let people know that other viewpoints are valid; and it showed that their newspaper does care about their community" (personal communication, March 8, 2002).

THE CINCINNATI ENQUIRER:
"NEIGHBOR-TO-NEIGHBOR: COMMUNITY CONVERSATIONS ON RACE"

Focus Groups and Community Partnerships

In April 2001, Cincinnati, Ohio, was the scene of race riots after a white police-
man shot and killed a black youth. The incident, however, was only the spark
that ignited a long-smoldering anger among some groups in the city. Rosemary
Goudreau is the managing editor of *The Cincinnati Enquirer*. With the support of
her editor Ward Bushee, she and her staff wanted to address the potentially ex-
plosive race issue. They knew that many people were afraid to talk about it, and
the newspaper staff had already initiated conversations with community leaders
on the topic. In fact, on the night of the riots, newspaper employees were meeting with some grassroots community leaders, she said.

"Before the riots, we had brought together leaders to put the race issue on the
agenda, but people backed away from it. It was the same old sources and the
same old faces, so we decided to bring real people into the conversation,"
Goudreau said (personal communication, March 8, 2002). The paper decided
to engage the community in a conversation about the racial issues dividing
them. To do this, the staff began a series of facilitated neighborhood discussions
designed to probe the underlying tensions and explore ideas about what citizens
could do. Goudreau said that, at the time, many people, especially African
Americans, were frustrated by what they saw as "lots of talk" but little action.

For help in structuring the conversations, the newspaper turned to the
Charles F. Kettering Foundation in nearby Dayton, Ohio. The Kettering Foundation is an international research organization that studies democracy. It
works with the National Issues Forums (NIF), a nonpartisan network of community organizations that has developed a model to help citizens talk and deliberate about complex issues. The NIF researches and writes deliberation
guidebooks on numerous community and national issues and already had one
available that dealt with community race relations. The NIF model creates
structured conversations on specific topics. Forum participants are asked to
read an issue book that provides information on the particular topic. The issue
book presents several choices that represent various perspectives on the issue,
and a moderator guides the group through the discussion of each choice. It is
through this choice work that deliberation ensues, as citizens began to grapple
with the complexities involved in each choice. Deliberation is different from ordinary conversation or debates. It is a dialogue for weighing options (Mathews
& McAfee, 1997). *The Enquirer* took the NIF model and used it as a guide, cre-

ating their own methods to fit their research or news needs, Goudreau said (personal communication, March 8, 2002).

The newspaper started by forming a citizens' steering committee. The goal was to hold solutions-oriented meetings in every neighborhood of Greater Cincinnati. It was an ambitious undertaking, Goudreau said. Even some committee members expressed doubts about being able to accomplish the goal. Yet soon other community organizations offered help. The Cincinnati Chapter of the American Marketing Association volunteered to provide some of their trained facilitators, and the National Conference for Community and Justice also helped find people to serve as facilitators. Altogether, more than 100 facilitators went through training in how to help citizens hold a deliberative conversation, a process that created trained moderators. The use of trained moderators correlates with standard focus group methodology requirements.

The newspaper's staff began working on organizing the neighborhood groups in July 2001. In August, the newspaper also conducted a community poll of 1,112 adults living in Greater Cincinnati. Although not part of the project itself, the polling data helped inform citizens about people's attitudes toward race—in housing, the workplace, in schools, and in personal relationships. This resulted in a five-part series, "Divided By Race" (Goudreau, 2002). In November 2001, the paper launched its "Neighbor-to-Neighbor" project, a series on the community's conversations about race relations.

In all, the newspaper brought together approximately 2,100 people in 148 meetings over a period of 5 months, from November 2001 to March 2002. Each of these meetings had at least one, and more often two, trained facilitators, most often one white and one African American, Goudreau said. From the beginning, Goudreau and the steering committee recognized that they needed professional guidance in organizing this endeavor and found partners with various civic and service organizations in the community. Ultimately, the neighborhood project was endorsed by 111 community groups, corporations, and faith groups, and more than "300 people volunteered more than 4,000 hours" to host or lead the discussions (Thompson, 2002, p. A1).

The newspaper sponsored four training sessions for the facilitators who learned the NIF deliberative model of discussion. The meeting agendas were structured to identify areas of agreement and disagreement among the participants and also to ascertain what citizens and leaders needed to do to address the racial issues confronting their community. "We wanted them to discuss the kinds of action that needed to be taken and what the priorities were," Goudreau said (personal communication, March 8, 2002).

Finding meeting locations took a great deal of time. Appeals were made in newspaper stories and in mass mailings, but ultimately it took hours working the phones to get a sufficient number of host locations. The places most eager to serve as hosts were faith organizations and schools, she said. "An open invitation just didn't do it. People needed to have personal contact. It took a good bit of time and handholding," she said (personal communication, March 8, 2002). These duties were assigned to one editor who was responsible for identifying and contacting civic-minded people or groups in each neighborhood to see who would agree to host a meeting. The newspaper's reporters and editors spent many hours in getting to know the key contacts, preparing for the community conversations, finding and training facilitators, and coordinating the meetings. At the end of each meeting, the chief facilitator submitted a report on what happened and any agreed-upon courses of action, Goudreau said. As part of the "Neighbor-to-Neighbor" project, the newspaper published one of these reports on the front page of the Metro section every day for nearly 4 months so people could stay informed about what was being discussed.

Although the project focused on deliberation, Goudreau said that at its conclusion more than 45 percent of the participants decided to continue to meet to discuss what kind of action needed to be taken. In this overall endeavor, the newspaper used a variety of methods, including a quantitative poll and structured group conversations, and the results of the project extended beyond the original research goal of conversations. The project brought together diverse segments of the community; fostered partnerships among the newspaper, community civic organizations, and academic groups; and the project stimulated more discussions about translating talk into constructive action. For their efforts in bringing together thousands of people to talk about race, *The Enquirer* was named runner-up for the 2002 Batten Award for Excellence.

CONCLUSION

Journalists have transformed the focus group model into a hybrid blend of group methodologies in their effort to get more ideas and voices into news reports and to address real problems facing their communities. Journalists use variant forms of group conversations to collect data that help add depth and new information to their stories. In addition, the conversations serve to educate the journalists, as well as the participants and sometimes have an added benefit of encouraging citizen-based action. Although the focus groups created by journalists may not always meet stringent scientific methodology requirements, the process itself and the information obtained follow standard qualitative research criteria and appear to serve the journalistic community well.

When journalists organize neighborhood conversations or backyard barbecues, they fulfill some of the basic research requirements for group methodology. They have identified the research questions and the population and placed the groups in familiar settings so the discussions can take place in a friendly environment. As participants begin to talk, the group interaction itself has value, and members begin to identify with the project and issues at hand. During the conversations, reporters take a back seat to listen, take notes, and identify patterns about the issues of concern being expressed. They also meet new sources in the community to help shift news coverage from the expert mode to a more egalitarian perspective, to include the middle ground of diverse voices.

Some newspapers also are reconnecting with some of the civic organizations in their communities. These loosely formed partnerships enable reporters to draw on expertise that may not be available to reporters and to use this knowledge to enhance the validity of the report. The partnerships, along with citizen interaction within the group discussions, may help form relationships among diverse peoples, creating and building the linkages Putman (2001) called social capital.

Throughout the process, journalists report on the community meetings and discussions. They write stories that provide background information on the issues so the citizens are able to better understand the complexities involved. In some instances, group participants have continued the discussions after the reporting project ended, and some groups have transformed into action-oriented groups. The group newsgathering methods discussed here rarely stand alone; rather, they complement the more traditional methods of newsgathering. Reporters continue to tap the quantitative information from surveys or polls. They also research documents and conduct individual interviews for their stories, creating a triangulation of information gathering methodologies that strengthen validity.

REFERENCES

Agar, M., & MacDonald, J. (1995). Focus groups and ethnography. *Human Organization, 54,* 78–86.

Argyris, C., Putnam, R., & Smith, D. M. (1990). *Action science: Concepts, methods, and skills for research and intervention.* San Francisco: Jossey-Bass.

Bloor, M., Frankland, J., Thomas, M., & Robson, K. (2001). *Focus groups in social research.* London: Sage.

Coghlan, D. J., & Brannick, T. (2001). *Doing action research in your own organization.* London: Sage.

Fern, E. F. (2001). *Advanced focus group research.* Thousand Oaks, CA: Sage.

Fielder, V. D. (1995, March 6). Speech presented to the Newspaper Association of America (NAA) research conference, Orlando, FL.

Flores, J. G., & Alonso, C. G. (1995). Using focus groups in education research: Exploring teachers' perspectives on educational change. *Evaluation Review, 19,* 16–29.

Frey, J. H., & Fontana, A. (1993). The group interview in social research. In D. L. Morgan (Ed.), *Successful focus groups: Advancing the state of the art* (pp. 20–34). Newbury Park, CA: Sage.

Greenwood, D., & Levin, M. (1998). *Introduction to action research: Social research for social change.* Thousand Oaks, CA: Sage.

Goudreau, R. (Winter 2002). Race conversations blitz Cincinnati. *The Civic Catalyst Newsletter*, Washington, DC: Pew Center for Civic Journalism.

Knodel, J. (1993). The design and analysis of focus group studies: A practical approach. In D. L. Morgan (Ed.), *Successful focus groups: Advancing the state of the art* (pp. 35–50). Newbury Park, CA: Sage.

Krueger, R. A. (1988). *Focus groups: A practical guide for applied research*. Newbury Park, CA: Sage.

Krueger, R. A. (1993). Quality control in focus group research. In D. L. Morgan (Ed.), *Successful focus groups: Advancing the state of the art* (pp. 65–85). Newbury Park, CA: Sage.

Lambeth, E. B., Meyer, P. E., & Thorson, E. (1998). *Assessing public journalism*. Columbia, MO: University of Missouri.

Mathews, D., & McAfee, N. (1997). *Making choices together: The power of public deliberation*. Dayton, OH: The Charles F. Kettering Foundation.

Merritt, D. (1998). *Public journalism and public life: Why telling the news is not enough* (2nd ed.). Hillsdale, NJ: Lawrence Erlbaum.

Merton, R. K. (1987). The focussed interview and focus groups: Continuities and discontinuities. *Public Opinion Quarterly, 51*, pp. 550–566.

Morgan, D. L. (Ed.). (1993). *Successful focus groups: Advancing the state of the art*. Newbury Park, CA: Sage.

Morgan, D. L., & Krueger, R. A. (1993). When to use focus groups. In D. L. Morgan (Ed.), *Successful focus groups: advancing the state of the art* (pp. 3–19). Newbury Park, CA: Sage.

Plaut, T. S., Landis, S., & Trevor, J. (1993). Focus groups and community mobilization: A case study from rural North Carolina. In D. L. Morgan (Ed.), *Successful focus groups: advancing the state of the art* (pp. 202–217). Newbury Park, CA: Sage.

Putnam, R. D. (2001). *Bowling alone: The collapse and revival of American community*. New York: Simon & Schuster.

Rosen, J. (1999). *What are journalists for?* New Haven, CT: Yale University Press.

Stringer, E. T. (1999). *Action Research* (2nd ed.). Thousand Oaks, CA: Sage.

Thompson, R. (2002, April 7). First, we talk. The *Cincinnati Enquirer*, p. A1.

Willey, S. (1997). Civic journalism in practice: Case studies in the art of listening. *Newspaper Research Journal, 19*, 16–29.

Yankelovich, D. (1991). *Coming to public judgment: Making democracy work in a complex world*. New York: Syracuse University.

6

Oral and Life Histories

Giving Voice to the Voiceless

Renita Coleman
Louisiana State University

In many ways, social science research is an extended form of journalism. Both observe, record, analyze, and report findings. Social scientists, however, are largely free of the deadline pressures that define news work. Nevertheless, journalists can benefit from learning about the more methodical approach of social science research and adapting it where possible to their own work. The method of oral or life history, mostly practiced by historians, sociologists, and anthropologists, is one research method that closely mirrors what journalists do. In fact, many texts on the oral history method draw on the work of journalists in describing the practices of this method and recounting its history. Journalists are credited with popularizing the technique of interviewing significant people about their lives. Some say Horace Greeley of the *New York Tribune* started the trend when he went to Salt Lake City to interview Mormon patriarch Brigham Young in 1859 (Ritchie, 1995).

However, journalists working on deadline are not doing the same thing as oral historians even though the techniques bear many similarities. Journalists have no time for multiple, lengthy interviews, typically use only a few short quotes, do not always record the interview, and rarely transcribe tapes and archive them in a library for others to examine. Interviews become oral history only when these criteria are met, according to Ritchie (1995). Nevertheless, for longer journalistic projects the oral history method can be adapted to suit journalists' work and can enhance the credibility of their reports with the more rigorous attention to issues of validity and reliability, and greater focus on interpretation and analysis that is the hallmark of social scientific research.

ORAL HISTORY DEFINED

What is oral history if not just an interview? As the name implies, there must be some historical component to a project in order to separate it from the social scientific method of in-depth interviews. Neither can the oral history interviewer "visit the scene" being recalled by the interviewee as in ethnographic research (Hoopes, 1979, p. 9). Most oral history projects take place years after the event being examined. There is no strict time limit and even recent events can be the focus of oral history projects, the Vietnam War of the 1970s or the civil rights movement of the 1960s, for example. Some element of passing time is required to get the kind of reflection and analysis of the event from those who lived through it. That is what makes oral history unique. Also, oral history is particularly interested in people's interpretations of these events years later, not just the facts of the events themselves. How events have changed in people's minds reveals how people have tried to make sense of their past.

Oral histories are often organized around an event or a subject—the history of a certain ethnic group or community, for example. Life histories are defined somewhat differently from oral histories in that they are autobiographical, recounting people's entire lives. Usually fewer people are interviewed but more time is devoted to each interview. Otherwise, the procedures of life and oral history are the same. Both methods are particularly focused on the personal experiences and inner feelings of the people involved, not just external facts. Oral history has focused on ordinary people and those whose stories are not often told in mainstream media and books. "Giving voice to the voiceless" is the phrase most often used to describe oral history. Inclusion of overlooked groups of people helps construct a more specific and credible history. This goal of oral history also reflects journalists' growing awareness of the importance of diversity in sourcing. Using real people, as well as officials and experts, has been popularized by the civic or public journalism movement and mirrors the interest of oral historians.

ADVANTAGES AND DRAWBACKS

One of the advantages of the oral history approach is the ability to fill in gaps left by reporting norms of the time or history written from the perspective of the dominant social groups. The stories of African American communities that were ignored until the 1960s is one example (Hoopes, 1979). The method has its drawbacks as well. Memories fade. People's stories are, by nature, quite subjective. In the interest of scientific validity, oral historians have addressed these criticisms, but not eliminated them. The Oral History Association has developed standards and guidelines (Ritchie, 1995), and with training and practice, anyone can conduct a successful oral history project. This method is often recommended to graduate students doing a thesis or dissertation, and even high school students have undertaken oral history projects—the *Foxfire* collection of mountain folklore being the most notable example (Wigginton, 1972).

ORAL HISTORY STEP BY STEP

Designing the Project

Almost any person, group, event, or subject with a past is fodder for an oral or life history project. Most projects are broadly conceived—Ellis Island immigrants, for example, American Indians, contemporary religious, ethnic, and racial groups, social and occupational groups, or topics from the perspective of women have all been the subject of oral histories. Any group of people who share a common identity, whether it is location, race, ethnic group, religion, organization, occupation, or families, can be examined through oral histories. Some recent civic journalism projects that examine past events in the context of present problems of a neighborhood resemble oral histories.

Probably the best known examples of oral history as journalism are the books of Studs Terkel. The Pulitzer Prize-winning author captured the voices of ordinary people who lived through the Depression in *Hard Times* (1970), and World War II in *The Good War* (1984). Researchers advise selecting a fixed period to study, as Terkel did. A historically identifiable period or distinct time of social change helps set limits and focus the project (Lance, 1984). Another approach is to select a topic rather than a time period, as Terkel did for his book *Working* (1974), in which he recorded how ordinary people thought and felt about their jobs. Groups of people are also excellent for oral histories as Alex Haley showed when he wrote about descendants of slaves in *Roots* (1976) as did Iorio (1999) when she told the story of a group of Mennonites. Events can also be chosen for an oral history project, as Tom Wicker did with his story of the Attica prison uprising, *A Time to Die* (1975).

When choosing a topic, the researcher should always ask, "Is this reasonable?" It would not be reasonable, for example, to do a project that required interviewing former slaves or Civil War soldiers since no firsthand witnesses are alive today. Perhaps the most common problem is choosing a subject that is too broad. Narrowing the topic ensures a thorough treatment of what is chosen. After the field of study is chosen, it should then be broken down into specific main areas to be examined in detail—work life, family life, social life, education, and dress, for example (Lance, 1984). The areas will depend on the topic chosen, and choice of areas will be guided by an intimate knowledge of the subject.

Sampling

One of the great strengths of the oral history method is that it includes the stories—called evidence or accounts in social scientific terms—of ordinary people, not just the rich and powerful. While the first oral history projects recorded events from the perspective of elites—presidents, congressmen, celebrities, and millionaires—oral history has grown to be known as a method that concentrates mostly on the poor, working class, and minorities. Such groups are so often the subject of this method that oral history has become synonymous with what one author calls "the underside" (Thompson, 1988, p. 7). While these groups of people who have traditionally been marginalized in mainstream history are typically easier to meet and interview than the rich and famous, that is not the primary reason why oral histories continue to focus on them. Instead, the value of adding these voices and experiences to our knowledge of history and social change remains the driving force behind selection of whom to interview. While it is traditional that oral histories focus on everyday people, some researchers caution against an attitude of reverse snobbery that excludes the middle class from such projects; they can be just as interesting and colorful, and their stories just as valuable, as those of poor people (Hoopes, 1979, p. 71).

When choosing the people to sample, as it is called in research, designers of an oral history project should also be concerned with representativeness—that is, making sure that the people interviewed represent the entire range of roles or social strata in the group being studied. A project about the history of an occupation—journalism, for instance—should include people from executive editor to news clerks. Consciously including those typically excluded is important in oral history; in the past these groups have included women and minorities, but there are other, less obvious groups who are frequently forgotten. In a study of journalists, for example, polls and studies typically focus on reporters and editors—the word people—with photographers, artists, and layout people all but ignored. Representativeness helps the project reveal the variety of social experience that comes with different roles and also helps guard against possible bias. Selecting only reporters and editors might result in bias, for example. Of course, no generalizations can be made on the basis of one or two interviews, but representativeness can be high with a small number of sources if the collection is balanced and the sources are knowledgeable.

It may be hard to calculate in advance how many people to interview. The range of informants, research terminology for the people interviewed, can be anywhere from 2 or 3 for a term paper to more than 100 as in Terkel's *Hard Times* (Hoopes, 1979). The rule of thumb for knowing when enough interviews have been done is this: When no new information is being revealed, do one more interview, and if nothing new results, stop.

It is standard in oral history research to interview the oldest and most significant people first and move on to younger and more secondary sources later. Not only does this strategy help guard against interviewees dying and the effects of aging, but the more important sources can also help identify and persuade others to cooperate. Asking sources to recommend others who could be sources is known as snowball sampling in research. Of course, as with any project that relies on cooperative subjects, it is easiest to start with people who are most willing to participate and work toward the more reluctant sources. For his book on death, Terkel interviewed his friends and physician, as well as people he had interviewed for previous books. When many people have cooperated, it seems less threatening for others.

Besides word-of-mouth referrals, successful oral history projects have located participants by putting ads in newspapers, newsletters, and locations that are likely to be seen by those who could serve as sources. Researchers also recommend contacting people by whatever means is most comfortable for them. For some, a formal letter stating the nature of the project and purpose will work best; for others, a phone call or in-person request may be more effective. In any case, a follow-up letter is recommended so the interviewees will have the researcher's contact information, and the researcher will have a record for the files. It's also not a bad idea to call and remind sources of the interview a few days before it is to take place.

Preparing for the Interviews

As with all news stories or academic papers, it is necessary to do the homework. Doing plenty of background research before the first interview question is ever asked is important on many levels. It helps in the construction of meaningful questions, makes interviews more efficient (no wasted time asking, "What year did that happen?"), and allows researchers to recognize bad answers and poor memories. Background research makes interviewers well enough informed to establish rapport with their interviewees and get the interesting stories and inwardly reflective thoughts that make an oral history project come alive. Unlike the question of how many people should be interviewed, it is easier to answer how much background research should be done for an oral history project—only when the researcher has become thoroughly steeped in the subject matter should interviews begin. Some scholars even suggest 10 hours of background work for every hour of interviewing as a general guideline (Ritchie, 1995).

Sources of background information include everything that could possibly have been published about the topic, including primary documents such as birth and death records and secondary documents such as old newspaper articles. Some possible places to search include libraries, newspapers, churches, museums, courthouses, city halls, schools, genealogies, even attics and basements. Oral history researchers often forget an obvious source—other oral histories. Historical societies archive oral history projects' tapes, transcripts, and written reports. Other sources of oral history collections can be found in reference books such as *Oral History Collections* by Meckler and McMullin (1975), and *Oral History in the United States* by Shumway (1971). A useful list of contacts of oral history associations can be found in Perks and Thomson (1998).

The final step in using background research to prepare for the interviews is the construction of an interview guide. This can be anything from a list of specific, open-ended questions to a set of broad topics to be covered. Seasoned oral historians recommend open-ended questions such as "Tell me about what it was like growing up there?" when seeking broader, longer, and more interpretive answers. Open-ended questions often include how and why. Some specific questions will be necessary; they can be used to show the interviewer's knowledge, for example. Interviews, however, should consist mainly of open-ended questions that encourage the interviewees to reminisce and go where they please. Short answers from sources are a sign of too many specific questions and not enough open-ended ones. Questions or topics should be put in an order that reflects their logical relationships; one question should lead naturally to the next and avoid abrupt changes of topic. Life histories can proceed chronologically while event-centered projects should be arranged by topic. The beginning of the interview should start broadly rather than jumping right into the main questions. One oral historian developed a two-sentence format for questions and believes it works best (Morrissey, 1987). The first sentence states the problem and the second poses the question: For example, "The records show you were a leader in establishing better race relations. Why was this your objective?"

Confrontational or controversial questions should be saved for the end. If bitterness over a question results, that line of questioning should be shifted until better rapport has been established. One technique for getting over this hurdle is to quote someone else and then ask the interviewee to give his or her side of the story. For example, "At the time, the newspapers were reporting you had a conflict of interest. What was your take on that?" Interviewers can always return to controversial or important topics later, approaching them from a different angle. A wrap-up question should end the interview—asking people to reflect or draw conclusions, or look ahead to the future, for example. Finally interviewers should ask if there is anything that has been left out; people should be encouraged to put what they consider important into the record.

Recording the Interviews

It is tempting for seasoned journalists to want to forgo the tape recording of interviews—do not do it. If the project is truly to be an oral history, albeit one adapted for a journalistic production, then recording the interviews is important. Like any qualitative social science method, oral history is defined by the depth of the project. True qualitative methods depend for their veracity on the researcher being deeply immersed in the subject. To carry the weight of a social science methodology, oral history adapted for journalistic purposes should be more in-depth than the typical media story, even the weekenders and enterprise stories that are typically longer and more expansive than weekday news articles. To achieve the kind of credibility that social science methods have, journalistic oral histories must be more in-depth in the research and reporting phase, something along the line of the kind of time devoted to investigative reporting. The sheer number of interviews and their lengthy duration make tape recording a necessity. Even journalists who have become adept at distilling the essence of someone's quotes in notes and recalling them nearly verbatim will be daunted by the size of the task posed in an oral history project. Note-taking is simply not up to the task. The longer the interviews last, the more the note-taker will miss. Recording allows interviewers to focus their attention and listen to what is said, think ahead to the next question, and formulate unexpected questions rapidly. Recordings also serve as a form of self-protection. In fact, there is no reason not to record and take notes at the same time, using the recording to pick up what the notes missed and quote more accurately. Transcribing of tapes is recommended because of the deteriorating quality of tapes, but not required (Ritchie, 1995). If tapes are not transcribed, an abstract or index is recommended, and the notes taken during the interviews can serve this function.

Taping interviews requires a good deal of attention to technology. First, only good quality portable tape recorders should be used. It is nice to have one that signals when the end of the tape is about to be reached. High quality tapes—60 to 90 minutes long—and an extra supply of batteries are also important. Good microphones—never the built-in kind—should be used, and many interviewers prefer the lavaliere mikes that clip onto clothing. Equipment should always be tested before every use and back-up equipment available. If the project does have the resources for transcribing the tapes, transcribing machines with foot pedals make the task easier.

Collecting the Data—Also Known as Interviewing

When it comes time to sit down and interview someone, the specific techniques that can ensure the success of the interview will vary depending on the person being interviewed and the interviewer. However, there are some general guidelines that have been shown to work well most of the time. Since oral history researchers advise using interviewing techniques perfected by journalists, most seasoned reporters will already be aware of most of these suggestions.

A quiet location that is comfortable for both interviewer and interviewee is preferable. Having a desk between the two is almost never a good idea because it creates psychological distance. The tape recorder and microphone should be placed where the interviewer can see it to check its function, but out of the direct line of sight of the interviewee. It should never be concealed. Beginning with small talk about some points the interviewer has in common with the interviewee will usually help put the person at ease and begin the crucial process of establishing rapport. Listening carefully and encouraging candid responses is also crucial. Since the point of oral history is to record another person's point of view, even if it seems exaggerated or boastful, it is essential to encourage people to be honest, accurate, and revealing. One of the hardest tasks is to move people beyond their natural reluctance to give an honest and critical evaluation of the past (Ritchie, 1995).

Oral histories are also focused on ideas, emotions, and behavior (Hoopes, 1979), so questions should probe these areas, as well as historical facts. Observations and opinions that are not already well documented should be collected—a goal that fits well with the purposes of civic journalism projects. So interviewers should leave room for people to talk about what is on their minds, abandoning prepared questions and following some unexpected paths if necessary. Interviewers will want to watch out for rehearsed or often-told stories, and try to move the person beyond them. Questions should guide without leading. As polls and surveys have shown, the way a question is worded can change the answer. Naturally, loaded questions—questions that lead a person to give an answer the interviewer expects—should be avoided. Interviewers should never interrupt, but still keep the dialogue moving. One technique interviewers sometimes use is to fill in names, dates, and other information that the person being interviewed cannot remember. This is one place where the background research will come in handy. Some people may try to test the interviewer's knowledge of the subject by pretending not to know some information to see if the interviewer will offer the correct answer. If the answer to a fact question is unknown, other sources can provide the who, what, when, and where. Keep interviews focused on getting insights into how and why. Only one question should be asked at a time, and follow-up questions should always be included. One technique for thinking of these questions is for interviewers to put themselves in the position of the person being interviewed, visualize the world from his or her perspective, and think of questions that shed light on that place and time.

It is natural for people to be reluctant to talk about difficult issues, so interviewers need to be prepared to ask about painful and embarrassing topics in a sensitive way. If the answers are less than forthcoming, this should be pointed out respectfully. Little is gained in oral histories by going off the record. If the purpose of oral history is to make known what is not, keeping this information confidential will not advance that goal. Instead, it is recommended that interviewers stop the tape and hear the person's problem without having those thoughts recorded, but not allow the information to be off the record. A technique many journalists use to encourage people to expand on ideas is the pregnant pause—remaining silent indicates the interviewer expects more and often people will give it.

In oral histories, unlike journalism, more than one interview is usually conducted. Among the many benefits, it establishes more intimacy between interviewer and interviewee. There is no ideal number of interview sessions to have with each person; some people have more to contribute than others. Each interview session should be limited to 1½ to 2 hours to avoid tiring everyone. Interviews are best done one-on-one to establish a relationship; group interviews can be fruitful because people will feed off each other's memories, but these should be considered supplements to individual interviews.

Analyzing, Interpreting, and Writing Up the Data

First-time oral historians will be amazed—and daunted—by the amount of material they have collected. Now, the problem is where to begin analyzing and writing. Most researchers using any qualitative method recommend not waiting until all the data are collected to begin analyzing. As soon as an interview is finished, the researcher should go over the notes or tapes and fill in the details—the environment, significant body language of the interviewee, general impressions of the interviewer, etc. (Hoopes, 1979). This is also the time for the researcher to begin writing the reflective and analytical interpretations that will form the basis of the report. Analysis should focus on the larger questions and meanings in broad context, critical thinking about the evidence and interpretation of it (Hoopes, 1979). Such journal-like entries make the writing task much easier in the end.

This aspect of interpretation may be the hardest part for traditionally objective journalists to reconcile when using oral history methods. There is controversy within the social sciences over whether people's stories should be interpreted by another person—the writer. The consensus seems to be that no interpretation adds little to our knowledge, and the Q&A format that is left is unlikely to be interesting enough for many people to use. Thus the voiceless would remain so. The harshest criticism of oral history sans interpretation is that it represents a "cowardly reluctance to think" (Johnson, 1994, p. 14). The minimum, says one expert, is that authors "should provide some background for their interviews to place the interviewees in context" (Ritchie, 1995, p. 104). This background and context can be achieved by relating the stories to the broader culture and society, offering insights into the cultural significance of an event, or relating the evidence to wider patterns and theories (Hoopes, 1979). Said Thompson, "The ability to make connections between separated spheres of life is an intrinsic strength of oral history" (Thompson, 1988, p. 257).

A more subjective approach to interpretation taken by oral historians is to look for hidden and half-conscious meanings in people's statements, or to interpret what has been said through a specific theoretical lens. For example, oral histories of workers talking about their jobs could be interpreted using a Marxist perspective, or women's stories could be examined through the eyes of feminist theory. Interpretations of oral history evidence should not distort people's stories so much that they no longer recognize them, however. While the people who give their accounts for an oral history project may not interpret them the way the interviewer does, they should at least recognize their stories and agree that the interpretation is one that can truthfully be told.

In writing oral histories it is important to devote no more than half the report to interpretation with at least half or more devoted to the quotes of the interviewees. This fulfills the requirements of letting people tell their own stories. Editing and rearranging for clarification is allowed so long as the original meaning is retained. It is also recommended that questions, as well as answers, be included in the write-up lest it appear that people were raising these issues themselves rather than being prompted by questions.

Other Issues

Oral history is often criticized on grounds of validity or credibility because people's accounts are subjective. Scholars celebrate this, saying that:

the credibility of oral sources is a *different* credibility … The importance of oral testimony may often lie not in its adherence to facts but rather in its divergence from there. (Portelli, 1998, p. 68)

They have also addressed ways to improve this reliability. As with any research method, no single piece of evidence should be trusted alone; everything needs to be compared against other evidence (Ritchie, 1995). Two corroborating statements should be collected for every fact, and oral testimony should be checked against written records. Using statistics to set the narrative in a context is also helpful. The general rules in examining evidence are "to look for internal consistency, to seek confirmation in other sources, and to be aware of potential bias" (Thompson, 1988, p. 102). The real goal should be "to *reveal* sources of bias, rather than pretend they can be nullified" (Thompson, 1988, p. 117).

While journalists do not often use legal release forms, it is necessary to do so with oral histories. The law grants copyright automatically to people whose words are recorded for 50 years after their death; there is no need for them even to register it. A deed or gift of contract is usually collected at the time of the first interview (see sample in Appendix 6.1). It is customary in oral history research to present the interviewees with a gift, usually copies of the tapes or transcripts, book, or article (Ritchie, 1995). Archiving of tapes and transcripts is another issue that specifically concerns oral history, and some say it is one of the defining characteristics of this method. Placing the tapes in a library for others' use is customary, but new technologies are presenting other means for saving the entire record, such as CD-ROM and Web sites.

AN ORAL HISTORY PROJECT

In May 2000, *The Wichita Eagle's* general assignment reporter and columnist Roy Wenzl wrote a series that serves as a good example of the adaptation of the oral–life history method to journalism. While Wenzl said he did not approach it with oral history in mind (personal communication, April 17, 2002), many characteristics of his series about a runaway girl fit the description of this qualitative research method.

The eight-part series told the story of Karen Irene "Reenie" Countryman, whose mother killed herself when Karen was 13. After 3 years in and out of foster care and the Wichita Children's Home, Karen persuaded a judge to free her from state custody and allow her to live on her own—at age 16. Eventually, Karen went back to the Children's Home to work and joined the outreach program riding around searching for troubled kids. She pestered the street kids, trying to help them, and convince them to help themselves. She even saved a few lives.

The series is more a melding of oral history about a topic (the social problem of runaway teens) and life history (the story of Karen's short but eventful life) than purely one or the other. The choice of subject matter is in keeping with the oral history method's concentration on marginalized groups of people; in mainstream reporting, it is usually officials and experts who tell us about runaways, not the runaways themselves. While officials and experts get their say in the series, this story does indeed give voice to the voiceless by focusing on the perspective of the runaway children. The life history aspect of the project is that it concentrates on one person's life as an example, but rather than covering Karen's entire life history, it focuses on 4 or 5 years.

The project fulfills the requirement of representativeness in its use of sources from all strata of this social circle—stories from the judge, court employees, social workers, Children's Home staffers, volunteers, and runaways keep the story balanced with other viewpoints. Dozens of different people appear in the stories, and Wenzl interviewed even more who did not appear in the series. "I didn't want to accept the story at face value from just her, so I spent a lot of time getting somebody to confirm everything," Wenzl said (personal communication, April 17, 2002). This helped the story be more fully representative of the issue, but it also added to the reliability of the report by corroborating all statements.

Wenzl also did plenty of background research, and some of it shows up in the articles in the form of statistics about troubled teens, suicide, and homelessness. Most of the research remains in the background, but was crucial for the story. Wenzl spent 15 months working on the story, allowing him to become deeply immersed in the topic. "I didn't work on it full-time, but a lot of time was spent on it. There was a lot of interviewing, her and others," he said. "I lost count of how many times I interviewed her, maybe 30 or 50 times. Some were really long, and some were short" (personal communication, April 17, 2002). Other people were also interviewed more than once, but not as many times as Karen. In the case of this private and wary 18-year-old, Wenzl found that numerous interviews were needed to establish the trust and intimacy necessary for Karen to open up and offer a true and searching account of her life (personal communication, April 17, 2002). Still, Wenzl found her reluctant to talk about certain difficult issues. In one story, Wenzl wrote:

> Before the beating, she'd been sleeping in a shed in Haysville, living on the streets with her older brother Jeremiah. She'd run away from the foster family that took her in after her mother's suicide. She doesn't want to say why. (Wenzl, 2000, May 9, p. 1A)

Karen herself acknowledged this reluctance, so typical of life histories, in a piece that was published at the end of the series:

> Deciding whether to share my life with the world was one of the hardest decisions I have ever made. All of us are a bit afraid to share the intimate experiences of our lives. (Countryman, 2000, May 14, p. 11A)

A veteran reporter, Wenzl did not use an interview guide, nor did he tape record the interviews. That is a method he has grown comfortable with, and it was necessary to put the main subject of the story at ease. "A list of questions is intimidating with somebody like her," Wenzl said. "Sometimes I wouldn't even have the notebook out. I'd pull it out later and write it down" (personal communication, April 17, 2002).

In addition to corroborating Karen's statements with others' Wenzl overcame validity issues by including information from written records. In addition to statistics about suicide and runaways, Wenzl included information from court records, which was problematic since juvenile records are sealed. "After a lot of negotiation we worked out a deal where the state and court people would look in the records and tell me if something was in there and was true or not," said Wenzl (personal communication, April 17, 2002). Another, more unusual document source Wenzl included in the series was lengthy excerpts from Karen's own journal, with each entry dated in the series. Each story is made up mainly of direct quotes, supplemented with details that Wenzl reconstructed to paint a picture and make the series come alive:

> So when Reenie pulled open the back door at 418 N. Spruce, the smell would float out like a wave. And she could smell the floral shampoo in Mom's hair when they hugged. (Wenzl, 2000a, May 7, p. 3A)

Feelings such as grief, anger, and guilt also figure into the stories, either in the quotes or in the interviewee's self-reflections. Karen said:

> It hurts so much. What happened to me and (my brother) Jeremiah, what happened to my Mom, it hurts too much. (Wenzl, 2000b, May 7, p. 1A)

Finally, the topic of analysis and interpretation, so ingrained in journalists to avoid, was skillfully handled in this series by allowing the people in the stories to offer their own interpretation and analysis. "I didn't try to editorialize. I didn't try to put my own spin on it. I just tried to do justice to what was a great story because of what happened to her and what she did," said Wenzl (personal communication, April 17, 2002). This reporter maintained his objectivity and provided background for broader cultural and social patterns, but incorporated interpretation and analysis provided by others, not himself. For example, one of the reflections by Judge Bacon, who emancipated Karen, on her decision-making process, said:

This child, thought the judge, was giving her facts. Not empty promises, as so many other runaways make when asking for their freedom. Real information. The girl had submitted eight full pages of apartment price comparisons and weekly shopping lists, showing how she'd care for herself if freed from custody.... In those pages of lists, Bacon saw the threads of an unfinished tale. It was the tale of a Mom and a little girl, a story embedded in sheet after sheet of paper, typed out or written in Karen's fluid hand. (Wenzl, 2000, May 12, p. 1A)

Then there are reflections from Karen herself:

We all have a choice," Reenie would say years later. "When the bad things come, we can decide to be bad, or we can decide to be good. (Wenzl, 2000, May 8, p. 1A)

Also:

I guess what I want people to know by me sharing my life is this: There is hope. I have gone through a lot in my life, and I feel I have turned that around to use it towards my strength and happiness. My pain has helped me find my passion. No matter how hard your life is, you can survive. (Countryman, 2000, May 14, p. 11A)

Finally, Wenzl narrated:

But for all the memories, for all she shares with Mom, Karen has been able to say something new in the last year. 'I'm NOT my Mom.' (Wenzl, 2000c, May 14, p. 1A)

CONCLUSION

As this series shows, good, in-depth journalism and social science methods such as oral history have many similarities. Oral historians have studied the practice of journalism and incorporated techniques from it into their method of research. Now it is time for journalists to do the same. Writers who make an effort to learn about these social science methods and work to incorporate appropriate techniques from them into their journalistic practice will find themselves with more confidence in the credibility of their work because they will have adhered to respected scientific methods for assuring validity and reliability.

REFERENCES

Countryman, K. (2000, May 14). A message from Karen. *The Wichita Eagle*, p. 11A.

Haley, A. (1976). *Roots: The saga of an American family*. Garden City, NY: Doubleday.

Hoopes, J. (1979). *Oral history: An introduction for students*. Chapel Hill, NC: The University of North Carolina Press.

Iorio, S. H. (1999). *Faith's harvest*. Norman, OK: University of Oklahoma Press.

Johnson, D. (1994, April 10). I, the jury: Why this novelist can't resist a good book panel. *New York Times Book Review*, p. 14.

Lance, D. (1984). Oral history project design. In D. K. Dunaway & W. K. Baum (Eds.), *Oral history: An interdisciplinary anthology* (pp. 116–123). Nashville, TN: The American Association for State and Local History.

Meckler, A. M., & McMullin, R. (1975). *Oral history collections.* New York: R. R. Bowker.

Morrissey, C. T. (1987). The two-sentence format as an interviewing technique in oral history fieldwork. *Oral History Review, 15,* 43–53.

Perks, R., & Thomson, A. (Eds.) (1998). *The oral history reader.* London: Routledge.

Portelli, A. (1998). What makes oral history different. In R. Perks & A. Thomson (Eds.), *The oral history reader* (pp. 63–74). London: Routledge.

Ritchie, D. A. (1995). *Doing oral history.* New York: Twayne Publishers.

Shumway, G. (1971). *Oral history in the United States: A directory.* New York: Oral History Association.

Terkel, S. (1970). *Hard Times: An oral history of the Great Depression.* New York: Pantheon.

Terkel, S. (1974). *Working: People talk about what they do all day and how they feel about what they do.* New York: Pantheon.

Terkel, S. (1984). *"The Good War": An oral history of World War Two.* New York: Pantheon.

Thompson, P. (1988). *The voice of the past: Oral history* (2nd Ed.). Oxford, England: Oxford University Press.

Wenzl, R. (2000a, May 7). Reenie and mom. *The Wichita Eagle,* p. 3A.

Wenzl, R. (2000b, May 7). Karen lost and found. *The Wichita Eagle,* p. 1A.

Wenzl, R. (2000, May 8). Childhood lost. A girl's life unravels after her mom's suicide. *The Wichita Eagle,* p. 1A.

Wenzl, R. (2000, May 9). Good girl, bad girl. A pot-smoking kid finds trouble on the street. *The Wichita Eagle,* p. 1A.

Wenzl, R. (2000, May 12). Judgement Day. A 16-year-old asks the court to grant her freedom. *The Wichita Eagle,* p. 1A.

Wenzl, R. (2000, May 14). "I am not my Mom." *The Wichita Eagle,* p. 1A.

Wicker, T. (1975). *A time to die.* New York: Quadrangle.

Wigginton, E. (Ed.) (1972). *The Foxfire book.* Garden City, NY: Doubleday.

APPENDIX 6.1

DEED OF GIFT TO THE PUBLIC DOMAIN

I, (interviewee), do hereby give to (organization), the tape recordings and transcripts of my interviews conducted on (date). I authorize use of the tapes and transcripts in such a manner as may best serve the educational and historical objectives of this oral history program. In making this gift, I voluntarily convey ownership of the tapes and transcripts to the public domain.

_____   _____   _____
        (Agent)   (donor)   (date)

(From Senate Historical Office, Ritchie, 1995, p. 213)

7

Focused Interviews

Sharon Hartin Iorio
Wichita State University

One time-honored tradition of journalism is the street interview. To do a street interview, a reporter goes to a public place, stops people by chance, and asks each one a single question about an important issue of the day. This very simple form of reporting community reaction illustrates three pivotal features of the qualitative research method called focused interviewing. First, the reporter seeks out everyday citizens, not government officials, high-ranking business leaders, or social elites. Second, the reporter asks each person the same question in the same way. Third, the resulting news report comes directly from the words of those interviewed. The social science method of focused interviews, however, is not merely an extended form of the street interview.

The street interview can produce no more than the brief, snapshot opinions of those willing to share their views. Focused interview methodology is a qualitative research tool that can elicit in-depth responses and identify commonalities among the replies people give. The off-the-cuff comments picked up from street interviews are merely interesting opinions of individuals. The purpose of the focused interview is not only to identify and report, like the street interview, but also to interpret and show any shared insights found among the individuals' replies. The focus is to uncover accurately how a group of interviewees understand a problem or what they believe about a certain topic. The actual interview process is personal and conducted one-on-one to draw out each individual's unique viewpoint (Merton, Fiske, & Kendall, 1956/1990).

The focused interview makes a specific contribution to social science research and journalism. It enriches information gathered by other methods through revealing subjective responses—that is, answering what and how people think about a particular subject. The method, sometimes described as "guided conversations" or "conversations with a purpose" (Gollin, 1956/1990, p. x), can produce accurate information about the context of political, social, and economic life for individuals. The focused interview is a valuable tool for the journalist.

IN THE BEGINNING:
EARLY USE OF FOCUSED INTERVIEWS

In the early 1940s, both academic and commercial investigators began to develop sophisticated methods of conducting surveys. Working with newly developed quantitative, statistical designs, techniques to survey individuals accurately were studied and refined. The beneficial result was that the surveyed reactions supplied by a limited number of people could be generalized to that of a larger population of similar individuals. In other words, if conducted correctly, the survey of a small group would produce results that could (within statistical and other limitations) predict the overall responses of a much larger group. As might be expected, the survey method blossomed as business and political interests recognized its benefits.

Research priorities, however, shifted as war engulfed Europe and threatened the United States. One November evening in 1941, Paul Lazarsfeld, a professor at Columbia University, took time from his busy, war-related research agenda to invite Robert Merton, his new colleague at the university, to dinner. Lazarsfeld was so engrossed in his challenging work that before the first course was served; he suggested that he and Merton visit the studio where Lazarsfeld was testing responses to several radio morale programs for the U.S. Office of Facts and Figures, the predecessor of the Office of War Information (Merton et al., 1956/1990). When the two arrived at the studio, the research was in progress. While the test-groups stated what they did and did not like about the program, the on-site researchers lacked an empirical method to explore what those interviewed did or did not like and "why." Merton was enticed. He began working the next week on a report that developed techniques for in-depth questioning of interviewees and launched the first focused interview strategy.

Through much of World War II, Merton and Lazarsfeld continued their collaboration on communication research projects and the methods to build more effective research designs. They were joined by another communication research pioneer, Carl Hovland, who was on leave from Yale University during the war. Hovland understood the benefits of qualitative interviews as adjuncts to the experiments that he designed (Merton et al., 1956/1990). Hovland's and Lazarsfeld's contributions led to quantitative methods, but both emphasized the balance and importance that the qualitative work of this period brought to their ground-breaking research. Lazarsfeld (1944) laid out the aims of the focused interview as follows:

1. to clarify the meanings of common concepts and opinions;
2. to distinguish the decisive elements of an expressed opinion;
3. to determine what influenced a person to form an opinion or to act in a certain way;
4. to classify complex attitude patterns; and
5. to understand the interpretations that people attribute to their motivations to act.

Lazarsfeld's purposes, first published in 1944, remain, despite the intervening years, the foundation of focused interviewing (Lindlof, 1995).

Merton's projects during World War II included a study of Army training films and the charisma of Kate Smith, a popular singer of the day who raised more than $39 million in pledges to buy war bonds. Working with Kendall and Fiske, Merton published an article and a book about how to use focused interviews (Merton et al., 1956/1990; Merton & Kendall, 1946). These publications laid out the principles and procedures of interviewing that Merton, Fiske, and Kendall had developed by examining the persuasiveness of propaganda efforts during the war years (Morgan, 1988). The overall criteria they developed are paraphrased below as:

1. Range. The interview should enable interviewees to maximize the variety of elements and patterns in the situation or topic the interviewees are asked to describe, as well as document, the full array of responses they may give.
2. Specificity. The interview should elicit highly precise reports of the different aspects of the situation or topic to which interviewees are asked to respond.
3. Depth. The interview should help interviewees to describe their emotions, evaluations, and their reasoned analysis of the situation or topic as well as the degree of their involvement with it.
4. Personal Context. The interview should bring out the prior experience of interviewees and their personal attributes that give the situation the distinctive meanings they express (Merton et al., 1956/1990).

Merton's et al. (1956/1990) focused interview guide included information on a related method, focus groups, that were first introduced in the 1920s. Soon, commercial researchers found that interviewing in groups made for faster data collection and was less expensive than personal interviews. The focus group technique was quickly incorporated into commercial marketing research that grew exponentially from the 1950s to the end of the 20th century and remains an extremely popular tool for marketing and media research today.

Post-World War II, Merton and his colleagues continued their work, but little research that used the interview method they proposed was published by them (Morgan, 1988), nor has it been widely used by sociologists in general. One example of a published focused interview study in social science research is Zuckerman's "Interviewing an Ultra-elite" (1972), an article that revealed sequences in the careers of Nobel laureates. Another is "Media Consumption and Girls Who Want to Have Fun" (Peterson, 1987).

Despite the focused interview's lack of attraction as a social science research method, Merton, Fiske, and Kendall fueled the popular trend in focus group research, and, over time, the contribution of the focused interview method as a research tool has been far reaching. The method has informed the interview process in major branches of social science research within both the public and private sectors. In the preface to the second edition of *The Focused Interview* (Merton, Fiske, & Kendall) published in 1990, Merton wrote that he could not:

> presume to say how much of the seeming discontinuity between the focused interview and its modified version in the form of focus groups is actually another instance of obliteration by incorporation ... If the focused interview has experienced even occasional obliteration by incorporation in the originating field of sociology, one is inclined to suppose that it is all the more (a fortiori) likely to have occurred in other fields into which it had diffused. (p. xxx)

The concepts and techniques underlying the focused interview process can be found repeated and extended in related qualitative interview methods including the personal or intensive interview, in which in-depth responses are elicited but uniform interview guides are not employed (e.g., Brissett & Edgley, 1990). The diffusion Merton noted also can be observed across the social science disciplines. For example, the permeation is seen in works on the sociological interview (Fielding & Fielding, 1986; Maso & Wester, 1996; McCracken, 1988), in publication on social science and education interviewing (Seidman, 1998), in government studies (Nathan, 1986), and in communication research (Berger, 2000; Lindlof, 1995; Potter, 1996; Wimmer & Dominick, 2002).

COMPARING FOCUSED
AND JOURNALISTIC-SOURCE INTERVIEWS

Journalists who work on deadlines and do interviews daily use many of the principles and techniques of the focused interview, even though they may use them in a different way or for a different purpose. Whether by infusion from the methods of social science or diffusion of sound journalism practice, basic tenets of the focused interview are also essential elements found in reporting texts and other books specifically targeted to those interested in learning about the media interview (Adams, 2001; Biagi, 1991; Gibbs & Warhover, 2002; Metzler,1997; Paterno & Stein, 2001). In these publications, reporters, like focused interviewers, learn how to seek specific rather than general information. Reporters are directed (as Merton et al., 1956/1990, pointed out) to seek a range of responses from their sources and to interview for responses that reveal deep emotions and strongly held attitudes; reporters learn to probe. They are taught techniques, such as using transitions, and ways to avoid abrupt shifts in the interview that might break the source's train of thought. A journalist is educated, like the researchers Merton and his colleagues trained, to look "beyond limited, one-dimensional reports of 'positive' or 'negative,' 'favorable' or 'unfavorable' responses ... to obtain a maximum of self-revelatory reports of how the situation under review was experienced" (Merton et al., 1956/1990, p. 95).

Traditional news reporting, however, differs greatly from focused interviewing. First and foremost, the news reporter almost always has a frame or "lede" or starting point for a story. The reporter is interested in finding details that will build the story or in some cases reject the story as a news item. Reporters are strategic (Paterno & Stein, 2001). They size up the interview source and push ultimately for the source to reveal the information sought. The focused interviewer will not build a sequence of leading questions to ferret out facts or test a possible conclusion. The focused interviewer encourages general discussion as a way to identify and extrapolate newsworthy concerns that come from the lives people lead. Metzler (1997) marked the distinction between the focused method and the traditional interview by labeling the two types of interviewing as directive and nondirective in his journalistic writers guide, *Creative Interviewing*.

Second, the reporter writes a traditional news story or feature using a lede and builds the body of the story from direct and indirect quotes drawn from multiple sources. In many instances, the comments frame the story from opposing viewpoints. In other instances, the comments provide a variety of viewpoints. Focused interview findings may be the starting point for traditional news or feature story or may stand alone as a news story. In any of these cases, a story that results from focused interviews will report and quote sources, but the reporting will be based on shared perspectives that underlie multiple opinions collected on a particular topic. The point is not to publish many voices on an issue or problem but to compare and analyze many voices to find commonly held points of view. The identified themes are the point of the news story, and the writer supports the themes with quotes taken from the interviews. To illustrate, one newspaper series was launched when editors and reporters found, through focused interviews, that local citizens' concerns prior to an election were not the same campaign issues that the candidates emphasized (the example that follows later in this chapter describes this project in detail).

THE ADVANTAGES AND DISADVANTAGES OF FOCUSED INTERVIEWS

The focused interview does not replace the standard journalism interview that has for decades served as the basis of the majority of news stories that are read or viewed by the public daily. Nor does the focused interview substitute for the benefits of the occasional well-timed street interview that was discussed at the beginning of this chapter. The focused interview is an effective newsroom tool when used to

1. identify budding political issues;
2. understand individuals' interpretation of highly publicized issues; and
3. learn the connection between personal affairs and larger social problems.

Researchers and journalists can use focused interviews prior to surveys to help identify broad or untapped concerns that can then be translated to specific questions. Focused interviews can also be used to follow up on the limited findings of quantitative studies such as public opinion polls. When Merton queried soldiers after they rated training films, he was following up on quantitative research findings.

Moreover, the focused interview method can stand on its own as the primary method for a project. For example, a focused interview project can gather and analyze information from a wide cross-section of people (the example that follows later in this chapter used a large, countywide sample). Focused interviews with a small number of people also can be useful (Poindexter & McCombs, 2000). Interviews with small numbers of respondents are appropriate when the individuals interviewed have access to information that average people do not have. For example, a study might query the presidents of national corporations on their view of accounting consultant practices or the appropriate level for executives' salaries. Focused interview projects with limited numbers of respondents are also suitable when those interviewed, because of their positions, can be obstacles to, or influences on, change. Interviewing community church leaders on the subject of religious tolerance or school superintendents on their views of affirmative action are just two examples at the local level in which small numbers of respondents could provide desired information. Depending on the sample size needed, focused interviews can be conducted by one researcher or reporter or by a team of reporters or researchers.

The advantages of the focused interview method are that it provides unfiltered information from first-person accounts; it offers early identification of common concerns; and it identifies grassroots issues at the point where the problems are located. These advantages come into play when deciding whether to use focused interviews or focus groups. The focus group provides good feedback when the topic is not extremely broad; whereas, the focused interview is ideal for soliciting comprehensive, multilayered responses.

There are also technical advantages that the focused interview has over the focus group. The success of the focus group rests on the ability of a well-trained moderator to draw full responses from each of the participants in a short amount of time without allowing any one person to dominate the group. Furthermore, focus group participants generally are paid for their time, thus presenting an unanswerable question about the underlying validity of the data. The aforementioned challenges usually are not associated with one-on-one interviewing.

In a focused interview, the interviewer has time to devote to a single individual. That time can be used to help set each interviewee at ease with the process, repeat or rephrase questions, and draw out complete answers. There is no threat that one person will drown out another's attempt to contribute information or that a group mentality can develop to stifle opposing opinion, as can happen in the focus group interview. In addition, the focused interview can be conducted when circumstances prevent bringing a specific group, such as decision makers who may be in scattered locations, together at one place and time (Poindexter & McCombs, 2000). Interviewees need not be paid, and most reporters have the basic skills required to conduct the interviews.

Disadvantages of the method, however, should be considered before entering a focused interview project. Sample sizes should be chosen with regard to researching the question(s) posed for the project. Small samples, chosen without regard to the scope of the data needed to answer the research question(s) and merely due to time and cost constraints, limit the reliability of the data collected. An additional disadvantage is that within the interviewing process some respondents may concentrate only on their personal relationships with other individuals; this limits the ability to analyze the information they provide (Iorio &

Huxman, 1996). For the most part, however, it is the time and cost involved in conducting first-person interviews that make their frequent use difficult for deadline-driven media industries. With effort, focus group data can be obtained quickly, even overnight. Focused interviews generally take longer to conduct and analyze. Focused interviews may be better suited for enterprise stories and political campaign coverage.

In summary, the focused interview should be used when the project calls for methods to go beyond simply naming topics of interest to individuals—when reporters, pollsters, and researchers need to explore brief, scattered comments—when a simple answer may not convey a complex viewpoint. Focused interviews work well when a nontraditional approach is required to get at the qualifications and caveats people place around their opinions. The focused interview is ideally suited to augment the more limited findings of survey research. The benefit of the focused interview is its ability to collect unfiltered insights and unadulterated opinions people hold in common but are often overlooked by focus groups and surveys.

PLANNING AND CONDUCTING A FOCUSED INTERVIEW PROJECT

Purpose of the Research

In the fall of 1991, a focused interview study was conducted in Wichita, Kansas through a partnership between *The Wichita Eagle* and faculty at the Elliott School of Communication, Wichita State University. What evolved became a large-scale study and a long-term *Eagle* reporting venture. The overall project will serve as both an example of the focused interview method and a guide to its implementation, even though focused interview projects can be large or small, conducted by a single interviewer or a team, and developed by a newsroom on its own or by partnerships among news organizations and academic researchers. In this example, the university faculty and *Eagle* representatives jointly planned the project. The faculty designed the research and supervised the graduate-student interviewers. Then, the *Eagle* reporters, editors, and designers used the interviews as a springboard for a special eight-part series and for general election coverage in the year that followed.

The basis of all social scientific research holds true for journalism projects in general and for the WSU/*Eagle* project. That basis is the recognition of a core issue, topic, or problem and the will to address it (Wimmer & Dominick, 2002). Among the reasons for the *Eagle* management team's interest in the partnership with WSU was:

1. to help plan the newspaper's coverage of the 1992 elections by learning citizens' concerns and
2. to validate questionnaire construction for subsequent telephone interviews on these topics.

The initial step in this and any focused interview research (Hsia, 1988) was to address the research problem by formulating a series of clear and compelling research questions. After a plenary session with faculty and newspaper management, the following interrelated questions emerged:

1. What are Sedgwick County residents most worried about these days in their communities, neighborhoods, and day-to-day lives?
2. How do those concerns relate to political concerns?
3. Which of the concerns are underexposed by our elected officials and in media coverage?

Sample Selection

The next step in planning a project is to select a sample. Some focused interview projects are characterized by a sample that is intentionally or purposively chosen, in other words, developed through informal contacts or networking (Wimmer & Dominick, 2002). In different circumstances, the best sample of interviewees is a probability sample. A probability sample is chosen in a manner that can be calculated statistically to reveal the probability that the sample is representative of the larger population of people that the interviews hope to reflect. The statistics are used only to describe the sample and not to draw conclusions about the data that will be collected later. For the *Eagle*/WSU project, a randomly drawn sample was deemed necessary because the newspaper staff wanted to learn about the concerns of a particular and sizable population—more than 350,000 residents of the county that encompasses the city of Wichita. After deciding on a sampling method, the next step was to obtain willing participants. One popular way to draw probability samples designed to reflect large populations is random-digit dialing, and it was used by *Eagle* employees to identify 270 county residents who were willing to participate.

Preparing for the Interviews

With the sample drawn and the research problem in mind, the research team began to work on the interview guide. The goal was to build on the basic criteria of focused interviews—range, specificity, depth, and personal context (Merton et al., 1956/1990). The guide was designed to help interviewers collect detailed personal experiences and comprehensive opinions on a maximum number of topics. The guide was based on the Merton et al. (1956/1990) procedures and supplemented by other publications on interviewing (Labaw, 1980; McCracken, 1988). Within the guide, the interviewers received information on how to initiate the interview session, help put the respondent at ease, and probe for full responses. Material on interpersonal skills involved in conducting interviews was distributed to the interviewers.

Except for demographic data, all questions were open-ended (Merton, 1987; Merton et al., 1956/1990; Mishler, 1986). The guide was written to allow free discussion and questions to be asked by the respondent. The questions on the guide were sequenced. The first question asked respondents to identify their concerns, then interviewers were instructed to probe for how respondents specifically viewed those concerns. Next, interviewers asked respondents to indicate at what level (personal, neighborhood, community, state, national, and international) their concerns existed. This was followed by a question designed to establish the locus of responsibility of their concerns. The researchers sought to know who or what institutions respondents believed were responsible for addressing their concerns. Finally, interviewers asked respondents how they kept informed. The guide called for respondents to be assured anonymity at the beginning of the interview, but each was asked at the end of the interview whether he or she would be willing to be interviewed by a reporter for a newspaper story. The interview guide was prepared, pretested, and revised prior to conducting the first interview. To assure uniformity across the interviews, the interviewers attended two training sessions and conducted practice interviews. The interviews were scheduled to last 30 minutes. They were tape-recorded, and the interviewers took supplemental notes. Each of the 17 interviewers conducted approximately 12 interviews. The use of multiple interviewers established one form of triangulation (or multiple cross-checks) for the study.

An important part of the preinterview process involved informing the respondents about the project and assuring that the respondents were aware of the kind of information they would be asked. Those who agreed to be interviewed were mailed a letter explaining the project. Respondents were then contacted by telephone by one of the graduate students. The call reiterated the purpose of the project. A framework was created through the letters and phone calls to heighten the conscious awareness of the respondents so that they would be ready to talk when they arrived at the interview site (Labaw, 1980). In consideration of the respondents' travel time, interviews were held at one of five locations scattered across the county.

Determining the Project's Validity and Reliability

To ensure the validity, or accuracy, and the reliability, or consistency, procedures for each part of the project were stringent. Then after the project was completed, all the procedures were reviewed and any possible limitations were noted. To assure an adequate and representative sample, repeated telephone calls were made to prospective subjects to schedule interviews and later to reschedule broken interview dates. As a result, 192 people out of the sample pool were interviewed for a completion rate of 88 percent. Despite the high response rate, convenience appeared to play a role in garnering participation. A substantial representation of those with discretionary time or flexible schedules, such as housewives, professionals, and shift workers, were interviewed. The young, the elderly, the handicapped, and the poor may have been underrepresented. To be interviewed, one needed a telephone and transportation to the site. Was the sample an accurate representation of the county population? To find out, a profile of those interviewed was compared to U. S. census data. Comparisons based on age, gender, length of residence in the county, and voter registration did not prove the sample to be a mirror image of the general population neither was it grossly misrepresentative.[1]

Clear-cut, on-site interview procedures were followed. Diversity of responses was solicited through a heterogeneous group of interviewers; both genders and a variety of ages were represented. Yet, despite the precautions, the presence of the interviewer may have affected how some subjects responded to questions. In a few cases, respondents apparently tailored their responses to conform to the perceived personal attitudes of individual interviewers. For example, interviewers who were international students reported a higher rate of discussions centered on global concerns than did the other interviewers. Interviewers who were African American and Hispanic reported more discussions on racial and ethnic issues than did interviewers whose appearance did not identify them as minorities. A few interviewers commented that some of the respondents appeared to try to make a good impression by voicing only positive statements or expressing only normative ideas. These anomalies were noted in the final report.

Mortality rates for this kind of study are always a concern. The long duration of an interview time frame is often cited as a threat to a project's validity (Campbell & Stanley, 1963). The *Eagle* interviews took place over a 6-week period, and the time lapse may have contributed to a change in attitudes among those interviewed earlier and those interviewed near the end of the project. Then again, no spectacularly dramatic news event occurred during the interview period, so time was eliminated as a mitigating factor, and all the interviews were analyzed together.

Coding and Analyzing the Interviews

As the interviews were being conducted, the coding began. Using a matrix patterned after Miles' and Huberman's (1994) designs, each interviewer coded the interviews that he or she conducted by putting the responses in a category for each of the questions asked. After the initial coding, the interviewers broke down each category into subcategories based on broad themes found among the answers. One general debriefing session was held where preliminary findings were discussed and compared for verification. Finally, the coded data was reduced to summary sheets and a comprehensive analysis was prepared by the WSU faculty. The researchers' analysis based on grounded theory did not impose any preconceived theory on the data; instead, the findings emerged from the "ground," that is, from coding and summary sheets (Glaser & Strauss, 1967). The report was written directly from the comments that appeared in the categories.

The composite portrait revealed most respondents as registered voters who looked to the mass media for their source of information, had lived in the county for more than 5 years, and had some college education. Respondents addressed how the *Eagle* covers issues in an informed manner. In general, when the interviewees talked about their everyday lives, they did not speak in terms of legislation, governmental policy, or party endorsements. They told researchers their individual hopes, expectations, and fears. What they did not tell researchers was how their attitudes and opinions translated into political strategies or party platforms. In short, they raised a large number of issues and discussed them in disparate fashion. Personal concerns did not appear to translate directly into political solutions.

The exception to this was the topic of education. The respondents were more confident in offering solutions to educational woes. Respondents' suggestions included: design better teacher education, explore alternative teacher certification, increase teacher salaries, reduce the number of students in classes, extend the school year, and adopt national tests. When respondents were asked, "[Overall] which do you think is the most important concern of all you've named," the concerns mentioned were crime, 32; education, 26; taxes, 21; the economy, 20; abortion, 10; family life, 6; status of government and leadership, 5; health care, 5; drugs, 4; and the future of children, 4.[2] These same concerns have appeared, in roughly the same form, in public opinion polls for years. A review of Gallup poll surveys shows similar concerns coded as far back as 1975. Except for abortion, family life, and the future of children, the items on the Gallup list of the 21 most important problems in 1991 showed up again in 1993, and they were among the 10 most often mentioned by respondents.[3] It is not surprising that most of the same issues also turned up in later surveys

(Kohut, 2002). The importance of the *Eagle* research was that it revealed "how" those interviewed viewed the issues.

Overall, the *Eagle*/WSU research discovered that people's concerns related to an issue were often not entirely the same as government administrators or politicians view of that same issue, and, at times, were quite different. Recent research also has noted the multifaceted and personal-level responses people give when asked to comment on their political concerns. In mid-September 2002, a poll asked Americans whether they favored using U.S. military force to remove Iraq's leader, Saddam Hussein. The poll reported support (64%) for military intervention, but looking beneath the easy thumbs-up, thumbs-down characterization, a complex picture of public opinion appeared. Kohut (2002) discovered a conflicted public that voiced many qualifications and limitations about their vote on this particular issue, just as the earlier *Eagle*/WSU research uncovered multifaceted responses when individuals spoke about their concerns.

It was clear to the interviewers and principal researchers in 1991 that a new and different kind of research report was needed. The team wanted to show how stability across major topics voiced by people breaks down into problems that link issues and choices to individual's personal lives. The researchers began by providing the *Eagle* with a list of the most often mentioned topics together with selected verbatim accounts that showed how people spoke about their personal concerns. Attached to the report was a list of news story ideas generated by the student interviewers and faculty researchers. These were posed as questions. The news story ideas came directly from the words of the interviewees and corresponded to the eight top concerns found in the interviews. The *Eagle* management team was surprised by the topics and noted it was doubtful that reporters and editors could have come up the topics by just kicking around ideas. At the time, none of the general topics in the local and national news were being addressed from the particular viewpoints voiced across the interviews. Some of the interviewees' highly ranked topics were not being covered at all.

How the Newsroom Used the Findings

The eight major topics of concern named in the interviews are followed by some proposed news story ideas (questions) the research team found associated with that particular concern. They are:

1. Crime: Is crime really higher in the parts of the city where most people think it is higher? Do more people support gun control now that so many fear random and crime-related shootings? How can we learn to feel safe in

our city? Should we? How can we reclaim victims' rights? What exactly is the relationship between drugs and crime in Wichita?

2. Education: See findings discussed previously in this chapter.

3. Taxes: Why are taxes rising, and who is to blame?

4. The economy: How many businesses have failed in the past year? How many surviving businesses have had layoffs? How many vacant business properties are there? How does the high interest paid on credit-card debt affect the pocketbook of the average family and our nation? How many homeless are there in Wichita, and what is being done to help them?

5. Abortion: Wichita had been the scene of a Right to Life protest in the summer of 1991 that lasted more than 40 days. Media coverage was extensive; therefore, story ideas were not suggested for this topic.

6. Family life: Why cannot quality day care be affordable? How do strong families get that way? Stay that way? What family values are attacked most these days?

7. Health care: Why will not some doctors take Medicare and Medicaid patients? In what specialties is it most difficult for these patients to find help? Why? What are the best health care plans for workers among companies that employ locally?

8. Future of our children: What does cultural diversity mean? How can we regain community connectiveness? How at the community level, can we better combat loneliness ?

After receiving the report, the *Eagle* launched a major eight-part, page-one series based on the interviews. Titled the "People Project," the series ran as a comprehensive package that included in-depth reports, new interviews with citizens, further interviews with some of the original respondents, photos, explanatory graphics, an overall thematic design, and an identifying logo. The series was widely reviewed and became labeled as one of the first of many public or civic journalism projects to emerge in the early 1990s. The initial report also served as background information for public opinion telephone surveys conducted by the *Eagle* prior to the next general election, and, over the ensuing months, the *Eagle* addressed many of the 26 story proposals in separate news stories.

As the research results were put into practice, the newspaper staff learned that covering many of the story suggestions required innovative strategies. Following up on the suggestions involved building new networks of informants, many of whom did not qualify as credible sources in the traditional sense of that term. One staffer offered that a reporter simply could not rely on cultivating a single source or calling an established agency to get the scoop.

Second, the researchers and newspaper staff acknowledged that the project was time-bound. Over time, some of the concerns identified matured then faded away, others grew in intensity, and new issues appeared. The research findings and the People Project that followed were a freeze-framed picture of one community at one point in time.

CONCLUSION

When a project calls for an interpretative technique—that will gather specific data and at the same time reflect on the lives, circumstances, and distinctiveness of a populace (whether large or small)—the results of focused interviews are helpful. Developed during World War II for use in conjunction with quantitative studies, the focused interview method solicits in-depth, personal remarks. Because they are conducted one-on-one, focused interviews offer benefits over focus groups and shore up deficiencies of opinion polls that identify popular issues without checking what the issue-labels mean to individuals. Focused interviews involve many of the same techniques journalists use in daily reporting, but focused interviews are conducted according to a protocol that can be reviewed to discover commonalities among those interviewed. Among the comments collected in a focused interview project conducted by *The Wichita Eagle* and WSU researchers were expressions of gratitude from respondents for having an opportunity to be heard out in the interviews and appreciation for being made to feel important. Many said they were surprised that anyone, much less those in charge of the city's newspaper, would be interested in what they had to say. The results of the project show that how people talk about issues can turn out to be much more meaningful than what people identify as the issues. Use of qualitative methods such as the focused interview can dramatically shift political coverage and open doors for a new kind of interactive journalism.

ENDNOTES

[1] Of the Sedgwick County residents interviewed who gave their age, there were 9 (5%) between 18 and 24 years as compared to 14% of the total population who comprised that age group, 39 (23%) between 25 and 34 years as compared to 27% of the total population, 64 (37%) between 35 and 44 years as compared to 21% of the total population, 23 (13%) between 45 and 54 years as compared to 13% of the total population, 29 (17%) between 55 and 64 years as compared to 10% of the total population, and 7 (4%) who claimed to be more than 65 years old as compared to 16% of the total population (Census of Population and Housing, 1990). As for gender, 55% were male as compared to 49% of the total population and 45% were female as compared to 51% of the total population (U.S. Census, 1990). Five said they had lived in Sedgwick County less than 5 months, 26 less than 6 years, 15 less than 11 years, and 116 had lived in the county more than 11 years; 146 reported they were registered voters.

[2]Other concerns deemed most important were named by fewer than four respondents. Those named ranged from culvert repair to personal problems such as protecting one's children from violence at school.

[3]Data gathered by the American Institute on Public Opinion show results from a representative sample of the U.S. population asked at regular intervals an open-ended question: What is the most important problem facing the nation? Recurring as major categories are politics, economics, international relations–defense, the environment, health, poverty, race relations, crime, and morality. Most often mentioned in November 1991 were: (a) the economy in general, 32%; (b) unemployment, 23%; (c) poverty–homelessness, 16%; (d) drugs, 10%; (e) health care, 6%; (f) crime, 6%; (g) dissatisfaction with government, 5%; (h) AIDS, 5%; (i) insurance–Social Security, 5%; (j) federal-budget deficit, education quality, ethics–moral decline, trade relations–deficit, all 4% (Saad, 1993).

REFERENCES

Adams, S. (2001). *Interviewing for journalists.* New York: Routledge.

Berger, A. A. (2000). *Media and communication: Research methods.* Thousand Oaks, CA: Sage.

Biagi, S. (1991). *Interviews that work.* New York: Wadsworth.

Brissett, D., & Edgley, C. (1990). *Life as theater: A dramaturgical sourcebook.* New York: Aldine de Gruyter.

Campbell, D. T., & Stanley, J. C. (1963). *Experimental and quasi-experimental designs for research.* Skokie, IL: Rand McNally.

Census of Population and Housing. (1990). *1990 census of population and housing. Wichita, KS MSA.* Washington, DC: U.S. Government Printing Office.

Fielding, N. G., & Fielding, J. L. (1986). *Linking data.* Beverly Hills, CA: Sage.

Gibbs, C. K., & Warhover, T. (2002). *Getting the whole story: Reporting and writing the news.* New York: Guilford.

Glaser, B. G., & Strauss, A. L. (1967). *The discovery of grounded theory.* Chicago: Aldine.

Gollin, A. E. (1990). Foreword. In R. K. Merton, M. Fiske, & P. L. Kendall, *The focused interview* (pp. ix–xii). New York: The Free Press. (Original work published 1956)

Hsia, H. J. (1988). *Mass communications research methods: A step by step approach.* Hillsdale, NJ: Lawrence Erlbaum Associates.

Iorio, S. H., & Huxman, S. S. (1996). Media coverage of political issues and the framing of personal concerns. *Journal of Communication, 46,* 97–115.

Kohut, A. (2002, September 29). Simply put, the public's view can't be put simply. *The Washington Post,* p. B05.

Labaw, P. J. (1980). *Advanced questionnaire design.* Cambridge, MA: Abt Books.

Lazarsfeld, P. F. (1944). The controversy over detailed interviews. *Public Opinion Quarterly, 8,* 38–60.

Lindlof, T. R. (1995). *Qualitative communication research methods.* Thousand Oaks, CA: Sage.

Maso, I., & Wester, F. (Eds.). (1996). *The deliberate dialogue: Qualitative perspectives on the interview.* Brussels, Belgium: VUB University Press.

McCracken, G. (1988). *The long interview.* Newbury Park, CA: Sage.

Merton, R. K. (1987). The focused interview and focus groups. *Public Opinion Quarterly, 51,* 550–566.

Merton, R. K., Fiske, M., & Kendall, P. L. (1990). *The focused interview.* New York: The Free Press. (Original work published 1956)

Merton, R. K., & Kendall, P. L. (1946). The focused interview. *American Journal of Sociology, 51,* 541–557.

Metzler, K. (1997) *Creative interviewing* (3rd ed.). New York: Allyn & Bacon.

Miles, M. B., & Huberman, A. M. (1994). *Qualitative data analysis: An expanded sourcebook.* Thousand Oaks, CA: Sage.

Mishler, E. G. (1986). *Research interviewing.* Cambridge, MA: Harvard University Press.

Morgan, D. L. (1988). *Focus groups as qualitative research.* Beverly Hills, CA: Sage.

Nathan, H. (1986). *Critical choices in interviews.* Berkeley, CA: Institute of Governmental Studies University of California Berkeley.

Paterno, S. F., & Stein, M. L. (2001). *Talk straight listen carefully.* Ames, IA: Iowa State University Press.

Peterson, E. E. (1987). Media consumption and girls who want to have fun. *Critical Studies in Mass Communication, 4,* 37–50.

Poindexter, P. M., & McCombs, M. E. (2000). *Research in mass communication.* Boston: Bedford/St. Martin's.

Potter, W. J. (1996). *An analysis of thinking and research about qualitative methods.* Mahwah, NJ: Lawrence Erlbaum Associates.

Saad, L. (1993, January). Most important problem. *The Gallup Poll Monthly, 328,* 31–32.

Seidman, I. (1998). *Interviewing as qualitative research.* New York: Teachers' College Press.

Wimmer, R. D., & Dominick, J. R. (2002). *Mass media research* (7th ed.). New York: Wadsworth.

Zuckerman, H. (1972). Interviewing an ultra-elite. *Public Opinion Quarterly, 36,* 159–175.

8

Ethnographic Journalism

Janet M. Cramer
University of New Mexico

Michael McDevitt
University of Colorado, Boulder

Ethnography is primarily concerned with uncovering meanings—in particular, the meanings inherent to a particular group and its practices. The ethnographer accomplishes this awareness through a process of immersion into the life, routines, and rituals of the social setting under study. We describe in this chapter the principles and techniques of ethnographic journalism, but we are well aware that the method could put reporters in an awkward position in relationship to "sources." Reporting as social immersion would seem to violate the traditional understanding of objectivity as detachment from sources and subjects. However, we placed quote marks around the word "sources" for a reason—to emphasize that the task of grafting ethnography onto journalism requires us to revisit the author-subject relationship of reporting.

We offer what we hope is a persuasive rationale as to why journalists should use this powerful tool for observing and documenting social life. As we describe, ethnography is really not the alien concept that some in a newsroom might imagine; its narrative scheme and observational methods are close kin to long-respected journalistic practices. However, in providing practical suggestions for how to conduct this type of reporting, we will contemplate some of the ethical dilemmas that arise out of this blending of social science with journalism. We conclude with a description of a case study involving ethnographic reporting of panhandlers in a Northern California community.

PRINCIPLES AND TECHNIQUES OF ETHNOGRAPHY

Drawing on the root meanings of the words "ethno" (people) and "graphy" (describing), Lindlof (1995) explained that an ethnographer traditionally tries to describe all relevant aspects of a culture's material existence, social system, and collective beliefs and experiences. Thus, the more detail an ethnographer supplies and the more in-depth the encounter with a particular group, the greater the chances for a reader to understand that group and its members' feelings, thoughts, values, challenges, and goals.

Sociologists have used ethnography as a method in the field since the early 19th century (Gold, 1997; Marcus & Fischer, 1986/1999), but the best-known early study might be Bronislaw Malinowski's visits to the Trobriand Islands in the 1920s (Lindlof, 1995). In his research, Malinowski exhibited the value of sustained, firsthand experience with a group's environment, language, rituals, social customs, relationships, and experiences in the production of a truthful, authentic, and comprehensive account of that culture (Berger, 2000; Keyton, 2001; Van Maanen, 1988). Other examples include ethnographies of such groups as street gangs (Conquergood, 1994), witches' covens (Lesch, 1994), and Vietnam veterans' meetings (Braithwaite, 1997). In each case, the ethnographer was immersed in the group's activities to provide an insider's standpoint. Such thick description (Geertz, 1973) provides a perspective that emerges from within a group rather than being imposed from the observer's point of view. Ultimately, ethnography as exploration and investigation of a case in detail results in an analysis that involves explicit interpretation of the meanings and functions of human actions (Atkinson & Hammersley, 1994).

This explicit interpretation, however, is only achieved through close contact with the group being studied. Ethnographers are cautioned against imposing their own views on the data they collect (in the form of observations, conversations, and participation in the group's activities). Weber (1947) argued that only from a group member's perspective could an authentic account be achieved. The observed group keeps the ethnographer in check by validating or challenging the ethnographer's interpretation of events, because members of that group are considered the ultimate authorities regarding the significance of events and practices pertaining to the group (Gamble, 1978; Glaser & Strauss, 1967; Gold, 1997).

An ethnographer may participate in the life of a group at various levels, either as a complete participant, a participant as observer, an observer as participant, or as a complete observer (Atkinson & Hammersley, 1994; Gold, 1958; Junker, 1960). We discuss in a subsequent section the practical and ethical considerations of enacting these roles in journalism. The complete participant is fully functioning as a member of the scene, but others are not aware of the ethnographer's role (Keyton, 2001). A participant as observer acknowledges his or her observation role to the group under study but participates fully in that group's culture or activities. The observer as participant has the primary goal of observation and only a secondary role in participation, usually because of a lack of full access to or membership in the group, as Lesch's (1994) study of witch covens illustrated. The complete observer blends into the surroundings or is hidden completely from the group. There is no participation in the group's activities by the ethnographer and no awareness of the ethnographer's presence by the group being studied.

In addition to the selection of a participant–observer role, the practice of ethnography typically entails extensive use of field notes and may additionally include interviews with group members. An extended period of immersion is usually required, although specific time frames are dependent on the situation under study and other potential limiting factors, such as money or access. Typically, data are collected over a period of several days, but in certain cases, ethnographers have devoted years to collecting information. It may take many visits to understand fully why a group does what it does or to understand the thoughts, feelings, and attitudes of the members of a particular subculture. In the case of Conquergood's (1994) study of street gangs, the author decided to relocate to the neighborhood he was studying.

A RATIONALE FOR ETHNOGRAPHIC REPORTING

Ethnographic reporting challenges journalists' understanding of objectivity, neutrality, and balance, but it should appeal to professionals' commitment to enlighten rather than to obscure in the portrayal of everyday life. In fact, serious contemplation about the appropriateness of ethnography in journalism would suggest that the telling of authentic stories requires some rethinking about the relationships between reporters and sources.

To protect their objectivity, journalists are urged to keep some social and emotional distance between themselves and the people they write about. From an epistemological perspective, of course, the fact-value dichotomy is problematic at best. With respect to ethnography, the principle of detachment must be revisited if journalists are to embrace this method as a way to know, in intimate detail, the perspectives of groups that are otherwise invisible or stereotypically portrayed in the news.

While maddening to academic critics who highlight its problematic—if not delusional—implications, objectivity in journalism is not a static orientation to news work; perceptions about it have evolved in recent decades as professionals have come to appreciate its limitations (Ettema & Glasser, 1998). Within the profession itself, the norm of objectivity has shifted to an emphasis on more realistic goals such as neutrality, balance, accuracy, and fairness (Durham, 1998). This is reflected in the principles identified by reporting textbooks (e.g., Fedler, Bender, Davenport, & Kostyu, 1997), and in evidence of increased reflection about the routines of news production (e.g., Kovach & Rosenstiel, 2001).

One advantage of ethnographic reporting is how it portrays in a responsible manner the lives and cultures of groups that are typically marginalized through mainstream journalism practices. While most journalists do not refer to in-depth feature reporting as ethnographic, an abiding goal of the profession is pluralism in the portrayal of a culture's diverse groups. The Hutchins Commission, for example, advocated the "projection of a representative picture of the constituent groups in the society" (1947, p. 26). Responsible performance means "that the images repeated and emphasized be such as are in total representation of the social group as it is. The truth about any social group, though it should not exclude its weaknesses and vices, includes recognition of its values, its aspirations, and its common humanity." The commission expressed faith that if readers were presented with the "inner truth of the life of a particular group," they would develop respect and understanding for that group (p. 27). Inner truth is a key concept because an understanding of a group on its own terms is the very purpose of ethnography.

What is still lacking from the journalistic ethos, according to Durham (1998), is the recognition that representations of the truth about a group depend on the reporter's social location. Granted, the obligation to seek out oppositional views alleviates professional concerns about the inevitability of subjectivity. Thus the recent emphasis on balance is a more realistic goal than the pursuit of objectivity as value-free reporting. In practice, however, this creates a kind of crippling relativism that enforces dominant ideologies by defining the limits of acceptable public discourse.

Durham advocated "standpoint epistemology" as an escape from "the intellectual quicksand of relativism and the indefensible territory of neutrality and detachment" (p. 126). Standpoint epistemology requires a reformulation of objectivity, directing it away from the unrealistic erasure of bias toward the purposeful incorporation of subjective perspectives. Borrowing from feminist theory (Harding, 1991) and sociological models of knowledge production (Mannheim, 1952), Durham (1998) argued that people inside the dominant social order collect and interpret information about those who are either inside or outside it: "It is my contention here that news stories are journalistic because it is journalists who relay them" (p. 130). Geertz (1973) recognized the same problem in the ethnography of anthropological research, arguing that accounts of events or of people are ultimately interpretations of outsiders, casting suspicion on the realism or authenticity of such accounts. In response to this critique, ethnographers in recent years have become more reflexive about their social positions as observers of others, and now Durham advocates the same for journalists.

This reflexivity requires that reporters become self-conscious about their social locations in relation to the individuals and groups they write about. Autonomous reporters would realize that to pursue ethnographic journalism, they must in some ways transcend not only professional conventions and reporting habits but also their own demographic profiles. As a first step, Durham advocated strong objectivity, in which journalists would approach reporting from the vantage point of marginalized groups to counterbalance the dominant perspectives of mainstream news media. This approach becomes problematic, to say the least, in light of the formal education, training, and professional socialization that positions many reporters closer to the insider views of dominant groups than the views of the disadvantaged or the politically disengaged.

The context in which most journalism is practiced, in highly bureaucratic and corporate settings, further restricts the realization of strong objectivity. Glasser (1992) noted that the very purpose of professional socialization is to obliterate diversity in journalistic values and reporting practices, so that the only diversity that remains is of the token variety, with the primary concern being the ethnic breakdown of the editorial staff. What we need, Glasser contended, is diversity in the true sense of the word, so that journalists bring a wealth of cultural perspectives, not only to the newsroom itself but also to their methods of newswriting. Ethnography provides what is perhaps the most effective method for enacting strong objectivity.

Thus, one advantage of the ethnographic method is accurate portrayal of various groups in society that may not be realized when adhering to traditional methods or newsmaking criteria. Another advantage is a rethinking of the problematic notion of objectivity. However, ethnographic reporting raises some ethical considerations that are in some ways representative of the profession but also unique in the application of ethnographic techniques. We consider next common areas of concern, along with some divergence in thinking, in the ways that journalism and ethnography address ethical issues involving verification, bias, disclosure of intent to sources, and confidentiality.

ETHICAL CONSIDERATIONS

Objectivity as Verification

For journalists, objectivity is typically construed as detachment from the object or persons being reported, along with the assurance of balanced perspectives. Ethnography, however, represents the antithesis of this with its emphasis on immersion and its goal of telling a story as intimately as possible from the standpoint of the group being studied. Immersion into the life of those observed can invite a certain measure of idealization. As Keyton (2001) observed, the researcher's "value and belief system becomes so integrated with the value and belief systems of those being observed that the researcher loses the ability to believe that a degree of objectivity is attainable" (p. 275). Rather than detachment, however, the purpose of objectivity, with respect to ethnography, is faithfulness to the real world under study. What is sought is the retelling of a story as it actually occurs, not as the ethnographer interprets it. Thus, procedures are used to maximize observational efficacy, minimize investigator bias, and allow for replication or verification or both of the ethnographer's observations (Gold, 1997, p. 397). Objectivity is achieved when the ethnographer's report and the participants' experiences are in agreement.

Journalists are urged to check facts for accuracy and to protect sources if there is potential harm that might occur as a result of publication (e.g., Fedler et al., 1997). However, the verification of explicit and uncontested facts is too limiting as a prescription for ethnographic journalism. If journalists are to tell stories from the standpoint of a particular group, the individuals observed must participate to some extent in verification of how the meanings of their lives are portrayed. Allowing this would require some rethinking of journalistic habits, such as the norm that reporters should not allow a source to read a draft prior to publication.

Avoiding Bias

A compatible goal of the ethnographic method and the craft of journalism is the absence of intended bias. Both the ethnographer and the journalist strive to avoid applying their own frame of reference to the events and people observed. Because the purpose of ethnography is to portray a group accurately and intimately, the imposition of the ethnographer's point of view would corrupt the final product.

However, when applied to the organizational context of journalism, the evaluation of bias must extend beyond the individual reporter to the news production process itself. Ethnography in journalism, for instance, requires an abandonment of routines such as the reliance on official sources and the goal of creating balance by juxtaposing conflicting views of ideological elites (Gans, 1980; Tuchman, 1978).

Covert or Overt Observation

Another ethical consideration is whether to inform those being studied of the intent of the ethnographer to observe certain practices. Although one of the roles an ethnographer might assume is that of pure observer—in which the presence of the ethnographer is unknown to those being observed—such practices are prohibited when federal funding is used to support research (Punch, 1994). Still, the necessity to receive the consent of those observed might prevent many useful projects. As Punch (1994) observed: "a strict application of codes will restrain and restrict a great deal of informal, innocuous research in which ... explicitly enforcing rules concerning informed consent will make the research role simply untenable" (p. 90). Therefore, ethical considerations regarding covert observation should be considered guidelines and not strict rules.

A distinction is made, however, between informed consent and deception regarding one's purpose. Deception seems to be most common when an ethnographer embarks on research intended to expose corrupt practices or to advocate for reforms. Researchers disagree on where and when to draw this line. The benefits of particular kinds of knowledge might outweigh the potential or actual harm of methods used to obtain that knowledge, according to some researchers. Most scholars agree that the rights of subjects take precedence and should guide one's moral calculations.

Attempts to justify deception in journalism typically derive from the premise that unusual reporting techniques are necessary to expose certain types of corruption (Elliott & Culver, 1992). By contrast, we envision ethnographic reporting as a commitment to portray people and perspectives usually ignored in mainstream media. Apart from the ethical implications, deception restricts the capacity of the observer to create an authentic portrait. Concerns about privacy, along with the need to include group members in the story verification process, require that a journalist openly declare her intentions.

On the other hand, it is possible to envision ethnography used in investigative journalism with the goal of exposing corruption. Whether in conventional or investigative journalism, the motivation to conceal a reporter's intention stems from the assumption that one's identity as a reporter alters naturally occurring behaviors. The immediacy and audience size associated with publication, coupled with the public's increasing cynicism about journalistic motives (Cappella & Jamieson, 1997), often produces guarded or artificial behavior. Awareness of ethnographic techniques, however, could encourage journalists to think of alternatives to concealment or to outright stealth. Whereas social scientists are trained in methods that address threats to inference such as the Hawthorne effect, journalism education provides little guidance beyond interview techniques that might put a source at ease (e.g., Rich, 2000). If journalists were trained in techniques that reduce—or at least accommodate—the influence of their presence on others, they might be less tempted to conceal their identities.

Confidentiality

A related concern is the preservation of confidentiality. An ethnographer's assurance of confidentiality provides some safeguard against invasion of privacy. According to Punch (1994): "There is a strong feeling among fieldworkers that settings and respondents should not be identifiable in print and that they should not suffer harm or embarrassment as a consequence of research" (p. 92). To observe this standard requires some sensitivity to what might be considered embarrassing and what might be considered public as opposed to private. Journalism entails a larger and more diverse audience in comparison to academic research, making the protection of confidentiality all the more important for ethnographic reporting. Publication in mainstream media represents a magnitude of potential harm that far exceeds the damage that might arise from private behavior revealed in a scholarly journal. A reporter should discuss with group members—and perhaps negotiate—the kind of information that should be revealed. While a reporter might assure that an individual remains anonymous, certain actions or statements could become public, with possible harm to the group's reputation.

HOW TO CONDUCT ETHNOGRAPHIC REPORTING

To illustrate the process of ethnographic reporting, we include Table 8.1 that pinpoints key differences between in-depth feature reporting (the closest relative in conventional journalism to the method described in this chapter) and ethnographic journalism on three levels: conceptualization, reporting, and writing.

Conceptualization

In traditional conceptions of newsworthiness, journalists focus on extraordinary events and the actions and decisions of politicians, business leaders and celebrities. By contrast, ethnographic reporting aims for pluralism in its coverage of everyday people, stressing individual character and quotidian victories over

TABLE 8.1

Differences Between Conventional and Ethnographic Reporting

	Conventional In-depth Features	Ethnographic Portraits
	Conceptualization	
Newsworthiness	• Change	• Adaptation
	• The unusual	• Hidden meanings
	• Celebrities and elites	• Rituals and practices
	Reporting	
Relationship with sources	Autonomous professional	Socially acceptable incompetent
Observation	Deductive	Inductive
Interviewer	The miner	The traveler
	Writing	
Narrator	Journalist	Group
Epistemology	Balance	Authenticity

bureaucratic or political achievements. The notion of change as a criterion for newsworthiness helps us to make this distinction. While a conventional journalist will look for social eruptions or gradual trends that signal change, a reporter pursuing ethnography examines change in a different sense. According to the perspective of structural functionalism, social systems do change but for the purpose of adaptation and continuity. The paradox of this dynamic becomes manifest in rituals and practices that help a group to cope with external pressures while preserving identity and values. These practices can involve hidden meanings that must be understood by a journalist if the group's story is to be told accurately.

Reporting

A journalist interviewing for an in-depth feature would seek to establish rapport with sources while maintaining some distance as an autonomous observer and recorder. Reporters are sometimes advised to demonstrate knowledge about a topic while conversing with a source, in the hope that the interviewee will reciprocate and offer valuable insights. In ethnographic journalism, however, the reporter must not let professional expertise impinge on her effort to observe and gather information in a natural setting. Lofland and Lofland recommended that a field researcher act as a "socially acceptable incompetent" (1995, pp. 56–57) as a technique for gaining access to groups without altering their behavior.

In conventional journalism, reporters usually have in mind the basic theme of their stories before most interviews are conducted. With space to fill and a deadline to meet, an editor might insist that a reporter essentially have the nut graph (the paragraph that distills what the story is about) written before beginning research. This deductive approach—in which interviews are conducted to confirm the story initially imagined by the reporter—is not compatible with the inductive techniques of ethnography. Only after a process of discovery does the writer contemplate the meaning of what she observed.

Kvale's (1996) portrayal of the interview as a miner or a traveler highlights how these contrasting approaches are played out during interviews (Babbie, 1998). Miners assume that their role is to dig out nuggets of information, along with lively quotes, because the source is essentially used to extract information. A traveler wanders without a map through unknown territory and asks questions "that lead the subjects to tell their own stories of their lived world" (Babbie, 1998, p. 5).

Some of the best examples of in-depth and literary journalism in the United States reflect ethnographic principles (e.g., Berner, 1999; Connery, 1992; Sims, 1990; Sims and Kramer, 1995), and practitioners have on occasion explicitly described their work as ethnographic (e.g., Kramer, 1995; Sims, 1995). As explained by Harrington (1997), the techniques of producing narratives of ordinary lives are similar to the ethnographic method: writing the story from the point of view of one or several subjects; gathering details from subjects' lives; gathering real-life dialogue; gathering "interior" monologue, such as what subjects are thinking, dreaming, imagining, or worrying about; gathering physical details of places and people; and immersing temporarily in the lives of subjects.

Immersion and what ethnographers would call participant observation are the primary techniques used to gather data. For instance, Kidder watched a design team build a computer to write his Pulitzer Prize-winning book, *The Soul of a New Machine*, and for another story, spent a year in a nursing home, taking notes and listening to conversations to collect material (Sims, 1995). In an interview with Norman Sims on the subject, Ted Conover said:

> Participant observation ... is the way I prefer to pursue journalism. It means a reliance not on the interview so much as on the shared experience with somebody. The idea to me that journalism and anthropology go together ... was a great enabling idea for my life—the idea that I could learn about different people and different aspects of the world by placing myself in situations, and thereby see more than you ever could just by doing an interview. (Sims, 1995, p. 13)

Writing

The goal of literary journalism, according to Kramer (1995), is to broaden "readers' scans" and allow them to see other lives and contexts, thereby moving readers—and writers—"toward realization, compassion, and in the best of cases, wisdom" (p. 34). Ethnography takes this principle a step further by insisting that the subjects written about are the actual narrators of the story. The writer becomes a medium through which the group's story is told. The close examination of a group ensures that it is not the ethnographer's point of view but the actual experiences, values, and goals of the group that are communicated (Blumer, 1969).

In this regard, the epistemological goal of the ethnographic reporter is authenticity in the portrayal of a group's perspective. By contrast, the knowledge produced in a conventional feature originates from attempts to create balance, whereby competing ideologies or other perspectives are juxtaposed. Kovach and Rosenstiel (2001) provided evidence that many journalists do realize the limitations of the concepts of objectivity, neutrality, and balance. The authors reported on a study they described as the most comprehensive examination ever conducted by journalists of news gathering and its responsibilities. "After synthesizing what we learned, it became clear that a number of familiar and even useful ideas—including fairness and balance—are too vague to rise to the level of essential elements of the profession" (p. 13). We want to emphasize that Kovach and Rosenstiel are describing a critical perspective expressed by journalists themselves, rather than a critique originating from academic theory.

A CASE STUDY: SIDEWALK STANDOFF

How the ethnographic method might be applied is illustrated next in the description of a case study conducted in Palo Alto, where college journalists produced stories on the homeless population.

Coverage of homeless people illustrates the potential harm of conventional reporting, as well as the value of an ethnographic alternative. In the late 1990s, for example, the City Council in Palo Alto enacted a ban on sitting or lying on downtown streets. Merchants had complained about homeless people hovering outside their storefronts and aggressive panhandlers scaring off customers. Local newspapers provided extensive coverage when about 200 citizens, in opposition to the ordinance, staged a sit-down protest outside downtown shops on the evening the law went into effect. However, in a university town that views itself as a tolerant community, the subsequent news stories seemed to enflame outrage on both sides.

The case study described here outlines how a political communication course at Stanford University, taught by one of the authors of this essay, sought to contribute to public knowledge and constructive dialogue about panhandling. In a project that became known as *Sidewalk Standoff*, students adopted a three-stage model. They developed goals based on evaluation of prior news coverage; generated stories using ethnographic methods; and assessed the community's reaction to the project. Ethnographic journalism obviously takes more time than the typical deadline-oriented coverage, and the class took advantage of the 10-week academic quarter to pursue activities associated with each of the three stages. Students eventually contributed multiple features and sidebars for the *Palo Alto Weekly*, an off-campus, locally owned paper.

Stage One: Evaluation

In content analysis or other methods, an evaluation of prior news coverage, particularly in its depictions of a particular subculture, can provide a rationale for ethnographic approaches. An analysis of coverage may reveal that the local press virtually ignores certain groups, or that it perpetuates stereotypes despite the lack of purposeful bias. This realization is itself an important outcome of educational training for future journalists because it might counteract the common scenario in which a student's psychological need to identify with a profession fosters a rigid loyalty to conventional notions of detachment and autonomy (McDevitt, Gassaway, & Perez, 2002).

For the Palo Alto project, students noticed that news sources rarely expressed outright hostility toward panhandlers, but reporters tended to lump homeless people together: as a collective problem, as an embarrassment for the community, as a curiosity for the upscale town, or as objects of sympathy. The local press dutifully provided what may have appeared to be a balanced account of the debate between merchants and community activists, but virtually absent were perspectives of homeless individuals themselves. Students resolved to understand the meanings that homeless people themselves bring to their lives and to share these insights with readers. This became the overriding goal of the class, and the next step was to choose the appropriate reporting techniques.

Stage Two: Ethnographic Reporting

The class initially decided on a team approach to reporting, which seemed to alleviate the unstated but obvious apprehension of some students about interacting with homeless people on their own turf. About a dozen students arrived together at a homeless shelter one morning to meet several men and women who were waiting for donuts and coffee. The team approach also allowed the class to distribute questionnaires efficiently to 33 homeless persons to produce data that would eventually supplement qualitative descriptions. Individual students then worked on their own to write intimate portraits of homeless people. Meanwhile, a few students tried their hands at first-person journalism by living the life of panhandlers for 1 day and experimenting with passive and aggressive approaches to begging.

In interviews and in observations of panhandling, students began to appreciate the diversity of life experiences and outlooks within the homeless population. In one news story, for example, a student explained that many homeless people never panhandle, consider such activity to be demeaning, and resent the negative image panhandling imparts to homeless people in general. Many of the panhandlers, in turn, described themselves as long-term, stable members of the community, and they expressed resentment toward newcomers who had engaged in aggressive begging.

In aggregate, the reporting seemed to challenge most directly the perception that homeless people were outsiders, rather than members of the community. Data from the survey distributed at the shelter supported the various narratives produced by the students. For example, the average number of years respondents had lived in Palo Alto was 15, about 55 percent of the respondents indicated that they had relatives in the San Francisco Bay Area, and 52 percent said they felt comfortable living in the area. Anecdotes from personality profiles portrayed the subjects with cultural traits, values, and parochial perspectives similar to other residents with monthly mortgage payments. Data from the questionnaires encouraged readers to come to the same conclusion.

Stage Three: Recording Community Response

The primary goal was to contribute to readers' understanding of panhandlers, not to influence policy at City Hall directly. The class did conclude the series, however, with a roundtable discussion held at the newspaper's office, to which public officials, activists, and merchants were invited. Most importantly from an ethnographic perspective, a member of the homeless community attended the discussion to confirm or challenge various portrayals in the students' news coverage. The hope was that insight from the published series would contribute to a constructive dialogue directed toward consensus on how to alleviate various concerns about panhandling.

The content of the newspaper's letters to the editor and of 110 telephone interviews conducted by students with residents following the coverage offered insight about the complexity of perspectives in the community. Indeed, many respondents expressed ambivalence about panhandlers: While 59 percent indicated that they had spoken with a homeless person, more than 40 percent said they would cross a road to avoid a panhandler. The class could not assert with certainty that its series contributed to this ambivalence, but if it did, this would be considered a positive outcome in light of prior research showing that the process of coming to judgment requires a reconsideration of assumptions prior to the attainment of a refined perspective (Yankelovich, 1991). The telephone survey design was not intended to produce inferences about the influence of news exposure on readers' knowledge and attitudes, but 55 percent of respondents agreed or strongly agreed with the following statement: The news reports "made me think more about possible solutions to the homeless problem."

A final outcome of the project concerned the influence of ethnographic reporting on the students themselves. The desire of some students to join the ranks of the panhandlers, if only for 1 day, and the nuanced manner in which they portrayed homeless individuals suggest that these journalists-in-training were embracing an empathetic approach to the craft. They seemed to be experiencing journalism as a form of citizenship, in which they were coming to know, perhaps for the first time, the true complexity of their community. They had certainly stepped beyond—both physically and psychologically—the privileged setting of the university campus.

However, if ethnography directs student journalists to a kind of immersion into the lives of marginalized groups, it also challenges the perception that professional autonomy is equivalent to social detachment. Students are encouraged to decide for themselves whether any ethnographic experiences they might have cross the line into advocacy. At the very least, a reflective response to this question encourages students to consider the limitations of what is typically considered objective, value-free reporting.

CONCLUSION

In the construction of authentic and empathetic portrayals, journalists are aided by employing ethnographic methods in their work. Such techniques entail immersion in a community or culture to reveal as deeply and as accurately as possible group members' feelings, thoughts, values, challenges, and goals.

These journalistic accounts, then, are drawn from perspectives within a group rather than interpretations imposed from the outside. Such perspectives reflect the strong objectivity described by Durham, which is not a detached viewpoint but a purposeful incorporation of subjective perspectives. It is an objectivity based on accuracy, rich description, and an insider point of view.

The aim of some community-oriented newspapers seems compatible with the ultimate goals of an ethnographic journalism—that is, to have a newspaper be of its community and let members of the community tell their stories through a journalist immersed temporarily in their culture (e.g., Hindman, 1998). While we recognize the hazards of adopting what may seem to be advocacy journalism, we contend that journalists can adopt ethnographic methods without sacrificing the essential values of the profession. Indeed, through ethnography, journalists might recover a core, but perhaps neglected, principle of their craft. As Harrington (1997) suggested: "The stories of everyday life—about ... people as they seek meaning and purpose in their lives, stories that are windows on our universal human struggle—should be at the soul of every good newspaper" (p. xiv).

At a practical level, we also recognize that reporters cannot practice ethnography on deadline. Like civic journalism or investigative reporting, ethnographic journalism requires a project approach based on substantial planning and management support. Indeed, it might require a fundamental change in a newsroom's culture. Civic and investigative journalism have become institutionalized as regular practice at a relatively small percentage of newspapers in the United States. We invite students as future professionals to consider whether ethnography also provides a compelling reason to slow the frenetic pace of daily news coverage.

Educators and students, meanwhile, can experiment with a three-stage curriculum strategy that initially asks students to evaluate conventional coverage. Students should then appreciate the value of ethnographic principles as they begin the reporting stage. Finally, students reflect on how their reporting might empower not merely their subjects, but themselves as storytellers now more deeply engaged in a community.

Through ethnographic journalism, students and professionals edge closer to portraying the inner truths of society's constituent groups (Hutchins Commission, 1947). Spradley (1979) wrote that ethnography represents "the one systematic approach in the social sciences that leads us into those separate realities that others have learned and used to make sense out of their worlds" (p. iv). However, if these separate realities are systematically excluded in news coverage, journalists must rethink the methods they use to describe the social world, and they must revisit the professional values that legitimize these methods.

REFERENCES

Atkinson, P., & Hammersley, M. (1994). Ethnography and participant observation. In N. K. Denzin & Y. Lincoln (Eds.), *Handbook of qualitative research* (pp. 248–261). Thousand Oaks, CA: Sage.

Babbie, E. (1998). *The practice of social research*. Belmont, CA: Wadsworth.

Berger, A. A. (2000). *Media and communication research methods: An introduction to qualitative and quantitative approaches*. Thousand Oaks, CA: Sage.

Berner, R. T. (1999). *The literature of journalism: Text and content*. State College, PA: Strata Publishing.

Blumer, H. (1969). *Symbolic interactionism: perspective and method*. Englewood Cliffs, NJ: Prentice Hall.

Braithwaite, C. A. (1997). "Were YOU there?" A ritual of legitimacy among Vietnam veterans. *Western Journal of Communication, 61*, 423–447.

Cappella, J. N., & Jamieson, K. H. (1997). *Spiral of cynicism: The press and the public good*. New York: Oxford University Press.

Charity, A. (1995). *Doing public journalism*. New York: Guilford.

Connery, T. B. (Ed.) (1992). *A sourcebook of American literary journalism: Representative writers in an emerging genre*. New York: Greenwood Press.

Conquergood, D. (1994). Homeboys and hoods: Gang communication and cultural space. In L. R. Frey (Ed.), *Group communication in context: Studies of natural groups* (pp. 23–55). Hillsdale, NJ: Lawrence Erlbaum Associates.

Durham, M. G. (1998). On the relevance of standpoint epistemology to the practice of journalism: The case for "strong objectivity." *Communication Theory, 82*, 117–140.

Elliott, D., & Culver, C. (1992). Defining and analyzing journalistic deception. *Journal of Mass Media Ethics, 7*, 69–84.

Ettema, J. S., & Glasser, T. L. (1998). *Custodians of conscience: Investigative journalism and public virtue*. New York: Columbia University Press.

Fedler, F., Bender, J. R., Davenport, L., & Kostyu, P. E. (1997). *Reporting for the media* (6th ed.). Fort Worth, TX: Harcourt Brace.

Gamble, D. (1978). The Berger inquiry: An impact assessment process. *Science, 199*, 946–952.

Gans, H. J. (1980). *Deciding what's news: A study of CBS Evening News, NBC Nightly News, Newsweek, and Time*. New York: Random House.

Geertz, C. (1973). Thick description: Toward an interpretive theory of culture. In *The interpretation of cultures* (pp. 3–30). New York: Basic Books.

Glaser, B. G., & Strauss, A. L. (1967). *The discovery of grounded theory: Strategies for qualitative research*. New York: Aldine.

Glasser, T. L. (1992). Professionalism and the derision of diversity: The case of the education of journalists. *Journal of Communication, 12*(2), 131–140.

Gold, R. (1958). Roles in sociological field observations. *Social Forces, 36*, 217–223.

Gold, R. L. (1997). The ethnographic method in sociology. *Qualitative Inquiry, 3*, 388–403.

Harding, S. (1991). *Whose science? Whose knowledge? Thinking from women's lives*. Ithaca, NY: Cornell University Press.

Harrington, W. (Ed.). (1997). *Intimate journalism: The art and craft of reporting everyday life*. Thousand Oaks, CA: Sage.

Hindman, E. B. (1998). "Spectacles of the poor": Conventions of alternative news. *Journalism and Mass Communication Quarterly, 75*, 177–193.

Hutchins Commission (1947). *A free and responsible press*. Chicago: University of Chicago Press.

Junker, B. (1960). *Field work*. Chicago: University of Chicago Press.

Keyton, J. (2001). *Communication research: Asking questions, finding answers*. Mountain View, CA: Mayfield Publishing Company.

Kovach, B., & Rosenstiel, T. (2001). *The elements of journalism: What newspeople should know and the public should expect*. New York: Crown Publishers.

Kramer, M. (1995). Breakable rules for literary journalists. In N. Sims & M. Kramer (Eds.), *Literary journalism* (pp. 21–34). New York: Ballantine.

Kvale. S. (1996). *InterViews: An introduction to qualitative research interviewing*. Thousand Oaks, CA: Sage.

Lesch, C. L. (1994). Observing theory in practice: Sustaining consciousness in a coven. In L. R. Frey (Ed.), *Group communication in context: Studies of natural groups* (pp. 57–84). Hillsdale, NJ: Lawrence Erlbaum Associates.

Lindlof, T. R. (1995). *Qualitative communication research methods*. Thousand Oaks, CA: Sage.

Lofland, J., & Lofland, L. H. (1995). *Analyzing social settings: A guide to qualitative observation and analysis*. Belmont, CA: Wadsworth.

Mannheim, K. (1952). *Essays on the sociology of knowledge*. London: Routledge & Kegan Paul.

Marcus, G. E., & Fischer, M. M. J. (1986/1999). *Anthropology as cultural critique: An experimental moment in the human sciences*. Chicago: The University of Chicago Press.

McDevitt, M., Gassaway, B., & Perez, F. G. (2002). The making and unmaking of civic journalists: Influences of professional socialization. *Journalism and Mass Communication Quarterly, 79*, 87–100.

Punch, M. (1994). Politics and ethics in qualitative research. In N. K. Denzin & Y. S. Lincoln (Eds.), *Handbook of qualitative research* (pp. 83–97). Thousand Oaks, CA: Sage.

Rich, C. (2000). *Writing and reporting news: A coaching method*. Belmont, CA: Wadsworth.

Sims, N. (Ed.) (1990). *Literary journalism in the twentieth century*. New York: Oxford University Press.

Sims, N. (1995). The art of literary journalism. In N. Sims & M. Kramer (Eds.), *Literary journalism: A new collection of the best American nonfiction* (pp. 3–19). New York: Ballantine.

Sims, N., & Kramer, M. (Eds.) (1995). *Literary journalism: A new collection of the best American nonfiction*. New York: Ballantine.

Spradley, J. P. (1979). *The ethnographic interview*. Fort Worth, TX: Harcourt Brace.

Tuchman, G. (1978). *Making news: A study in the construction of reality*. New York: Free Press.

Van Maanen, J. (1988). *Tales of the field: On writing ethnography*. Chicago: University of Chicago Press.

Weber, M. (1947). *The theory of social and economic organization* (1st American ed.). (A. M. Henderson & T. Parsons, Trans.). New York: Oxford University Press.

Yankelovich, D. (1991). *Coming to public judgment*. Syracuse, NY: Syracuse University Press.

9

Inventing Civic Mapping

Kathryn B. Campbell
University of Oregon

Some reporting assignments and research problems simply boggle the mind. How can a complicated social or political issue be investigated, understood in all of its complexity, and then communicated to an audience that may—or may not—be ready to consider and act on the information?

Part of the answer to this question is straightforward. To tackle complex research and storytelling about a community, a reporter can assess the qualitative and quantitative methods that have a documented history of successful implementation and then choose the method that appears best suited to the enterprise. Consider, however, the exciting and challenging notion that the best method may not have been devised yet. New research problems often call for the creation of new research methods, or for the combination of existing methods, to solve them.

The emerging practice of civic mapping is an example of such innovative thinking. At its most basic, civic mapping is a way for reporters and community researchers to find out who talks to whom about what. The "who" in this case could be an individual, community group, or government entity. The "whom" includes other individuals, groups, and organizations, as well as themselves. To "map" the patterns of communication, researchers systematically record information on the relationships among individuals and groups, paying special attention to the number and variety of the researchers' own sources. This map helps the researcher or reporter identify the gaps in communication channels, such as two groups working on housing issues who do not coordinate their efforts or entire neighborhoods whose residents are never interviewed for newspaper stories. Identifying such gaps is the first step toward closing them.

The journalists who decide to try civic mapping are indeed innovative. These mapping experiments, undertaken in about three dozen cities to date, have resulted in projects ranging from the creation of "expanded Rolodex" databases for reporters to multipart newspaper series on complex issues. Most often, however, the term mapping becomes a metaphor for a list, a database, or a chart, rather than being used in its more literal, traditional sense; and geographic maps have rarely been incorporated in the projects.

An exception is the case of civic mapping at *The Tampa Tribune* in Tampa, Florida. In 1999, two reporters at *The Tribune* wanted to find out how residents felt about a redevelopment plan that would encourage the restoration of charming but rundown houses in the Tampa Heights neighborhood. The assignment sounds deceptively simple. The reporters could have interviewed a couple of city officials, called three or four property owners, and written a solid news story about the pros and cons of the redevelopment plan. But they didn't. Realizing that they knew little more about the neighborhood than its name, they decided to experiment with civic mapping, immersing themselves in the Tampa Heights neighborhood until they developed a comprehensive, nuanced understanding of the community's concerns. Even though they were among the first to test this new research technique, what they learned has indelibly changed their own journalistic practice.

Another case of experimental civic mapping unfolded differently. To begin with, the research question was clearly complex. Reporters at *The Spokesman-Review* in Spokane, Washington, wanted to know why some children grow up to lead happy, productive lives and others simply end up on the streets, drug addicted, or in jail. More than that, they wanted to help Spokane families figure out how to help themselves raise successful children. Clearly, the issue could not be addressed by making a few phone calls and talking to a few parents. The Spokane journalists also decided to experiment with what they called civic mapping, inventing as necessary the methods they needed to research and report the enormously complicated story they had assigned themselves.

In Tampa and in Spokane, the experienced journalists assigned to these stories were familiar with many of the research techniques described in this volume. They were skilled, for example, in using focus groups and conducting in-depth interviews; and they were acquainted with the techniques of case studies, oral histories, ethnography, and issue analysis. They also had experience in using quantitative data in more traditional investigative reporting. Yet as they tackled their projects, they pushed themselves beyond the familiar to try to create something entirely new. In doing so, they were acting in the best tradition of the Chicago School—reaching across disciplines to try to develop ways of reporting and researching that are equal to the complexity of the problem at hand.

CONCEPTUALIZING CIVIC MAPPING

Civic mapping can be conceptualized in at least two ways: cognitively and structurally. The concepts are somewhat similar, but their differences lead quite naturally to different kinds of civic mapping. A brief introduction to these conceptual approaches may help explain how two experiments, both called civic mapping, differed so markedly.

Cognitive Mapping

Cognitive mapping is the kind of mapping previously described, which can be defined more formally as an attempt to catalog the actors in a community, their positions in the community and their relationships to each other, and their relationships to journalists. This is the methodology that was developed and disseminated by the Pew Center for Civic Journalism and The Harwood Group between 1999 and 2002. This method of civic mapping, which is described more fully later in this chapter, does not insist on the production of geographic maps; indeed, only one such set of maps emerged in the 3 years of the Pew–Harwood training seminars.

Structural Mapping

Structural mapping is more complex and thus better suited to complex research. Its hallmark is an attempt to capture graphically the social networks, layers of civic life, and the spatial relationships among people and institutions. Put another way, structural mapping literally uses maps of communities—streets and boulevards, bike paths and bridges, buildings and open spaces—to plot the pattern of community relationships. The central task of structural mapping is to

> demonstrate the complex set of interrelationships across the entire range of the multiple levels of society that make up the interlocking structure of public life. Individuals, small groups, larger groups and associations, and institutions all contribute to the structure of public life, and all must be considered in their interrelationships if we are to have any adequate working model of contemporary public life. (Friedland, Kang, Campbell, & Pondillo, 1999, p. 2)

These groups communicate with each other in a mediated atmosphere— that is, they construct an imagined community (Anderson, 1991) relying in large part on the media to circulate information about them. Using this kind of civic mapping, journalists can uncover the boundaries of communities—whether they are the boundaries of political partitions, the barriers of socioeconomic status, or the limits of common interest—and try to deduce how members of various communities get and use information about the others. The subsequent geographic display of detailed and comprehensive data on these patterns is critical for researchers to acquire an understanding of the whole, rather than simply the sum of the parts, of community life.

MAPPING IN HISTORICAL SOCIAL RESEARCH

Mapping is both an ordering and an orderly affair, and it has historically been seen as a way to reduce the amount of error present in calculations about the relationships among places and people. This was precisely the reason that Charles Booth, in the late 1800s, dedicated nearly two decades to mapping London. Booth's motives were clear: He wanted to demonstrate the correlations between poverty and wages, and between impoverished morality and organized religion, in order to provide social reformers with accurate information about the scope of the problems they were trying to solve. As noted in a previous chapter, the Booth method traveled well across the Atlantic, where social activists were dedicating themselves to research and reform. Jane Addams and Florence Kelley based *Hull-House Maps and Papers* (Residents, 1895) on the first volumes of Booth's study, *Labour and Life of the People in London* (1889, 1891). Booth's maps were also the model for dozens of graduate students whose research formed the core of the University of Chicago's version of sociology, commonly referred to as the Chicago School.

Mapping was central to all the research of the period and nowhere was it more important than in the Chicago School studies. Bulmer (1984) attributes to one monograph's author the recollection that "it was difficult as a Chicago sociologist in the 1920s to get a Ph.D. without doing a spot map" (p. 155). Indeed, graduate students from about 1922 to 1935 produced a series of studies that were not only illustrated by maps of their findings but used mapping as a crucial component of their methodology.[1]

One of these classic studies, *The Taxi-Dance Hall* (Cressey, 1925/1969), was completed under the direction of Professors Robert E. Park and Ernest Burgess. This study of the dime-a-dance halls of Chicago, which Cressey supplemented by research on similar establishments in other big cities of the 1920s, is an excellent example of the way the Chicago School used mapping to reveal relationships as well as to display the data in a published report. That is, mapping was a way of learning about the topic being studied, not just a graphic device to present what had been learned.

The taxi-dance halls, according to Cressey's analysis, had evolved in response to the social and economic needs of various groups: men who wanted female company, young women who wanted to earn more than factory wages, and
businessmen who wanted to make money. At a taxi-dance, men paid 10 cents
for dances with the women, who split the payment with the dance hall owners.
These taxi-dance halls were considered by most conventional people to be
breeding grounds for, at the very least, indecent behavior and interracial relationships, and, most probably, for prostitution and other illegal activities. As a
result, social workers were concerned with the morals of the young women who
worked as dancers, many of whom were in their middle teens, and law enforce-
ment agencies were concerned with crime and neighborhood safety.

The taxi-dance hall was not only a microcosm of the city itself; it was a product
of the city. Cressey investigated the taxi-dance halls socially, geographically, psychologically, and morally (through the voices of social workers, among others).
He concluded that taxi-dance halls filled legitimate needs for companionship,
commerce, and better wages in the city and that their more unsavory aspects
might be controlled through the efforts of "social engineers," his term for a collection of social workers, clergy, newspaper editors, police officials, and the like.

In the manner of the Chicago studies of the period, Cressey used a variety
of data from a variety of sources, trying to account for the structural changes
that rapid urbanization had brought to people's lives. He interviewed, at
great length, the girls and the men who paid for their company on the dance
floor. In addition, Cressey made maps. He plotted the locations of the dancers' homes, the customers' homes, and the dance halls. In doing so, Cressey
learned a great deal about the relationships among them, which he shared
with his readers:

> Compare, in the first place, the distribution of residences throughout the city. Al-
> though the girls come from homes in nearly all parts of the city, a large majority reside
> on the North and Northwest sides. Much more important, however, is the observation
> that the taxi-dancers appear to be persons somewhat detached from the communities
> in which they have lived. This is revealed through Map I.... Little evidence of neigh-
> borhood association was found, and as a result one is forced to the conclusion that the
> taxi-dancer's girl associates do not come from her own neighborhood within the city.
> When found in the dance hall, the taxi-dancer is already considerably detached from
> her early neighborhood ties.

> These maps also suggest something concerning the nationality and ancestry of these
> young girls. A surprisingly large number are from the Polish areas of the city. Hardly
> any girls come from the Italian areas or from the Jewish Ghetto. In the Jewish areas of
> second settlement, however, where the Jew moves first after leaving the Ghetto, one
> finds taxi-dancers. The striking contrast between the Polish group, on the one hand,
> and the Italian and the Ghetto groups, on the other, suggests the distinct cultural heri-
> tage of the Slavic group as compared with that of either of the latter two groups, and

suggests the apparent ease with which the girl of Polish parents may be absorbed into the life of the taxi-dance hall. (1925/1969, pp. 57–58)

In Cressey's *The Taxi-Dance Hall*, and throughout most of the monographs produced in the same manner, the spatial dimension of the data collected was crucial to the understanding of the whole. As Abbott (1997) puts it:

> The Chicago school thought ... that one cannot understand social life without understanding the arrangements of particular social actors in particular social times and places ... Chicago felt that no social fact makes any sense abstracted from its context in social (and often geographic) space and social time. Social facts are located. This means a focus on social relations and spatial ecology in synchronic analysis, as it means a similar focus on process in diachronic analysis. Every social fact is situated, surrounded by other contextual facts and brought into being by a process relating it to past contexts. (p. 1154)

Abbott (1997) argues, and it is true of most journalism as well, that "most contemporary sociology does not take the location or relationships of a social fact as central" (p. 1154). People, events, and processes, he says, are not located in time or in space. They are "units of analysis," rather than actors in a maze of social relations. "Yet," he adds, "throughout the Chicago writings ... we find map after map after map, dotted with brothels, schizophrenics, residential hotels, businesses, or whatever else was of interest. Throughout the Chicago writings, we find time and place" (p. 1156).

CIVIC MAPPING IN CONTEMPORARY JOURNALISM

The theory and practice of civic mapping is developing in two major directions that generally reflect the cognitive and structural concepts discussed earlier in this chapter. Each approach is remarkable for its initiative and inventiveness, and each is moving journalism toward a new reporting tool that may yet develop into a sustainable practice. These two approaches will be explored next by looking at mapping projects undertaken at *The Tampa Tribune* and *The Spokesman-Review*.

Although nearly three dozen newspapers have experimented with the cognitive approach to civic mapping, *The Tampa Tribune* is the only one that included a geographic mapping component. To date, the practice of civic mapping has not been studied systematically, but some evidence suggests that the practice has not yet gained widespread acceptance in newsrooms (Campbell, 2002). The case of *The Tampa Tribune* illustrates the successful application of the Harwood civic mapping method, as well as the challenges of sustaining it in daily practice, while the structural mapping suggested by the Chicago School studies inspired *The Spokesman-Review*'s civic mapping experiment.

The Harwood Method

The Pew Center for Civic Journalism began to develop its ideas about civic mapping in 1996 (Schaffer, 2001, May 22). Davis "Buzz" Merritt, editor of *The Wichita (Kansas) Eagle,* had a hand in it, too; he recalls that he asked Richard C. Harwood in the mid-1990s to help his newspaper "map" the "dark and trackless swamp of public life" (Harwood, 1996, p. 3). The Pew Center provided the funding for the Harwood study; and 5 years later, Pew was defining civic mapping as "a systematic search for alternative sources of knowledge—other than officials and quasi-officials" (Schaffer, 2001, Feb. 9–11). By then, the language of civic mapping officially included "charting community 'third places,' actively seeking out all stakeholders, using alternative story frames beyond simply conflict and controversy" (Schaffer, 2001, Feb. 9–11), and "building a database of people who know what's going on." (Schaffer, 2001, May 22).

To help newsrooms test the potential of civic mapping, the Pew Center contracted with The Harwood Institute for Public Innovation to provide basic training for journalists via a series of workshops. Founded and run by Richard C. Harwood, a public policy consultant with degrees from Skidmore College and Princeton University, The Harwood Institute worked closely with the Pew Center to develop the civic mapping seminars, a "how-to" workbook, and a boxed set of four training videos. Television, radio, newspaper, and web-based newsrooms applied to attend the seminars; attendees were selected based on their descriptions of a planned civic mapping project. The Pew Center distributed the videos and the workbook, now in its second edition, at little or no cost to journalists around the country.

The first Harwood civic mapping seminar was held in 1999, attended by journalists from five cities.[2] In 2000, two seminars were held to train journalists from 12 more newsrooms; and in 2001, another 12 newsroom projects were selected for the training workshops. Including another eight projects that were not directly tied to the Harwood seminars, a total of 37 newsrooms or media partnerships had tried, or were intending to try, a version of civic mapping by mid-2002.

The first Pew-Harwood workbook, *Tapping Civic Life,* was published in 1996 and introduced the concept of the layers of civic life, designated as official, quasi-official, third places, incidental, and private. These were the layers to be "mapped" by finding new sources of information and using that information to build a better understanding of a community. That is, reporters were encouraged to expand their understanding of their communities by walking their beats, talking with rather than interviewing people, and organizing the information they gleaned in a way that others in the newsroom could use. Some newspapers made lists; others drew charts on the walls of the newsrooms to track the emerging picture of the community. The Harwood notion of third places—locations such as coffee shops and beauty parlors where real people had real conversations—was quickly assimilated. Designating such places as rich and legitimate news sources gave reporters the time to do in-depth reporting, the permission to listen for more than a quote, and the luxury of gathering information that didn't have to show up in a story the next day.

The second edition of *Tapping Civic Life* appeared in April 2000, following the first round of workshops; it incorporated some of the experiences of the journalists who had participated, including those from *The Tampa Tribune* and its project partner, WFLA-TV. The second edition also laid out Harwood's new taxonomy of leadership layers, introducing terms that are still making their way into newsrooms: official leaders, civic leaders, connectors (people who interact with multiple organizations, institutions, or social groups), catalysts (people who exert influence through their networks of interpersonal relationships), and experts. The idea of civic mapping thus expanded slightly to add a new way of visualizing the connections that create a community.

Both editions of *Tapping Civic Life* (1996, 2000) provide step-by-step explanations of journalistic civic mapping and its associated terminology; the 2000 edition also offers specific examples of how newsrooms have collected and used this new kind of data. The workbook is available on the web at www.pewcenter. org/doingcj/pubs/tapping/toc.html

The Harwood Method in Practice

Executive Editor Gil Thelen arrived at *The Tampa Tribune* in May 1998 and promptly applied for admission to the first Harwood civic mapping seminar to be held the following year. Traditional journalistic practice at the newspaper was already being challenged by the unique partnership of *The Tampa Tribune*, WFLA-TV, and Tampa Bay Online. The three media outlets share a new campus of state-of-the-art buildings and a universal news–assignment desk. They also share their reporters and photographers. A daily news budget meeting pulls together 20 or more journalists, including representatives from each newsroom, where daily assignments and projects are "collaborated," that is, each story is evaluated for its potential in print, broadcast, and online.

Civic mapping was another new idea that the Tampa journalists were eager to try. After their Harwood training, editor Steve Kaylor and reporter Ken Koehn decided to test what they had learned for a series about a neighborhood slated for redevelopment. What the reporters uncovered was even more complex than they had anticipated. Following Harwood's injunctions to get beyond official and quasiofficial layers of civic life, they discovered that the residents of the neighborhood had very different goals, concerns, and fears—differences that actually separated rather than united the residents of what had always been considered a single neighborhood. Kaylor recalls:

> We went in thinking, "Tampa Heights: These are the Tampa Heights issues for the whole area up there." And the more time Ken spent in the neighborhoods up there, we realized there were very diverse subset areas along street boundaries. The people that live within the historic district, with the beautiful houses, obviously costing lots of money—their number one issue was historic preservation, making sure that the new houses going in maintained the character of their four-block area. Then we went three blocks away to this area that was slated for redevelopment and their number one issue was crime. The more reporting we did, the better picture we got of the neighborhood. They all may be a little bit concerned about all of the issues, but depending on where you were in that community, you can get an entirely different point of view. If your source is from the northeast corner, they may be worried about something completely different than a person in the southwest corner.[3]

Much of Kaylor's and Koehn's realization came from their decision to plot the information they were collecting on maps of the area. The maps served multiple purposes. They were a reporting tool, revealing key insights about the redevelopment stories as sources were plotted and updated; they were used as graphic illustrations for the stories that appeared in the newspaper; and they were to be made available, in slightly different form, to all the reporters and editors in the newsroom.

The Tampa Heights stories are an excellent example of the potential of civic mapping, and a training video produced by the Pew Center for Civic Journalism called "Tapping Your Community: What Don't You Know?" features interviews with Koehn and Kaylor about their experience.[4] Although the training materials were overly optimistic about the newsroom-wide use of the Tampa Heights prototype maps (indicating that intranet access was available, for example), the basic lessons learned about uncovering multiple layers of civic life are well explained.

It remains a challenge, however, to add the techniques of civic mapping to the everyday reporting in the Tampa newsroom. Ironically, innovations in convergence and collaboration that opened a receptive space for the idea of civic mapping have also distracted editors and reporters from pursuing this new practice. Newsroom leaders are still trying to find ways to institutionalize both the civic reporting methods and the knowledge gained from them, so that neither has to be rediscovered by new staff members. Top editors not only see civic mapping's promise as a reporting and editing tool, but also speculate that it could be useful in deciding how to allocate scarce newsroom resources and analyze their own use of sources.

Despite the philosophical commitment of the management, despite the benefit of outside training, and despite the demonstrated success of a newsroom mapping project, civic mapping remains on the shelf. Sidetracked by the challenges of multimedia convergence and further foiled by technology, even in a state-of-the-art newsroom with little staff turnover, plans to institutionalize the information gleaned from the Tampa Heights project have yet to materialize.

The Structural Approach

To the Pew Center for Civic Journalism, as well as to most of the Harwood seminar participants, mapping has remained a metaphor for the systematic recording of sources and other information about communities. Another approach was offered by Professor Lewis A. Friedland of the University of Wisconsin through informal conversations, conference presentations, and workshops in 1999 and 2000. Friedland envisioned a civic map that was geographically based, with multiple overlays revealing the pattern of community activities, liabilities, assets, and the networks of people and organizations that animate community life. He proposed that citizens could help gather data for such civic maps and that the maps could then be made available to the public as a resource to further encourage and inform community dialogue. In effect, Friedland was proposing a way to map and make public the interlocking networks of individuals and institutions that produce the social capital required for a vigorous and productive civic life.

The civic mapping experiment undertaken by *The Spokesman-Review* was grounded in Friedland's vision of civic mapping and reflected the historical perspective of the Chicago School's research methods. During the 2-year span of the project, led by then-editor Chris Peck, a newsroom team wrestled philosophically with ways to report an important and extraordinarily complex story about their community. They also wrestled with how to tell that story in a way that could be published. In the end, the civic mapping component of the project had produced some provocative discussion but did not produce newspaper copy in the way it had been envisioned.

Mapping Key Moments

Peck and his top editors had nearly a decade of experience in civic journalism when they decided to try to locate the holes that youngsters fall through on their way to growing up—the holes that drop them directly into prison. It quickly became clear that the project's working title, "Fixing Failing Families," was too negative in tone, and as the background reporting began, the idea of key moments emerged. Interactive editor Doug Floyd was instrumental in bringing together a number of professionals who work with children and adolescents to try to tease out the most common turning points in young lives. Working through a number of meetings with various groups, Floyd and his colleagues at the paper distilled what they found and agreed on 10 key moments that could be crucial in people's lives. They soon realized, too, that not all of the key moments were age-related, so they divided them into two groups: chronological and developmental. The chronological series included five key moments: conception to birth, bonding in infancy, age 10 (fourth grade), the first day of seventh grade, and rites of passage such as experimenting with alcohol and learning to drive. The developmental moments were collapsed into friendships, family moves, divorces and deaths, first failures and successes, and values development. Floyd, Peck, and others on the project team interviewed about 75 teenagers—from top students to juvenile delinquents—to test the fit of their key moments to actual experience and to try to identify the resources that were available to the youngsters as they were making life-changing decisions.[5]

Peck and Friedland hoped that the reporters would be able to plot the distribution of resources across the city and compare that map to a similar plotting of neighborhoods or elementary schools where successful lives were launched or troubled teens stumbled out and into jail (C. Peck, personal communication, January 6, 1999). Peck and Friedland were also interested in finding out how kids were socially connected to each other and how well the network of related social resources in the community was functioning.

Plans for the civic mapping component of the Key Moments project also included what Peck called maps of "civic assets, social assets, community resources, and reporters' beats." Recognizing that collecting this enormous amount of information would be labor intensive, Peck and Friedland anticipated that community volunteers from civic, church, and school organizations might help; in return, the community would have access to the data (C. Peck, personal communication, April 29, 1999).

During these early discussions of the project, Peck's voracious appetite for information and intellectual stimulation allowed him to acquire a relatively quick yet sophisticated understanding of social network theory; in addition, he looked to the early sociological studies at the University of Chicago for inspiration and understanding of the value of in-depth case studies. By June 1999, however, the pragmatic questions of what would be reported, what stories would be written, and what photos would be taken had become paramount. As photo editor John Sale put it toward the end of an intense discussion on the project on June 22, 1999, "Let's not let the mapping get in the way."

During the following summer, the Key Moments team refined its plans and the reporting got under way. Reporter Jeanette White and photographer Colin

Mulvaney found subjects for a yearlong story on a new seventh-grader and for an in-depth article on a homeless teen mother. White was also working on other key moments stories, including one about an adopted child struggling with the effects of fetal alcohol syndrome and another about adolescent best friends who had subsequently chosen completely different lifestyles. Meanwhile, one of the newspaper's editors, Rebecca Nappi, was working with fourth-graders who were writing and drawing about their own experiences; she was also reporting a story about the effects of divorce on one father and child. The Key Moments team hoped to have the series in print by the following spring.

As the project moved closer and closer to its deadline, however, it moved further and further away from a definable civic mapping component. Friedland and Peck still held on to the vision they had of the project, and Friedland visited Spokane to talk with the Key Moments team, as well as other reporters and editors, on November 5, 1999.[6] In three separate meetings, Peck and Friedland talked about ways to add some of the tools of social science research to the journalists' reporting skills. Peck described the Key Moments project as a laboratory where the idea of civic mapping was being tested in the hope that what was learned could be applied more generally in the newsroom. Friedland reviewed the principles of social network mapping, pointing out that the immediate reward was a deeper understanding of the complex relationships involved in a single story. The story can reflect that deeper understanding, Friedland said, but its full potential is not realized until it is, in effect, generalized:

> You can tell the story and the reader can identify with the problem, but it doesn't allow us to move it up to the next level of context. The goal is to try to develop a way to find the more general knowledge. By using [this particular] knowledge we can construct a generalized community knowledge that can be used again and again. Maybe there's a way to make sense out of it—to figure out a set of patterns. The general knowledge can be applied to other key moments as a follow up. Oftentimes you move on without extracting the more general lesson that would allow you to take your knowledge and use it in the newsroom, and in your own reporting and to share with fellow reporters. So it becomes a learning tool in the newsroom. You can pass on the knowledge of the beat.

Friedland framed this kind of civic mapping not only as a way of creating institutional memory but also as a way of reducing error. Error, in this context, he said, is not the error of a misspelled name or an incorrect date, but the error of omission—an incomplete picture of the complexity of any given story:

> It's not whether there's error—there's always error. The question is whether you deal with the possibility of error systematically or whether you deal with it simply as a kind of random, noisy intermix into your judgment. And right now, more often than not, error in reporting in communities is a matter of random noise. Here you're trying to reduce the random noise in the community information system so that you can do a little bit better

job of reducing error. It doesn't mean there isn't error—it just means you're controlling for error more systematically than you would be if you were just starting anew every time. [If] Jeanette does this for five years, she'll pretty much have this picture in her head ... But then somebody else comes in and they literally have to recreate this picture from scratch. They're introducing a whole new set of random errors into the knowledge system about the community that then gets filtered through this newspaper.

Peck was comfortable with the experimental nature of the mapping enterprise as infused with Friedland's social science:

What we're trying to do is use his social science background to see if there's actually a way you could institutionalize this in a newsroom. Maybe you can, maybe you can't. I'm not going to say we can do it. I'm sold on the idea though, on the possibility of it. I really think it is something you could build into a newsroom. It's bringing more focus, structure, attention, discipline to something we already do intuitively ... I think it would move the whole level of reporting up a notch. Ultimately it comes back to reporting. It comes back to saying, "This would help us be even better at our reporting."

In the final meeting of the day (November 5, 1999) the members of the Key Moments team were still struggling to find ways to apply what they were learning about civic mapping and social networks—and to get their stories published. Friedland suggested that one or two reporters could attempt a small experiment to determine the structure of juvenile peer networks. At first, even that limited task seemed overwhelming. Peck and Floyd recalled the prototype interview they conducted with a man named Rodney. The two editors had spent about 2 hours with Rodney, using an interview protocol they had developed to try to get him to pinpoint the key moments in his life where a decision or an event cleared his path to prison. The specter of conducting similar long interviews with various cliques of teenagers who might not be so self-reflective was at first quite daunting to Peck. "There's a lot there ... that's a lot of interviewing," he said. "You do five skinheads, five cowboys, five jocks, five nerds—that's ridiculous." But the paper's top editor was not easily dissuaded from an idea to which he had been committed for more than a year: "Well, if you did two hours a kid times 20 kids—that's 40 hours a week—that's doable." After a moment's thought, he turned to his colleague and added: "Right, Doug?"

The Key Moments series was published in June and July of 2000. White and Mulvaney had spent that year immersed in seventh grade when they weren't tracking the homeless teen mother at the downtown bus station or living through the trials of a family raising an adopted child with fetal alcohol syndrome. The project was huge, stretching across 2 months in 10 installments of 4 to 6 full pages each. Compelling journalism, the stories eschewed blatant attributions such as "experts say" or "psychologists believe"; the series was written from a position of authority, one earned by the in-depth research that preceded, as well as infused the reporting. Several of the installments featured sidebars on where to find out more information about particular issues. Following the series, Floyd hosted a public forum for parents and others who were interested in following up on the information; the newspaper printed a small brochure outlining available resources. But the civic mapping pieces, such as geographic plots of neighborhoods and social network analysis that could have helped reveal the holes in social and family support systems, were simply too much to be accomplished.

The Spokane case reveals quite clearly the challenges of devising a model of civic mapping that can produce newsroom knowledge as well as journalism. A strong tradition of innovative civic journalism was not enough; as the Key Moments team and other thoughtful journalists at the newspaper found, the social science research methods they were trying to adapt were fraught with complexity and distressingly plagued by unanswered questions. Managing editor Peggy Kuhr worried that they were trying to figure out too much of the story before they started the reporting; that is, she was concerned that the theory would drive too much of the practice. Reporter Kelly McBride raised a set of insightful questions about how journalists would be rewarded for participating in a civic mapping project, about who would own and control the data collected, and about how the mere existence of such data in a collected form might render it invalid. The Key Moments project, although it did not materialize in the way Peck and Friedland had envisioned, nevertheless produced remarkable, authoritative, meaningful, and top-caliber journalism. The lessons learned will help shape the practice of civic mapping as it continues to develop.

THE FUTURE OF CIVIC MAPPING

Refining the Practice

Researchers are continuing to test the potential of civic mapping as the methods to operationalize it are evaluated and revised. For example, a long-term project in civic mapping began in the fall of 2002 in Madison, Wisconsin, that used the combined resources of the Center for Communication and Democracy at the University of Wisconsin, the Center for Democracy in Action at Edgewood College, WISC-TV, and Dane County United Way. The planners developed a method in which the research would be conducted by the community partners, and the resulting data would be held in common for all to use.

The goals of the Madison project are to develop a picture of the community that reveals how people and organizations interact and to make that picture available to researchers, journalists, and citizens. To gather the basic information, 125 Edgewood College students were scheduled to interview about 1,000 community leaders about various civic associations and institutions with which they are affiliated. The interviewers planned to ask the leaders about each organization's mission and structure, which issues are the most important to it and to its work, and with whom it has worked on those issues during the past year.

At the end of the project, all of the data will be fed into a web-based software that can create a social network database from which graphic displays of the connections among people and organizations can be generated. This accomplished, the software will display the data using conventional GIS mapping techniques, enabling citizens to locate organizations and other community resources. The television partner, WISC-TV, planned to use the information to map the community in a way that reveals sectors not only where their own coverage is thin or nonexistent but also where it can be deepened or improved.

Enriching the Theory

The Spokane and Madison projects are the sole examples of structural civic mapping. All of the other civic mapping projects to date were built on the cognitively based Harwood model, and journalists and educators say they have found it to be instrumental in changing the way they see their communities and in reframing their stories as a result (Hetrick, 2001; Spurlock, 2001). Others have commented that dialogue in the community has been broadened, that new voices are being heard, that nontraditional sources have been found in third places, that catalysts and connectors are being identified, and that stories are now written with a more authoritative voice (Ford, 2000; Harwood, 1996, 2000).

The Harwood-inspired projects themselves have not been systematically examined, however. It is a daunting task. For example, many of the stated goals of the mapping seminar participants morph after they return to the newsroom. Their "maps" are often in their heads, perhaps on Rolodexes or in a modified database, occasionally brought together in a short document or wall chart. To date, no research has examined whether or how any of the self-reported accounts of the effectiveness in mapping correlate to measurable changes in news content, reader or viewer satisfaction, public opinion, cognition, civic participation, newsroom morale, or any of a host of other variables that have been used as traditional measures of media effects and journalistic practice.

The Pew–Harwood technique of civic mapping in the cognitive model has much to recommend it. Nevertheless, it might be improved if it incorporated more of the structural approach, that is, if it placed more emphasis on mapping itself and on the investigation of the nature of social networks at the levels of interpersonal, associational, and institutional life. Civic mapping models would be further enhanced if they specified a method, or a range of methods, to capture another critical dimension of the project: ensuring that the information so painstakingly gathered is collected, examined, updated, and institutionalized in a manner that increases the knowledge base in the newsroom and community as a whole.

A richer, more complex model of civic mapping may be needed to unpack the relationships among various layers of civic life. This "network of networks," as Friedland and McLeod (1999) contend, is the site of community revealed and understood in its most complex form. And community is not devoid of a geographic element; it can transcend environmental barriers, but it can be circumscribed by them as well. Illuminating the relationship of social networks to the geography that they inhabit or eclipse is a crucial piece of the community puzzle. The final piece is the critical role of the mass media. This single institution bridges the layers of civic life in ways that were not possible before cities with a single daily newspaper became the norm, before television invaded every home, and before the media became the primary creators of imagined community. The media are, in the end, the only place where members of a large and diverse public can "go" to see each other. Mapping the public space that they inhabit could become an invaluable tool for journalists to refine and improve their skill in understanding community life.

ENDNOTES

[1] It is worth borrowing a footnote here from Robert E. L. Faris, whose 1967 book, *Chicago Sociology 1920–1932*, rarely strays into the personal information he undoubtedly possessed as the son of one of the school's leading members. But in recounting the early attempts at preparing maps for display, Faris says: "Trial and error plays its part in most rapid developments of graphic devices. Some of the first spot maps were made by moistening and sticking onto the map little colored glue-backed dots. In addition to making an attractive display, the various colors provided highly visible distinctions which facilitated generalizations. But when a large map marked this way was taken out of a rack and unrolled, a cascade of colored dots broke loose and fell to the floor. Because there was no way of knowing where they had once been pasted, the whole map became worthless. This accident led to the use of ink for the spot maps—more work and less beauty, but they were durable" (p. 52, Footnote 2).

[2] This summary and analysis is based on materials drawn from the Pew Center for Civic Journalism's Web site, retrieved from www.pccj.org; and from its publications, including each edition of Civic Catalyst from Summer 1999 to Winter 2002. It also draws from two editions of *Tapping Civic Life* (Harwood, 1996, 2000), as well as the author's many years of participation, observation, and scholarship in the field of civic journalism.

[3] Unless otherwise noted, all quotes and information attributed to Steve Kaylor are from personal interviews conducted by the author, November 15–16, 2001, Tampa, Florida.

[4] For a critical analysis of the Tampa Heights project and in-depth interviews with Kaylor, Koehn, and their editors, see Campbell, 2002.

[5]This summary and analysis is drawn from the author's extensive research at *The Spokesman-Review* from 1999–2001.

[6]Unless otherwise cited, material in this section is based on the author's notes and transcriptions of tape recordings of the newsroom meetings held November 5, 1999, at *The Spokesman-Review* offices, Spokane, Washington.

REFERENCES

Abbott, A. (1997). Of time and space: The contemporary relevance of the Chicago School. *Social Forces, 75*(4), 1149–1182.

Anderson, B. (1991). *Imagined communities: Reflections on the origin and spread of nationalism.* London: Verso Books.

Booth, C. A. (1889). *Labour and life of the people: Volume I, East London* (2nd ed., Vol. I). London: Williams & Norgate.

Booth, C. A. (1891). *Labour and life of the people: Volume II, London continued* (Vol. II). London: Williams & Norgate.

Bulmer, M. (1984). *The Chicago School of Sociology.* Chicago: University of Chicago Press.

Campbell, K. B. (2002). *More than a metaphor: The challenge of civic mapping.* Unpublished dissertation, University of Wisconsin, Madison.

Cressey, P. G. (1969). *The taxi-dance hall.* Montclair, NJ: Patterson Smith. (Original work published in 1925)

Davis, A. F. (1967). *Spearheads for reform: The social settlements and the Progressive Movement, 1890–1914.* New York: Oxford University Press.

Faris, R. E. L. (1967). *Chicago Sociology 1920–1932.* San Francisco: Chandler.

Ford, P. (2000, Fall). Mapping pay off: Better stories. *Civic Catalyst, 22–23.*

Friedland, L. A., Kang, N., Campbell, K. B., & Pondillo, B. (1999). *Public life, community integration and the mass media: The empirical turn.* Paper presented at the Association for Journalism and Mass Communication, New Orleans, LA.

Friedland, L. A., & McLeod, J. M. (1999). Community integration and mass media: A reconsideration. In D. P. Demers & K. Viswanath (Eds.), *Mass media, social control, and social change: A macrosocial perspective* (pp. 197–226). Ames, IA: Iowa State University Press.

Harwood, R. C. (1996). *Tapping civic life.* Washington, DC: Pew Center for Civic Journalism.

Harwood, R. C. (2000). *Tapping civic life.* Washington, DC: Pew Center for Civic Journalism.

Hetrick, J. (2001, Fall). Students see value in civic mapping. *Civic Catalyst.*

Pew Center for Civic Journalism. (Summer 1999–Winter 2002). *Civic Catalyst.* Washington, DC.

Residents of Hull House. (1895). *Hull-House maps and papers.* Boston: Crowell & Co.

Schaffer, J. (2001, Feb. 9–11). *Civic journalism cycles-1990–2000.* Paper presented at the Civic innovations in newsrooms and classrooms workshop/seminar, Eugene, OR.

Schaffer, J. (2001, May 22). *Civic mapping.* Paper presented at the Morris Communications Workshop, Augusta, GA.

Spurlock, K. (2001, Summer). Community mapping reveals dire needs. *Civic Catalyst.*

10

Textual Analysis
in Journalism

John L. "Jack" Morris
Loyola University, New Orleans, LA

Textual analysis is sometimes called careful reading, and it is as important to a journalist as good listening. Textual analysis is a method that communication researchers use to describe, interpret, and evaluate the characteristics of a recorded message (Frey, Botan, Friedman, & Kreps, 1991). This type of qualitative research and analysis focuses on a particular text to determine its characteristics and place it in a category shared by other similar texts for comparison and contrast purposes. Qualitative textual analysis can lead to quantitative research methods such as content analysis (Krippendorff, 1980) or Q methodology (Brown, 1993; McKeown & Thomas, 1988), which can be used to analyze publications or opinions about texts.

For example, researchers might categorize the types of message strategies that politicians use in public campaign speeches as fear-appeals and reward-appeals by studying individual texts, and then conduct a quantitative study. This research project might study how the *New York Times* and the *Los Angeles Times* covered campaign speeches over the period of a year by focusing on the textual attributes of each paper's campaign coverage. Reporters who write the news stories also use some level of textual analysis to compare and contrast oral and written language. Reporters at the *Washington Post* use personal computers to search for key words in bills and legislation that indicate stakeholders—winners and losers—in the documents (see following examples).

Mass media textual analysis is closely related to literary criticism, which, broadly used today, encompasses any discourse on any literature, including three distinguishable but overlapping areas: history, theory, and evaluation. Many scholars view literature as part of an historical process, a phenomenon that can be described by internal principles such as types, techniques, and functions, or as objects to be studied, analyzed, and judged. Several methods and approaches to criticism fiercely compete for attention in the field. Wellek (1995) commented on this new age of criticism:

> The variety of voices today is so great that the situation has been compared to the Tower of Babel, with its mutually incompatible languages. Never before has there been such a ferment in criticism, and critics have never before attracted so much attention and fervent loyalty ... Indeed some scholars argue that this is the age of criticism, since literary critics now often function not only as specialists in literature, but also as general critics of society and civilization.

This chapter focuses on only the most common terms of textual analysis that are used by journalists. It addresses how journalists read, analyze, categorize, describe, and evaluate their own writing as well as the writing and oral language of others.

PURPOSES AND TYPES OF TEXTUAL ANALYSIS

There are two basic uses of textual analysis for practicing journalists. The first is to study the language of their sources for specific stories; the second is to study the language of journalism to refine their art of writing. This broad approach to criticism is relatively new; it has been advanced in recent decades by critiques of English composition and rhetorical analyses of speech communication. In their 1991 book, *Investigating Communication*, Frey and colleagues explained that textual analysis stems from a systematic attempt to understand how meaning moves from author to audience and how the text is related to other variables that precede it. Ultimately, textual analysis is a scientific attempt to evaluate a text based on a set of established standards or criteria. Several organizations and publications have begun criticizing the content of the news media on a regular basis for the general public. They include *NewsWatch, MediaChannel, Brill's Content, Fairness & Accuracy in Reporting, CounterSpin, Medianews,* and *Media Watch.*[1]

Textual analysis can be applied to any communications medium because photos, illustrations, graphics, and video images can be reduced to textual summaries before analysis. Some language theorists claim that history in general consists of texts to be analyzed (Iser, 1986). Scripts of radio and television news and entertainment are more readily available than ever, and they often can be secured over the Internet for textual analysis.

Five types of media criticism use textual analysis: Aristotelian, genre, historical, dramatic, and fantasy theme (Frey et al., 1991). The first is a return to Aristotle's judicial, logical, and formal analysis centered on the work itself rather than its historical, moral or religious context. Genre critics group texts that are similar in function, purpose, and form, and then evaluate each text based on the established attributes of the genre. An example of genre criticism is Cawelti's *Adventure, Mystery, and Romance: Formula Stories as Art and Popular Culture,* published by the University of Chicago Press in 1976.[2] Historical criticism consists of oral histories, case studies, bibliographical studies and social movement studies. The historical critic attempts to evaluate the influence of events on the creation of the text. Dramatic critics study principles drawn from theater—act, purpose, agent, agency, and scene—to evaluate texts. Finally, fantasy theme critics focus on stories with characters that symbolize cultural moral principles or philosophies. Examples of this type of criticism include Chance's *The Lord of the Rings: The Mythology of Power,* published by Twayne Publishers of New York in 1992.[3]

Each of these critical approaches used to study journalism and media share a common list of textual attributes that can be identified and then described, analyzed, and evaluated by a community of readers. Careful and comparative reading and analysis by knowledgeable critics help to create a richer understanding of the function and value of any single text, and such case studies contribute to the general knowledge in the field. While some media criticism attempts to measure the influence of the mass media on society, in general, textual analysis attempts to categorize, analyze, and evaluate one particular text. Visual forms such as the inverted pyramid (see Fig. 10.1) are tools of textual analysis that critics use to classify one piece of writing as a report, another as a story, and still another as an essay. Careless use of these forms contribute to confusion and imprecision in the profession.

Thus, textual analysis is an activity that reporters, editors, publishers, news directors, producers, media critics, and researchers use on a daily basis. For example, a reporter writes a 25-inch news story on Afghanistan, but how good is it? How can working journalists evaluate the quality of the texts they receive and create on a daily basis? Textual analysis can help. Attributes of nonfiction prose, including journalism, can be used to categorize, analyze, and evaluate any news report or feature story. Many of these textual attributes can be applied to texts of sources, too, but some other specialization, including terminology from a field other than journalism, may be required for such an analysis.[4]

Visual Forms of Textual Analysis

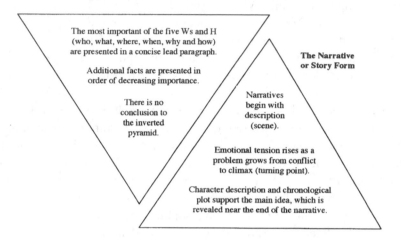

The Inverted Pyramid or Report Form

The most important of the five Ws and H (who, what, where, when, why and how) are presented in a concise lead paragraph.

Additional facts are presented in order of decreasing importance.

There is no conclusion to the inverted pyramid.

The Narrative or Story Form

Narratives begin with description (scene).

Emotional tension rises as a problem grows from conflict to climax (turning point).

Character description and chronological plot support the main idea, which is revealed near the end of the narrative.

The Three-Part or Essay Form

The beginning introduces the thesis or main idea of the piece of writing. A thesis statement is much like a summary lead.

The middle paragraphs present support for the main idea of the article. The body of an essay should focus clearly on the main idea.

The ending concludes the article by restating the thesis, main idea or lead.

Visual forms are structural aids to organizing, interpreting and evaluating texts. The inverted pyramid is well known to journalists, who often present factual reports, but the other two basic visual forms presented here are becoming more popular in news writing. Often associated with fiction and persuasive writing, the narrative and essay forms can be used to present objective, factual, nonfiction writing. For more about visual forms, see Brooks et al., *News Reporting and Writing*, 6th ed. (1999, 122-46) and Rackham and Bertagnolli, *From Sight to Insight: The Writing Process* (1999, 213-218).

FIG. 10.1.

TEXTUAL ANALYSIS OF NEWS WRITING

Evan Mahoney, a reporter for the Fund for Investigative Reporting and a professor at University of North Carolina at Asheville, uses the following terms when teaching, analyzing, and evaluating news writing (personal communication, February 21, 2002): abstraction, attribution, connotation, denotation, contrast, lead, nut graph, narration, exposition, form, induction, deduction, tone, voice, mood, style, thesis, quotation, and metaphor. Consistently careful use of such attributes of language can enrich the experience of reading in addition to simply informing the public.

For example, smell and fragrance have the same denotative (literal) meaning, but one has a positive connotative (suggestive) meaning while the other is negative. A quick reading, without textual analysis, can miss connotations. Exposition is logical explanation, and form is the overall structure of an article. Induction is reasoning that moves from specific details to a generalization, while deduction moves from a generalization to specifics. Tone and mood refer to word choices that indicate seriousness, humor, glee or depression, to name only a few emotions. Paying careful attention to these attributes of language can lead to an enriched understanding of a text. Mahoney urged writers to check for these attributes when revising their texts to enrich their writing and make it more engaging.

Diana Fishlock, diversity reporter for the *Harrison* (Penn.) *Patriot-News*, considered brainstorming, ambiguity, clichés, character, close-ups (concrete, sensory details), and editorializing when evaluating her own writing and the writing of others (personal communication, February 21, 2002). Brainstorming is a method for analyzing topics or ideas for a news story. It ranges from making simple lists of ideas and ranking them in importance to semantic webbing, in which the writer begins with a key word and diagrammatically connects it to another word, whatever comes to mind, and so on, through lines and circles. New connections are made in this playful act of discovery, and the process helps the writer see new possibilities for the article. Fishlock explains:

> Brainstorming often is extremely useful. Brainstorming and simply having time to let a concept percolate in my mind help me to explore more facets of the idea. Is there a historical context? What about religion? Given the time (or brainstorming input from other people) the story becomes much more complete ... Often character makes or breaks a story. If the character is compelling and the writer is able to show that, I'll read about someone doing almost anything—even something I may have no interest in.

Media criticism is growing as a classroom and newsroom practice, so news writers must become more sophisticated about their use of language. Textual analysis is a qualitative method that can be used to create, defend, and improve writing skills. "Making meaning clear does not mean making the copy tedious," Peter Jacobi explained during the Association for Education in Journalism and Mass Communication's Gannett Teaching Fellows Workshop at Indiana University (personal communication, July 22–28, 1990). "Exposition [information delivery] must go beyond a dictionary definition and be as bright and intriguing as narration [story telling]."

TEXTUAL ANALYSIS OF DOCUMENTS

In addition to enriching their own news writing, journalists can use textual analysis to understand complex legal, court, and corporate documents more completely as sources of news.

Washington Post reporters Helen Dewar and Bill Miller regularly analyze the texts of legislation, court opinions, and briefs. They have developed a method for finding the stakeholders of any government action based on the language of the official documents.

While analyzing the 2002 Energy Bill and Corporate Accountability Act, Dewar (personal communication, August 5, 2002) was forced to "read between the lines" of lawyers' "code language" to discover indications of permissive or mandatory requirements. Permissive requirements mean that the provisions of the bill allow lots of latitude in fulfilling them, whereas mandatory requirements are strict standards written into the bill that provide little or no wiggle-room. Words such as shall, may, or will are flags of intent that she carefully noted. She explained that reading between the lines meant talking to the lawyers who wrote the bill, as well as the critics who study the policies involved. She said some politicians and political critics use a form of textual analysis, too. They conduct computer searches of all new bills for key terms that signal their own interests to make sure an important issue is not buried in the wording of a seemingly unrelated bill. Dewar said she also looks for litigable language, which is language that would likely lead to lawsuits. Her reports explained the possibility and types of lawsuits that would likely arise if the bills were to become law.

While analyzing the 2002 Homeland Security Act, Miller (personal communication, August 5, 2002) said he looked for words that indicated authority to spend money or appoint staffs. More money and larger staffs usually appeal to bureaucrats regardless of the amount of public service they provide. A cost–benefit analysis can produce a valuable news story from a text that obscures its hidden purposes and powers. The boilerplate legal language of bills tends to cloud the political intentions of those who drafted them, Miller said, so he interviews the authors and critics about such issues. He also studied other analyses of the act, and he conducted computer searches for terms such as "National Guard," "budget," and "Civil Service." The search terms were based on hunches, hypotheses, or questions. Civil Service, for example, turned up all references to how the bill would regard or treat government employees. The references were scattered, but this method enabled Miller to gather and analyze them to produce an informative and engaging news story.

Both Miller and Dewar said they pay close attention to the beginning and end of a complex government document, and they underline or star highlights and meaningful passages. Every line, and even between the lines (what is not in the text), must be scrutinized because of the political nature of such documents. The following account is another example of how personal computers can be used to conduct key word searches that would be extremely tedious to do otherwise (Brooks et al., 1999):

> Kathleen Kerr and Russ Buettner of *Newsday* faced [this] sort of problem. Their goal: to discover whether New York City's criminal justice system discriminated against the poor. Their method: to acquire computer databases of city and state records on 27,810 prisoners, then to use their own computer to sort those cases by race and other criteria [including income level, jail time, bail, and verdicts.] Their findings: The poor, especially minorities, often were denied bail and forced to wait in jail for trials that often found them not guilty. (pp. 410–411)

Two obstacles to textual analysis are lack of time and money (Brooks et al., 1999). Reporters must carefully analyze all of the pertinent records or a scientifically selected sample. They also must ask the right questions and record data in a way that will answer them. Textual analysis is an invaluable qualitative method for understanding and evaluating police and court records, legislation, court opinions, and legal briefs, but it is more time-consuming and costly than the more traditional method of interviewing and quoting sources.

TEXTUAL ANALYSIS OF CIVIC JOURNALISM

Reporters conducted textual analysis of community conversations that were conducted with a wide range of citizens in Columbia, Missouri. The project began with University of Missouri School of Journalism Professor Edmund Lambeth who studied and taught civic journalism, a movement debated in research and trade journals throughout the 1990s (Coleman, 1997). Lambeth established the Civic Journalism Interest Group of the Association for Education in Journalism and Mass Communication and guided the university's *Columbia Missourian* newspaper staff through a civic journalism project that became known as "Faith in Our Community" (Morris, 2002, pp. 61–70). Lambeth (1998) said public journalism could be viewed as a form of journalism that seeks to:

1. Listen systematically to the stories and ideas of citizens even while protecting its freedom to choose what to cover.
2. Examine alternative ways to frame stories on important community issues.
3. Choose frames that stand the best chance to stimulate citizen deliberation and build public understanding of issues.

4. Take the initiative to report on major public problems in a way that advances public knowledge of possible solutions and the values served by alternative courses of action.
5. Pay continuing and systematic attention to how well and how credibly it is communicating with the public. (p. 17)

To test the effects of one of civic journalism's reporting tools, community conversations, a group of radio, TV, and newspaper journalists worked together to conduct a civic journalism project and publish a series of news stories during the week of May 26, 1996. With the support of their editors and station managers, the group planned a week-long collaborative strategy that included all three media because Lambeth's earlier research indicated that citizens learn more from multimedia presentations (Thorson & Lambeth, 1995).

Missourian Managing Editor George Kennedy (personal communication, April 30, 1996) said the media managers selected the topic during a discussion session. They settled on religion because it had high relevance to the community and inadequate coverage. He said the goal was to raise the level of public awareness concerning the relationship between religion and public life.

Research began in Fall 1995 when five resource panels were conducted. Each resource panel consisted of about five experts who were knowledgeable in some aspect of religion and public life. Media managers moderated the panels, and the audience consisted of reporters and editors. These panels were used for background information only.

Eight community conversations were planned. These, too, were used only for background information (Morris, 2002). Participants were told in advance that they would not be quoted in the newspaper or recorded for radio or TV, although minutes of the meetings were recorded and reported to project members.

Confidentiality enabled participants to speak more openly and freely, said a reporter (personal communication, April 20–21, 1996) who conducted the public policy conversation. Otherwise, the citizen-participants might have been reluctant to be honest and forthright about controversial issues, he said, adding that the conversations were good for generating sources and story ideas. One reservation was expressed by a reporter (personal communication, April 20–21, 1996) who said the time and effort required to organize, conduct, and analyze community conversations could be costly in day-to-day reporting. The advantage of using them on a collaborative project, he said, was that several reporters could attend and benefit from one community conversation.

Throughout the civic journalism project previously described, Lambeth met with graduate journalism students to study and analyze the significance of these practices to working journalists. One of his classes discussed a list of characteristics of civic journalism, which could be used to identify the language of civic journalism. These characteristic attributes of civic journalism were identified as coverage of citizen viewpoints, invitations to action in news stories, reporter-reader interaction, identification of personal and social values, identification of consequences associated with the events–issues covered, and identification of the stakeholders involved in the coverage. This list of attributes complemented the attributes of traditional news stories that researchers have previously identified as characteristics of news (Brooks et al, 1999): impact, proximity, timeliness, prominence, novelty, and conflict.

Two hypotheses emerged from this exercise: (a) Textual analysis of a civic journalism news story should produce attributes significantly different from those of a traditional news story; and (b) At least most of the attributes of civic journalism identified by Lambeth and his students should be found in civic journalism texts. The original list was modified according to suggestions in a memo from newspaper editor Davis Merritt (personal communication, September 2, 1996), one of the founders of the public journalism movement:

> The objective isn't to quantify things and make a judgment about whether or how much a newspaper is succeeding, though that might be a small side effect. Rather, the objective is to provide a list of traits that we think constitute public journalism and examples to illustrate those traits—and how they differ from traditional practice—as a step toward a working definition that journalists can understand.

A sample of readers was asked to rate these news criteria from low to high on a 7-point scale after reading several blocks of news coverage that resulted from the civic journalism project titled "Faith in Our Community" and samples of more traditional news coverage from the same period and newspaper. Some blocks contained traditional news coverage, some civic journalism style reporting, and some were mixed. The following are the textual attributes and their definitions that were rated in this pilot study (Morris, 2002).

1. Citizen viewpoints: Citizens are identified as contributors in solving a public issue.
2. Impact: Many citizens are likely to be significantly affected by this news.
3. Invitations to action: This news coverage presents ways readers can actively respond.
4. Proximity: This takes place close to readers' homes.
5. Reporter-reader interaction: This indicates reporters have communicated with citizens.
6. Timeliness: This news is based on recent events.
7. Values: The values (moral–ethical principles) underlying courses of action are explained.
8. Prominence: This news includes well-known personalities or celebrities.

9. Consequences: Consequences (the outcome or end results) of actual or possible decisions are explained.
10. Novelty: This news is based on the odd or unusual.
11. Stakeholders: Who (individuals or groups) stands to gain and who stands to lose are clearly identified (in the news story).
12. Conflict: This news emphasizes opposing sides. (p. 68)

A procedure was designed to test two hypotheses about the characteristics of the news coverage. The researcher (Morris, 2002) wanted to learn: (a) whether readers would identify civic journalism stories, and (b) whether readers would rate civic journalism stories differently from traditional news stories.

The readers for this pilot study consisted of 12, specifically selected journalism students who had completed a basic news writing course and were in a media history course. This sample was used because the members possessed a basic knowledge of the elements of journalism. Each subject was asked to read five to six blocks of news and rate each block, which represented part of a newspaper page and contained some of the "Faith in our Community" project. The block included headlines, teasers, photos, captions, and other news devices. The blocks were rated according to the 12 textual attributes previously listed.

At least two readers rated each block, and scores for each of the criteria were averaged for each copy block. The scores were grouped into a public journalism (PJ) index (statements 1, 3, 5, 7, 9, and 11 previously mentioned) and a traditional journalism (TJ) index (2, 4, 6, 8, 10, and 12). Each block received PJ index and TJ index scores. Scoring on a 7-point scale, the readers gave the public journalism blocks an average of 4.62 for public journalism and only 3.62 for traditional journalism; they gave the traditional journalism blocks a 4.16 for traditional journalism and a 3.67 for public journalism.

The public journalism index score was a full point above the traditional journalism index score for the blocks that contained the public journalism news. This shows that the readers correctly identified which news blocks contained more public journalism language attributes. They had identified public journalism by its textual attributes.[5]

CONCLUSION

Textual analysis can be useful to reporters, editors, news directors, and researchers, who use it to explain how mass media affect our everyday lives. Mahoney and Fishlock used textual analysis to help strengthen individual journalists' writing skills by offering models to identify, describe, and evaluate various types of news writing. Miller and Dewar used textual analysis of complex government documents to uncover important issues clouded by legalese. Finally, textual analysis offers benefits through identifying, describing, and evaluating various genres of journalism as shown by the civic journalism project in Missouri. That textual analysis revealed that a purposive sample of journalism students could identify public journalism texts by language attributes. Manzella (2002) frames the civic journalism debate of the 1990s as a battle between the news of record, inverted-pyramid journalists versus the narrative, storytelling journalists. Before deciding which is the one best style for journalism, media critics, editors, and news writers must carefully identify, describe, and evaluate the various genres of news writing. After seeing valid alternatives, the questions to ask, as Merritt (personal communication, September 2, 1996) suggested, involve the characteristics of various forms of journalism, and the set of circumstances that call for the use of each form.

The questions that can be addressed through textual analysis are qualitative. As researchers analyze a text, they ask the overarching question, "What are the qualities of this particular text, and how does this text compare and contrast to other texts?" Under this umbrella, they may ask other questions such as, "Can readers distinguish a public journalism text from a traditional journalism text?" or "What's the difference between a story and a report?" or "How does interactivity affect the language of journalism?" Textual analysis takes more time than routine reading, and it may require some computer hardware and software, but it is an effective method for understanding and evaluating news writing, complex documents and journalism genres.

ENDNOTES

[1] For an updated directory of media criticism, go to: http://journalismnet.com/media

[2] For more information about genre criticism, see: http://www.mbcnet.org/archives/etv/G/htmlG/genre/genre.htm

[3] For more examples of fantasy theme criticism, see: http://library.ci.scottsdale.az.us/web2/tramp2.exe/authority_hits/A0b8gujo.001?server=1home&item=1

[4] The following books contain explications of many journalism terms that can be used in textual analysis: *Assessing Public Journalism*, edited by Lambeth, Meyer and Thorson (1998); *News Reporting and Writing*, by Brooks, Kennedy, Moen and Ranly (1999); *Words on Words*, by John Bremner (1980); *The Public Journalism Movement in America*, by Don Corrigan (1999); *A Study of Attitudes toward Audience Interaction in Journalism*, by John Morris (2002); *From Sight to Insight*, by Rackham and Bertagnolli (1999); *A Glossary of Literary Terms*, by M. H. Abrams (1981); and *A Handbook to Literature*, by Holman and Harmon (1986).

[5] A t-test for statistical significance indicated the hypothesis was supported by the results ($p < .0004$).

REFERENCES

Abrams, M. H. (1981). *A glossary of literary terms* (4th ed.). New York: Holt, Rinehart, & Winston.

Bremner, J. B. (1980). *Words on words: A dictionary for writers and others who care about words.* New York: Columbia University Press.

Brooks, B. S., Kennedy, G., Moen, D. R., & Ranly, D. (1999). *News reporting and writing* (6th ed.). New York: Bedford/St. Martins.

Brown, S. R. (1993). A primer on Q methodology. *Operant Subjectivity, 16*(3), 91–138.

Cawelti, J. G. (1976). *Adventure, mystery and romance: Formula stories as art and popular culture.* Boulder: University of Colorado Press.

Chance, J. (1992). *The lord of the rings: The mythology of power.* New York: Twayne Publishers.

Coleman, R. (1997, August). *The treatment of public journalism in three media review journals.* Paper presented at the annual convention of the Association for Education in Journalism and Mass Communication, Chicago.

Corrigan, D. H. (1999). *The public journalism movement in America: Evangelists in the newsroom.* Westport, CT: Praeger.

Fishlock, D. *Harrison (Penn.) Patriot-News.* Personal communication, February 21, 2002.

Frey, L. R., Botan, C. H., Friedman, P. G., & Kreps, Gary L. (1991). Textual analysis. In *Investigating communication* (pp. 203–228). Englewood Cliffs, NJ: Prentice-Hall.

Holman, C. H., & Harmon, W. (1986). *A handbook to literature* (5th ed.). New York: Macmillan.

Iser, W. (1986). The reading process: A phenomenological approach. In R. C. Davis (Ed.), *Contemporary literary criticism: Modernism through post-structuralism* (pp. 376–391). New York: Longman.

Krippendorff, K. (1980). *Content analysis: An introduction to its methodology.* Newbury Park, CA: Sage.

Lambeth, E. B., Meyer, P. E., & Thorson, E. (Eds.). (1998). *Assessing public journalism.* Columbia, MO: University of Missouri Press.

Manzella, J. C. (2002). *The struggle to revitalize American newspapers* Lewiston, NY: Edwin Mellen.

McKeown, B., & Thomas, D. (1988). *Q methodology: Quantitative applications in the social sciences.* Newbury Park, CA: Sage Publications.

Morris, J. L. (2002). *A study of attitudes toward audience interaction in journalism: citizen-based reporting.* Lewiston, NY: Edwin Mellen.

Rackham, J., & Bertagnolli, O. (1999). *From sight to insight: The writing process* (6th ed.). Fort Worth, TX: Harcourt Brace.

Thorson, E. & Lambeth, E. B. (1995, August). *An evaluation of the cognitive, attitudinal and synergistic effects of a multi-media civic journalism project.* Paper presented at the annual convention of the Association for Education in Journalism and Mass Communication, Washington, DC.

Wellek, R. (1995). Literary criticism. In *The New Grolier Multimedia Encyclopedia* (p. 12). Danbury, CT: Grolier Electronic Publishing.

11

Scientists and Storytellers

The Imperative of Pairing Qualitative and Quantitative Approaches in Communication Research

Susan Schultz Huxman
Wichita State University

Mike Allen
University of Wisconsin, Milwaukee

From its inception, communication has been a complex, diverse, and rich cognate area, spanning the humanities (speech), fine arts (theater), social sciences (journalism; telecommunications), and natural sciences (communication disorders). It is little wonder then that the discipline has experienced a particularly lively and lengthy debate that began in the 1920s over its two research traditions: behaviorism and phenomenology.

The issue, which strikes at the heart of ontological and epistemological questions, has been posited in simple, polar extremes: Behaviorism is deductive, formal, functional, and quantitative in its quest to explain and predict human communicative behavior; phenomenology is inductive, interpretive, evaluative, and qualitative in its quest to understand and appreciate the meaning of human messages. This dichotomous mindset has led to entrenched and even combative views: "That which we cannot see, we cannot measure and so is meaningless"; versus "Attempts to find statistical correlation between discrete variables of a process, context-bound phenomena (i.e., communication) are hopelessly misguided." Increasingly, however, our discussions have been more inviting and collaborative. If the spirit of postmodernism has taught us anything, it is that dichotomies are often overdrawn—sometimes ridiculously so; a multiperspectivism enriches research findings; and paradoxes and ambiguities in the human condition should be celebrated.

This chapter, written by one author who practices qualitative research and the other who practices quantitative research, suggests that there is an imperative to pairing qualitative and quantitative approaches in communication research. It begins by revisiting the qualitative–quantitative debate, but argues that many of the dichotomies are overdrawn and that other real harms to the health of our discipline deserve our attention. From there, the chapter outlines the types, opportunities, and threats of triangulated research and introduces several case studies in communication that blend behavioral and phenomenological assumptions.

QUALITATIVE VERSUS QUANTITATIVE: ARE THE DISTINCTIONS OVERDRAWN?

When a person possesses only a hammer, [s/he] will view all problems as requiring the pounding of nails.

—Proverb

Quantitative research in communication takes its lead from the natural sciences. The outcome of a quantitative examination should be the estimation of an empirical relationship between or among abstract conceptual variables. The goal is to find a generalizable relationship that goes across context, time, and situation. For example, does the amount of political advertisements generate more votes for a candidate? The quantitative investigator would spend time generating a conceptual understanding of what is meant by the amount of paid political advertisements, and then compare that to the number of votes for a candidate.

While the term amount of paid political advertisements may first appear relatively simple, it carries with it a number of definitional issues. Does an attack advertisement on an opponent count toward the candidate's total or not? Do advertisements paid for by someone else count toward this total? Is a 15-second television advertisement the same as a 30-second advertisement? How do you total newspaper, radio, Internet, and television materials? As one can see, this simple set of problems related to the operationalizing or putting into practice the conceptual entity requires a great deal of effort. Such efforts are often acrimonious as scholars disagree about the conceptualization, as well as operationalization of various features. Yet this debate and explication, never fully settled, is an expected and healthy part of the process.

The second issue is that a single finding or study is subject to Type I (false positive) and Type II (false negative) error. The problem is that science operates in a world of probability. A single finding might be the result of random error. The search to estimate a single association necessitates dozens or even hundreds of attempts at replication. The replications are eventually summarized using meta-analysis to distill or generate a final association across the entire body of literature that often spans decades (in some rare cases we have more than 100 years of data). Science is a dynamic process of comparison of what we think we know to the current information collected by investigators and the theoretical predictions of what ought to be true.

Even when the scientific approach to understanding communication works (and it does), it does not supply meaning. We have several meta-analyses that demonstrate for public health messages that high fear messages are more persuasive than low fear messages (Boster & Mongeau, 1984; Mongeau, 1998; Sutton, 1982; Witte & Allen, 2000). This is an important and practical finding for those engaged in public health. However, the information is abstract and removed from the reality of crafting those messages. Sitting down to write a high fear message is difficult when research cannot provide instruction for how to do it. The problem of cultural instantiation is a fundamental limitation of quantitative methods in communication research (Allen & Preiss, 2002).

Another example of the blindness to understanding ethnographic factors in quantitative research is best expressed by Fisher (1994): "How appropriate is pre-test and post-test analysis in research assuming a process view of communication?" (pp. 3–4). Carey (1975) defined communication as: "a symbolic process whereby reality is produced, maintained, repaired, and transformed" (p. 17), and in 1989 pointedly encouraged mass communication researchers to abandon the discovery of laws and diagnose human meanings (see Leeds-Hurwitz, 1995, pp. 4, 7). Yet, behaviorists still feel compelled to treat complex and dynamic features of our communicative life as if they were well-defined variables entering into fixed relationships irrespective of context. Scholars have long suggested that prediction is flawed in the human sciences because we cannot shield the domain of human experiences from external influences. In short, interpretation of meaning does not allow for exactitude. Most important, if we grant that human beings are self-defining, it is much more accurate to understand communicative behavior after the fact than to predict. Human communication is "inescapably historical" (Polkinghorne, 1983, p. 229).

Qualitative research was born from these reactions to the limitations of quantitative design. Phenomenology takes its lead from the humanities, which are committed to celebrating the "wondrously uncommon creations as escape the generalizing mind because they are not, as the scientists say of their experiments, replicable" (Wayne Booth as quoted in Darsey, 1994, p. 171). Qualitative research, as Van Maanen (1983) articulated, is: "an umbrella term" covering a variety of interpretive methods that "seek to describe, decode, translate, and otherwise come to terms with the meaning, not the frequency, of certain ... naturally occurring phenomena in the social world" (p. 9). The qualitative researcher treats data as particular, continuous, and ambiguous; not discrete, replicable, and clearly defined. The emphasis is on description, analysis, and explanation, more than control, measurement, and prediction (Fitch, 1994, p. 32). In terms of the evidence of research reports, narrative excerpts often replace numerical charts.

In the communication discipline, qualitative researchers are committed to examining how agents produce meaning with words, written or spoken (Tomkins, 1994, p. 44). This means that communication is viewed as "a deeply cultured process," and the researcher must be a naturalist of sorts who "watches, listens, and records communicative conduct in its natural setting" (Philipsen, 1992, p. 7). Research questions that begin with how and why replace hypotheses that are driven by if-then connections. So, for example, qualitative researchers ask such questions as: How do advertisements that depict successful women corroborate and challenge theories of feminism? Why do presidential inaugurals sound so much alike? How does the music industry use Web sites to attract consumers? Why are people frightened of public speaking? These questions encourage communication researchers to personalize, localize, and particularize the implications of their findings. Unlike their quantitative counterparts, qualitative researchers do not claim to know what their observations mean "until they have developed a description of the context in which the behavior took place and attempted to see that behavior from the position of its originator" (Van Maanen,1983, p. 10).

Qualitative research does not require the sense of permanence necessary for scientific investigation. Philipsen's seminal work "Speaking Like a Man in Teamsterville," published in 1975, does not become flawed if we were to go back to that south-side Chicago neighborhood and found no one speaking like that in 2003. The requirement that replication of results be contextually and temporally invariant does not apply to qualitative research, nor should it. The value of qualitative research lies in creating an interpretation of the dynamics of a culture and the communication practices ongoing in that culture. However, cultures and practices change with time, experience, and circumstances.

Qualitative research is not without limitations. Interpreting meaning is messy and time-consuming, but the overriding concern is its proclivity to feature the human voice of the researcher. "Methods," as Black wryly noted: "admit of varying degrees of personality"(1965, p. xi). Qualitative research has personality because a lone researcher is generally the sole instrument of observation and the writing ability of the researcher is intrinsic to the validity of the findings. A qualitative researcher must bring the reader to corroborate an interpretive process. This means that the quality of the research is often dependent on the caliber of the researcher's own communicative performance (Black, 1965; Ivie, 1994). Unlike the quantitative researcher who purges style and supplants passive voice in order to distance the reader, the qualitative researcher tries to engage, even "enchant" the reader (Black, 1965, p. xiii) through persuasive "forensic reasoning" (Rosenfield, 1968, p. 10). These traits have led to criticism that the method lacks rigor.

With the defining characteristics, strengths, and limitations of qualitative and quantitative approaches in communication research established, one can see more clearly how the various practices of the two research traditions work. If you read a research report in an academic journal, how can you detect if the author is using quantitative or qualitative methods (procedures or practices)? A simple answer would be if there are numbers it is quantitative, no numbers qualitative (Frey, Boton, Friedman, & Kreps, 1992, p. 4). Yet as we discuss later in the chapter, more obfuscation than clarity comes from this distinction. A qualitative study would be interested in using some combination of interviews, observation, and analysis of texts to represent the communicative experiences of the persons studied. Sometimes called a thick description the report provides an attempt to capture the essence of what the person enacts or lives within a culture. Such descriptions attempt to represent the symbolic world of those under study with no attempt to predict or control the process.

A quantitative investigation is concerned with establishing and evaluating the relationship between or among conceptualized variables. The use of controls (like those in an experiment) and understanding the selection of samples for a survey (to estimate error from the group norm and to generalize to those not in the investigation) is critical to a quantitative investigation. The design may use experiments, surveys, or content analysis to extract information that assesses relationships among the variables under study. The effort is to find a mean (a central value) and the reason why individual scores deviate from that value.

Qualitative research is concerned with representations. Individual differences are not treated as part of the error term but encouraged to become part of the investigation. The representations in a qualitative investigation are the outcomes and may or may not have abstract implications that generalize to others.

Quantitative research views the particular participants as operationalizations of a context in which to examine relationships. Therefore, the statistics are intended to assess and evaluate those relationships. Qualitative research focuses on the accuracy of the representation of the participants' communication–culture without necessary regard to validation of external relationships or generalizability.

While there are many specific qualitative procedures that researchers use to uncover a research question, four common ones used in media research include: rhetorical criticism, content analysis, survey, and ethnography (Berger, 1998). Using rhetorical criticism (analysis of discourse), researchers perform a close, systematic inspection of messages with the help of a selected theory that serves as a lens. The aim is to describe, interpret, and evaluate message content (e.g., film, book, Web site, speech, and advertisement) in order to gain greater insight for how and why persuasion works. Using content analysis (measuring the amount of something in a representative sampling of discourse), researchers conduct a more sweeping, systematic examination of groups of discourse. The aim is to compare and contrast message form and content (e.g., television shows, newspaper coverage, and political campaign literature) in order to assemble frequencies and establish patterns of messages over time. Rhetorical criticism and content analysis are text-based and unobtrusive procedures for qualitative investigation. Content analysis, like survey research, is a hybrid procedure; it can be used for qualitative and quantitative purposes.

Using surveys (e.g., mailed questionnaires, telephone surveys, personal interviews, and focus groups), researchers ask people about themselves in order to draw conclusions about what the larger population thinks. Hence, gaining a representative sample is critical. The construction of the questionnaire or interview guide must be undertaken in a systematized way to maximize the accuracy and usefulness of the data gained. Using ethnography (participant observation), researchers enter the field to observe how people communicate with each other in their natural settings in order to understand the tacit rules that govern their communicative interaction. Survey and ethnography are subject, not text-based, procedures of qualitative investigation. Hence, they are often referred to as obtrusive methods that require subject consent. Survey and content analysis are used in quantitative or qualitative approaches to communication research and are typically marked by breadth of inquiry. Ethnography and rhetorical criticism are used strictly in qualitative approaches to communication research and are typically marked by depth of inquiry.

As we trot out these distinctions between the two research worldviews, and their corresponding methods of choice, we are mindful not to reify the very stereotypes we eschew. Many of the dichotomies between the methods are overdrawn.[1] For instance, quantitative research is usually equated with numbers, empiricism, objectivity, and deduction. Qualitative research conversely is equated with words, subjectivity, and induction. Upon close inspection, these grand either–ors collapse. All communication research is about words. "Words constitute THE data of interest to Communication scholars," wrote Liska and Cronkhite (1994, p. 59). In addition, many qualitative researchers count things. Some qualitative researchers have described themselves as "unwitting mathematicians" who notice rhetorical patterns, count things, and adhere to the law of "central tendency" (Hart,1994b, p. 75, 80). All communication researchers do empirical study. The critic–ethnographer and the scientist have in common two vitally important activities: "to see a thing clearly and to record what they have seen precisely" (Black,1965, p. 4). All communication research is rigorous and empirically based—though quantitative researchers practice it through research teams, random sampling and replication, and qualitative researchers practice it through purposive samples, lengthy immersion in a setting, and plausible argument drawn from reams of raw data. Perhaps the most curious distinction involves the deductive–inductive debate. Neither describes what researchers do. As Bavelas summarized it: "All researchers engage in a sequential process that includes both forms of reasoning" (1995, p. 54).

The harms of thinking that great chasms separate the two research practices are several-fold. First, differences of this magnitude breed hostility. Berger (1994) decried the tendency of the field's active researchers "to be occupied chronically with arguing about the relative merits of various methodological approaches for studying human communication" (p. 11). The intensity of the debate has sometimes degenerated into personal attack.[2] Second, turf wars also led to what Janesick aptly coined: "methodolatry"—"the slavish attachment and devotion to method" and "the almost constant obsession with the trinity of validity, reliability and generalizability" that overtakes the discourse (Janesick, 1988, p. 215). The temptation to become over involved with method means that researchers are prone to separate experience from knowing (p. 215). Burke (1969) referred to the phenomena of overzealous affirmation of a myopic skill set as a trained incapacity to see clearly. Third, the idolatry of a particular research paradigm has also led to a distressing tendency to sever research from theoretical advancements. Operational mastery does not in and of itself produce theoretical insights about human communicators. As Berger (1994) observed: "Atheoretical qualitative research is as uninformative as atheoretical quantitative research" (p. 14). Finally, looking at behaviorism and phenomenology as oil and water negates the entire possibilities of triangulation—of the postmodern impulse, of many fruitful interdisciplinary and academic-professional partnerships and the proposition to which these authors are committed.

HOW DOES TRIANGULATION WORK?
CASE STUDIES IN COMMUNICATION

The humanities without science are blind; science without the humanities may be vicious.

—Marie Hochmuth-Nicholas

When the word blended family first entered our lexicon to replace broken home, it was met with a mixture of relief and resistance. In some sense, the entrance of triangulation—a blending of humanistic and scientific research cultures—to replace the great qualitative–quantitative divide has met with a similar reaction in the academy. Paradoxically, the term triangulation has been used to describe precision, accuracy, and clarity, but also tension, duplicity, and obfuscation. Originally, the term came from the field of navigation to help describe how the use of multiple reference points could help investigators zero in on a precise location. The location of an unknown point can be found "*by the formation of a triangle* [emphasis added] having the unknown point and two known points as the vertices" (American Heritage Dictionary, 2001). This meaning of the term makes sense intuitively. As Singleton, Straits, and McAllister (1988) explained: "In their everyday lives, people frequently use more than one means to solve a problem" (p. 360). So, too, the reasoning goes, blending qualitative and quantitative methods can solve vexing research problems about communication. Yet in other contexts the word invites an opposite meaning. Visual communication scholars know that the shape of a triangle connotes tension and irresolution. The cliché love triangle reflects this mood. The Bermuda Triangle is a navigational nightmare, and the phrase has come to symbolize lost, misguided, or bungled scenarios. Communication consultants use the term triangulating to designate when two people are engaged in unhealthy conflict management—a dysfunctional communication pattern that involves sharing frustrations about another individual to a third person (Brenner, 2001).

This confluence of opposites can enrich the usage of the term in a research setting. Practicing triangulation is fraught with opportunities and threats, clarity, and obfuscation, the blending of views, and the breaking of traditions. As the title of our essay suggests, what the field of communication really needs are good scientists and storytellers. Scientists, who understand the importance of precision and measurement; storytellers, who understand the importance of engagement and reasoning. Communication research as a whole needs scope and generalizability, but it also must be vivid and particular. If we can frame our research from a triangulated perspective, we will yield explanation and insight; be true to the need of replication and receptivity; and present findings that are efficient and compelling. Neither worldview has a corner on relevance, validity, or significance. A "syncretic" (Polkinghorne, 1983, p. xi) or multiparadigmatic approach allows these staples of scholarship to flourish.

That said, where does one begin? The opportunities for triangulation are seemingly endless but because the path is not well marked, threats loom large. Janesick (1988) posited four types of triangulation: (a) investigator, (b) data, (c) methodological, and (d) theoretical, but published scholarship in the discipline tends not to reference this typology. We know that increasingly researchers advocate triangulation, but precious few practice it. Worse yet, graduate training in universities still tends to prepare students for one method or the other, not both (Jick, 1983, p. 135), and academic research publications still prefer singular methods, citing length and focus concerns. Yet, exciting models of blended scholarship exist on a range of communication topics from across the academic-professional landscape. The case studies examined below treat trends in presidential discourse from the 1960s through the 1980s, media coverage of character issues in the 2000 presidential campaign, viewer reactions to televised political debates in the 2000 election, and media coverage of the AIDS epidemic from its inception to the present by combining qualitative and quantitative research methods in sophisticated ways.

NEW DIRECTIONS IN CONTENT ANALYSIS

Content analysis is the oldest quantitatively driven method in mass communication research, extending back to the 1800s in this country, and even the 1500s in Europe. By the late 1960s, a few practitioners (Goffman, 1979; Holsti, 1969) embraced the radical notion that content analysis should become more qualitatively driven. Specifically, this nontraditional practice means that: (a) significance is not equated exclusively with frequency of occurrence; (b) content categories could and should be judgmental or interpretive; and (c) a discussion of latent meanings should follow the presentation of manifest content. In short, the research goal is to become adept at descriptive statistics and rhetorical analysis. Goffman's (1979) impressive studies of gender stereotypes and advertisements exemplified some of these new ideas. Few followed this lead.

A contemporary communication researcher, Hart, has won recognition for his sophisticated blending of content analysis and rhetorical criticism. In 1984, Hart published *Verbal Style and the Presidency: A Computer-Based Analysis*, a work that showcased his specially designed software package, DICTION. The work examined 800 presidential messages from John F. Kennedy to Ronald Reagan from 30 different language analysis vantage points. The study was both a humanistic and scientific examination of presidential rhetoric that in Hart's own words was "precise, comprehensive, comparative, and quantitative" (p.

14). The sampling methods, units of analysis, reliance on computer software, and, of course, the data presentation in the form of nearly 60 tables showing descriptive statistics and correlation among the language use of presidents, were quantitatively driven. The use of interpretative categories (activity, optimism, certainty, realism, embellishment, variety, human interest, complexity, etc.), the analysis of latent meanings, and the overall interest in presidential uniqueness (cleverness of symbolic choices), not just presidential conformity (frequency of symbolic choices), was qualitatively driven. The results of this two-pronged inquiry are broad (e.g., Presidents scored significantly higher in their use of optimism, self-reference, realism and caution than business, religious, and political leaders) and deep (e.g., Kennedy's rhetoric was least folksy, Johnson's least complex, and Nixon's most realistic of all other presidents' rhetoric). Hart captured the triangulated effort in this way:

> The purpose here is to show why the numerical data turned out as they did. Figure 1.2 is every bit as important as Table 1.1 since the former tears us away from the magic of numbers and forces us to deal, microscopically, with the structure of language. Such procedures return us to the lived reality of symbol-using and demand that we document for ourselves the facts unearthed by the computer. Throughout this book, therefore, examples of presidential persuasion will be used extensively. In almost all cases, I have confined the numerical data to the Appendixes so that words—not numbers—receive the attention due them. The numbers, of course, are indispensable, for they add the level of detail necessary to make sharp discriminations and valid comparisons. But every attempt will be made here to tell the *rhetorical* story of the modern presidency; to appreciate that story, we must listen, critically, to what our presidents have said. (1984, p. 34)

Increasingly, qualitative content analysis in communication is being practiced and finding a receptive audience. For example, The Project for Excellence in Journalism, funded by the Pew Research Center at Columbia University, released in their own words, an "unusual study of the character issue in the 2000 presidential election" (np, nd). The study was unusual in two senses. First, "character" is a variable that requires interpretive categories (in this case, the content categories included six themes: for Gore, "scandal tainted," "liar," "competence"; for Bush, "different kind of Republican," "unintelligent," and "coasts on family"). These character themes are difficult to isolate and quantify. Second, the content analysis was paired with a companion telephone survey to reveal how influential press coverage is in shaping public opinion of candidates. The study examined 5 weeks of stories in newspapers, television, radio, and the Internet between February and June of 2000. Drawn from a data set of 2000 print and Internet stories and 400 television and radio programs, the study suggested that character was a major focus of the coverage. Bush received more positive coverage, Gore more negative coverage; yet, as the survey data revealed, people form their own impressions of the candidates' character some-times in spite of the tendencies of press coverage.

In each case, the content analytic findings were enriched with the pairing of qualitative and quantitative data. Not only do we learn the what and where of a communication phenomena, but also the how and why. Breadth of discovery and depth of insight is a compelling, albeit difficult, research achievement.

NEW DIRECTIONS IN INTERVIEWS

The emergence of civic journalism has led to an unanticipated need for triangu-lation and an emphasis on qualitative approaches to newsgathering. Interview methods, for instance, have become much more complex, time-consuming, and context-dependent in an effort to generate relevant, in-depth stories from the local citizenry. Sophisticated interviewing methods that require profes-sional-academic partnerships are finding their way into television newsrooms especially during election coverage. The Interdisciplinary Communication Re-search Institute at Wichita State University devised a live debate tracker, a mo-bile automated response testing instrument (MARTI) that KSNW, the NBC affiliate, used in covering the 2000 presidential debates. Whether used for de-bate tracking, evaluating marketing strategies, testing advertising concepts, or even analyzing legal defenses, MARTI allows for focus group data to be gath-ered and processed in a more scientific way, according to the principle investiga-tor of the project, Philip Gaunt (personal communication, May 9, 2002). For the television station debate project, a random sample of area residents was conducted by a team of university researchers. Recruitment for the focus group involved screening for political affiliation, race, gender, income, and education. Once the scientifically selected focus group participants were identified, they met at the television station to view the debate live and were given responders that looked like walkie-talkies to record their impressions in real time. Each re-sponder had a numeric pad (to register discrete cognitive reaction) and a dy-namic control on the side (to register feeling states). Results were aggregated according to male versus female, and superimposed on the debate image at the bottom of the screen.

The novelty of the MARTI technology is that it recorded discrete and con-tinuous data in easy-to-process real time. In short, the blended research possi-bilities that this technology allowed were several fold. Quantitatively, the focus group was a representative sample. MARTI allowed for precision of analysis in numerical terms. The study controlled for gender and could con-trol for other variables. Finally, MARTI preserved the anonymity of the par-ticipants from the mass audience. Qualitatively, the focus group was debriefed after the live debate by a moderator who could ask such things as: Why did the women in the group respond so negatively to certain issues, while the men tended to respond positively? Many instances of a gender divide were recorded and the dialed intensity of feeling information generated more discussion than the pad presence or absence information. The event was live and allowed for continuous reaction thus lessening the artificiality of a traditional behaviorist study. Of course, the sophistication of this project required investigator triangulation, too. Engineers, technical directors, producers, and reporters at the television station worked with communication and education faculty at the university to pull off a first in local news programming anywhere in the country (Gaunt, personal communication, May 9, 2002).

A TRAJECTORY OF RESEARCH IN HIV EDUCATION AND MEDIA COVERAGE

More often, triangulated study of a research question comes indirectly from tracing the accumulated knowledge base of a subject over time. The fast changing world of how the media responded to what became known as the HIV epidemic is a case in point. A fundamental challenge to journalism and the practices of the mass media appeared in the early 1980s when groups of gay men started dying of rare diseases like Kaposi's Sarcoma in New York and San Francisco. The original label, Gay Related Infectious Disease (GRID), was eventually supplanted by the term Acquired Immune Deficiency Syndrome (AIDS) and the cause of the disease, Human Immunodeficiency Virus (HIV), was discovered. Critical questions about media coverage have emerged: (a) Did media coverage fuel a homophobic reaction? (b) Did media practices favor the political and scientific elite, and the status quo at the expense of change and intervention? and (c) Did media desire to avoid discussion of distasteful issues, marginalize persons (e.g., homosexuals and drug users) and practices (i.e., anal sex, breastfeeding, needle sharing, and promiscuity)?

Examination of media coverage in this arena exists from a variety of sources both quantitative and qualitative. One groundbreaking body of research on this topic, Elwood's (1999) *Power in the blood: A handbook on AIDS, politics, and communication*, is a compilation of behavioral and phenomenological approaches that taken as a whole exemplifies multiple types of triangulation.

Quantitative analyses in the book documents the kind, amount, trends, and impact of media coverage in a variety of settings, including such things as the number and types of guests on television programs (Wright, 1999), recall of public service announcements (Walters, Walters, & Priest, 1999a), and the rise of AIDS as a public issue (Walters, Walters, & Priest, 1999b). These investigations, using a variety of experimental, quasiexperimental, and survey methods respectively, provide a valuable set of quantitative inquiries on what the media coverage of this national epidemic looked like, as well as the impact of that coverage. In short, the accumulated research quantifies institutional bias on the part of media and points to the silences in the media at representing conditions afflicting the less popular segments of society (Fuller, 1999).

While media coverage of HIV was being documented in terms of quantitative research, additional study explored the undercurrent of frustration and fear expressed by marginalized publics. Qualitative essays in the Elwood anthology addressed these concerns. Haller (1999) pointed out that the change of AIDS to a legally defined disability carried a number of implications for how media covered such stories, not just how many stories were published. Rhetorical works in the series deal with the political issues involved in HIV (German & Courtright, 1999; McKinney & Pepper, 1998) and permit further understanding of the scientific investigations that preceded them. The backdrop of political and social forces that had labeled the disease represented a means to interpret the nature of the media reaction. The inability of the Reagan administration to acknowledge the disease and, as McKinney and Pepper (1998) pointed out, the distractions of the Clinton administration provides insight into the media practices documented in the quantitative studies.

The problem with any source of scientific or quantitative study is that the information must be understood in the environment in which those messages operate. When one understands the broader social, economic, and political context of the messages, then the quantitative data make sense. So, the impact of the announcement that NBA All-Star Earvin "Magic" Johnson had contracted HIV on public attitudes and behaviors (Allen et. al., 2001) provides an example of shifting attitudes in response to a single event. The problem with qualitative research, on the other hand, is that interpretive practices need a big picture perspective to validate the significance of their findings. The work by Knaus and Austin (1999) dealing with the impact of the AIDS Memorial Quilt required a context in which to interpret the meaning or symbolism of the quilt as a potential form of AIDS education and prevention. The pairing of qualitative and quantitative research permits an understanding of the quilt in personal and symbolic terms, as well as the social implications of the artwork as a force for change. Similarly, Shilts (1987), as a reporter, did not simply report just the facts but through personal in-depth interviews provides insight into those medical and scientific facts in the context of the gay community and represents the emotional and political struggles in which such facts take place.

Analysis is not confused with bias (an association often made by behaviorists to describe qualitative work) when the qualitative researcher can demonstrate that the conclusion reached carries a greater sense of universality than simply the perspective of the individual. All of the previously mentioned case studies are testament to the power of triangulated research methods to reduce the weaknesses of any one method, combine the strengths of multiple methods, and add sophistication (both scope and insight) to research questions in communication.

CONCLUSION

> In an age of mass media, a new and complex phenomenology reigns.
>
> —Rod Hart (1994, p. 310)

Ethnographers, wrote Philipsen (1992), must be good scientists and storytellers. That imperative, we have argued, should be true of all communication researchers regardless of perspective (behaviorism or phenomenology), field (journalism or telecommunications) research question (what, and where, or how, and why), or setting (laboratory or field). The pairing of qualitative and quantitative approaches in communication is necessary in a discipline that defines itself in process and context-dependent terms. The two approaches are also necessary for researchers who are committed to showcasing the human ingenuity of our symbol system and yet seek to theorize about the regularities of communicative patterns.

This chapter began by revisiting the qualitative–quantitative divide in order to capture the distinct strengths and weaknesses of each approach, but also to show that many of the dichotomies between the two research traditions are overdrawn. In recognizing that many of the differences are exaggerated, communication scholars can see more clearly the types, opportunities, and challenges of triangulation. At the same time, we acknowledged that the term itself is fraught with double meanings, requiring cautious venture into blended modes of inquiry. We highlighted new directions in communication content analysis and survey research, involving a range of communication topics (presidential speech patterns, media coverage of campaigns, televised debate response, and media coverage of AIDS). All used innovative triangulation (content analysis paired with rhetorical criticism; telephone surveys paired with content analysis; focus groups paired with a computerized survey instrument; and rhetorical criticism paired with personal interviews and tied to meta-analyses).

These kinds of studies should indicate that the outlook for triangulated research in communication is promising. In addition to the view already expressed in this chapter, researchers would be wise to note that the demands of postmodernism in the academy and cross-training in the workplace will continue to support a syncretic approach to research practice and a more complex phenomenological outlook. Foucault (1980) reminded us that the discursive turn of postmodernism privileges the power of words. Power is located in discourse; it is no longer the handmaiden of economic realities. Concomitantly, the rise of chaos theory, especially in the field of public relations (Murphy, 1996), reminds us that to capture the complexity and volatility of public opinion, prediction, and control models must give way to nonlinear, qualitative models.

The communication industry is also demanding that the academy produce graduates who are multiskilled. Employers in all types of communication-related fields expect, not just hope, that students can establish rapport with clients; craft compelling stories through articulate speaking, writing, and visual representation; decipher polling data, tables, and spread sheets; understand the research process; control for variables; and become immersed in communicative contexts by taking it to the streets.

ENDNOTES

[1]Curiously, these dichotomies still find their way into methods textbooks with great regularity. See Bavelas in Leeds-Hurwitz (1995) for an exceptional and witty discussion of many false dichotomies.

[2]See for instance the Darsey vs. Hart exchange in *Western Journal of Communication* (1994) the special issue devoted to qualitative and quantitative concerns. In addition, Polkinghorne (1983) and Cohen's (1994) work summarizing a century-worth of lively, and sometimes acrimonious, debate.

REFERENCES

Allen, M., & Preiss, R. (2002). An analysis of textbooks in interpersonal communication: How accurate are the representations? In M. Allen, R. Preiss, B. Gayle, & N. Burrell (Eds.), *Interpersonal communication research: Advances through meta-analysis* (pp. 371–388). Mahwah, NJ: Lawrence Erlbaum Associates.

Allen, M., Casey, M., Emmers-Sommers, T., Sahlstein, E., Degooyer, D., Dunn, T., Wagner, E., & Winters, A. (2001, April). When a celebrity contracts a disease: The example of Earvin "Magic" Johnson's announcement that he was HIV positive. Paper presented at the Central States Communication Association convention, Cincinnati, OH. (ERIC Document #453149).

American Heritage Dictionary (2001). 4th ed. New York: Dell.

A question of character: How the media have handled the issue and how the public has reacted (2000). *Project for excellence in journalism,* Pew Charitable Trusts, Columbia University Graduate School of Journalism.

Bavelas, J. B. (1995). Quantitative versus qualitative? In W. Leeds-Hurwitz (Ed.), *Social approaches to communication* (pp. 49–62). New York: Guilford.

Berger, A. B. (1998). *Media research techniques* (2nd ed.). Thousand Oaks, CA: Sage.

Berger, C. (1994). Evidence? For What? *Western Journal of Communication, 58,* 11–199.

Black, E. (1965). *Rhetorical criticism: A study in method.* Madison, WI: University of Wisconsin Press.

Boster, F. J., & Mongeau, P. (1984). Fear-arousing persuasive messages. In R. Bostrom (Ed.), *Communication yearbook* (8th ed., pp. 330–375). Newbury Park, CA: Sage.

Brenner, R. (2001). Emotions at work: The triangulation zone. *Point Lookout,* Chaco Canyon Consulting [on-line]. Available: http://www.chacocanyon.com

Burke, K. (1969). *A rhetoric of motives.* Berkeley, CA: University of California Press.

Carey, J. W. (1975). A cultural approach to communication. *Communication, 2,* 1–22.

Carey, J. W. (1989). *Culture as communication: Essays on media and society.* Boston: Unwin Hyman.

Cohen, H. (1994). *The history of speech communication: The emergence of a discipline, 1914–1945.* Annandale, VA: Speech Communication Association.

Darsey, J. (1994). Must we all be rhetorical theorists? An anti-democratic inquiry. *Western Journal of Communication, 58,* 164–181.

Elwood, W. (Ed.). (1998). *Power in the blood: A handbook on AIDS, politics, and communication.* Mahwah, NJ: Lawrence Erlbaum Associates.

Fisher, W. (1994). Genesis of the conversation. *Western Journal of Communication, 58,* 3–4.

Fitch, K. (1994). Criteria for evidence in qualitative research. *Western Journal of Communication, 58,* 32–38.

Frey, L., Botan, C., Friedman, P., & Kreps, G. (1992). *Interpreting communication.* Englewood Cliffs, NJ: Prentice-Hall.

Foucault, M. (1980). *Power/knowledge: Selected interviews and other writings, 1927–1977* (C. Gordon, Trans.). New York: Pantheon.

Fuller, L. (1999). Media manipulations and the AIDS/breastfeeding issue. In W. Elwood (Ed.), *Power in the blood: A handbook on AIDS, politics, and communication* (pp. 341–352). Mahwah, NJ: Lawrence Erlbaum Associates.

German, K., & Courtright, J. (1999). Politically privileged voices: Glaser and Fisher address the 1992 Presidential nominating conventions. In W. Elwood (Ed.), *Power in the blood: A handbook on AIDS, politics, and communication* (pp. 67–76). Mahwah, NJ: Lawrence Erlbaum Associates.

Goffman, E. (1979). *Gender advertisements.* New York: Harper & Row.

Haller, B. (1999). AIDS as a legally defined disability: Implications from new media coverage. In W. Elwood (Ed.), *Power in the blood: A handbook on AIDS, politics, and communication* (pp. 267–280). Mahwah, NJ: Lawrence Erlbaum Associates.

Hart, R. (1984). *Verbal style and the presidency: A computer-based analysis.* New York: Academic Press.

Hart, R. (1994a). Doing criticism my way: A reply to Darsey. *Western Journal of Communication, 58,* 308–312.

Hart, R. (1994b). Wandering with rhetorical criticism. In W. Nothstine, C. Blair, & G. Copeland (Eds.), *Critical questions: Invention, creativity, and the criticism of discourse and the media* (pp. 71–81). New York: St. Martins.

Holsti, O. (1969). *Content analysis for the social sciences and humanities.* Menlo Park, CA: Addison-Wesley.

Ivie, R. (1994). A question of significance. *Quarterly Journal of Speech, 80,* 1.

Janesick, Y. (1988). The dance of qualitative research design: Metaphor, methodology, and meaning. In R. Singleton, Jr., B. Straits, M. Straits, & R. McAllister (Eds.), *Approaches to social research* (pp. 209–229). New York: Oxford University Press.

Jick, T. (1983). Mixing qualitative and quantitative methods: Triangulation in action. In J. VanMaanen (Ed.), *Qualitative methodology* (pp. 135–148). Beverly Hills, CA: Sage.

Knaus, C., & Austin, E. (1999). The AIDS memorial quilt as a preventative education: A developmental analysis of the quilt. *AIDS Education and Prevention 11,* 525–540.

Leeds-Hurwitz, W. (Ed.). (1995). *Social approaches to communication*. New York: Guilford.

Liska, J., & Cronkhite, G. (1994, Winter). On the death, dismemberment, or disestablishment of the dominant paradigms. *Western Journal of Communication, 58*, 58–65.

McKinney, M., & Pepper, B. (1998). From hope to heartbreak: Bill Clinton and the rhetoric of AIDS. In W. Elwood (Ed.), *Power in the blood: A handbook on AIDS, politics, and communication* (pp. 77–92). Mahwah, NJ: Lawrence Erlbaum Associates.

Mongeau, P. (1998). Another look at fear-arousing persuasive appeals. In M. Allen & R. Preiss (Eds.), *Persuasion: Advances through meta-analysis* (pp. 53–68). Cresskill, NJ: Hampton Press.

Murphy, P. (1996). Chaos theory as a model for managing issues and crises. *Public Relations Review, 22*, 95–113.

Philipsen, G. (1975). Speaking like a man in Teamsterville: Cultural patterns of role enactment in an urban neighborhood. *Quarterly Journal of Speech, 61*, 13–22.

Philipsen, G. (1992). *Speaking culturally: Explorations in social communication*. Albany, NY: State University of New York Press.

Polkinghorne, D. (1983). *Methodology for the human sciences*. New York: State University of New York Press.

Rosenfield, L. (1968). The anatomy of critical discourse. *Speech Monographs, 25*, 55–69.

Shilts, R. (1987). *And the band played on: Politics, people, and the AIDS epidemic*. New York: Penguin Books.

Singleton, R., Straits, B., & McAllister, R. (1988). *Approaches to social research*. New York: Oxford University Press.

Sutton, S. (1982). Fear-arousing communications: A critical examination of theory and research. In J. Eiser (Ed.), *Social psychology and behavioral medicine* (pp. 303–337). New York: Wiley.

Tompkins, P. (1994). Principles of rigor for assessing evidence in qualitative communication research. *Western Journal of Communication, 58*, 44–50.

Van Maanen, J. (Ed.). (1983). *Qualitative methodology*. Beverly Hills, CA: Sage.

Walters, T., Walters, L., & Priest, S. (1999a). Life on the edge of the precipice: Information subsidy and the rise of AIDS as a public issue, 1983–1989. In W. Elwood (Ed.), *Power in the blood: A handbook on AIDS, politics, and communication* (pp. 257–266). Mahwah, NJ: Lawrence Erlbaum Associates.

Walters, T., Walters, L., & Priest, S. (1999b). What we say and how we say it: The influence of psychosocial characteristics and message content of HIV/AIDS Public Service Announcements. In W. Elwood (Ed.), *Power in the blood: A handbook on AIDS, politics, and communication* (pp. 293–310). Mahwah, NJ: Lawrence Erlbaum Associates.

Witte, K., & Allen, M. (2000). A meta-analysis of fear appeals: Implications for effective health campaigns. *Health Education & Behavior, 27*, 591–615.

Wright, K. (1999). AIDS, the status quo, and the elite media: An analysis of the guest lists of "The MacNeil/Lehrer News Hour" and "Nightline." In W. Elwood (Ed.), *Power in the blood: A handbook on AIDS, politics, and communication* (pp. 281–292). Mahwah, NJ: Lawrence Erlbaum Associates.

12

Academic/Professional Partnerships

Newsrooms and Community

Jan Schaffer

Pew Center for Civic Journalism, Washington, DC
J-Lab: The Institute for Interactive Journalism, College Park, MD

Over the past decade, news organizations have forged new relationships with various partners in their communities. Sometimes the relationships are with other news organizations, sometimes they are with community groups. Some of the most productive relationships, however, have been with local colleges and universities.

Whereas, in the past, universities have been aloof and often quite detached from their hometowns, they are now emerging to leverage their expertise in ways that can make a difference to their communities. Higher education articles have traditionally focused on town–gown tensions, binge drinking, or landlord–student tenant disputes—in addition to academic laurels or controversies. While not trying to abandon their watchdog roles, news organizations are reaching out to colleges and universities to add some additional juice to their journalism. Simply put, the news organizations are seeking to tap some of the academy's intellectual muscle in ways that build some capacity for addressing community issues or solving community problems. Moreover, the universities are looking for ways to be good corporate citizens.

These joint initiatives take many forms—from polling to training, from dialoguing to engineering, from beefing up stories to beefing up curricula. Many of these ventures have developed momentum and left lasting legacies in their towns. Usually neither the news organization nor the educational institution knew where the first overtures would lead, but the partnerships started out offering benefits to both parties and ended up generating win–win outcomes.

Some ventures show exciting promise. For instance, the energy simulator game developed by the University of Wisconsin for a Madison civic journalism partnership blended the newsroom's public-policy knowledge with the engineering department's technological expertise to advance new templates for public conversation, in this case, weighing the costs and choices affecting future energy supplies. The bottom line, as the following ventures demonstrate, is that these collaborations created new entry points for delivering information to people so that they do could their jobs better as citizens.

CUSTOMIZING SOFTWARE

Wisconsin State Journal and the University of Wisconsin–Madison

One of the most innovative partnerships occurred in Madison and involved using the university's computer software expertise to help people literally "play" with information to advance public dialogue. At issue were the state's energy options and the choices that would need to be made to ensure future supplies.

The news organizations had reported a fair amount of policy debate about the state's energy problems, said Tom Still, associate editor of the newspaper and president of the "We the People Wisconsin" civic journalism partnership (2002). "But it was clear to me that the average person wasn't tuned into this debate, had no real idea of the extent of the problem, probably thought they weren't part of the problem or part of the solution" (personal communication, February 19, 2002).

At an early brainstorming session, Still thought of the Sim City computer game, which lets players simulate different city-planning scenarios, and blurted out: "Why don't we turn it into a game?" A great idea, perhaps, but how to begin?

The partners decided to start with the university. Still went first to University Chancellor John D. Wiley, a physics professor who was part of a panel discussion Still moderated at a Fall 2000 economic summit sponsored by the university. "I knew he understood the nexus between science and public policy," Still said. Wiley hooked up the paper with a professor and two doctoral students in the engineering department. Still said they "were anxious to show they could be part of solving the problem even if it was just presenting information in an objective way" (personal communication, February 19, 2002).

Professor Jerry Kulcinski and the two students, Paul Meier and Paul Wilson, devised a user-friendly exercise to give the public a good look at their energy options. The result was "The Energy ED Simulator," a game that lets people select from different sources of energy and then see how each choice would impact people's future bills and future emissions of greenhouse gases. (See Fig. 12.1.) "It's been a great success with the public," Kulcinski said (personal communication, February 19, 2002). In addition to launching the game at a community conference, the engineers beta-tested it on a number of groups. "They all liked it and wanted to know how they could get it. We're now giving it to high school social studies teachers so they can use it with their students."

The "We the People Wisconsin" media partners—which also include WISC-TV and Wisconsin public radio and television—liked the interaction. "Bringing that issue home to people in a very hands-on way was important, and the role of the university was valuable," Still said. The university's participation also added credibility. Kulcinski called it a "provocative" partnership. "We don't normally do things like that. It was just something we did as a public service. No

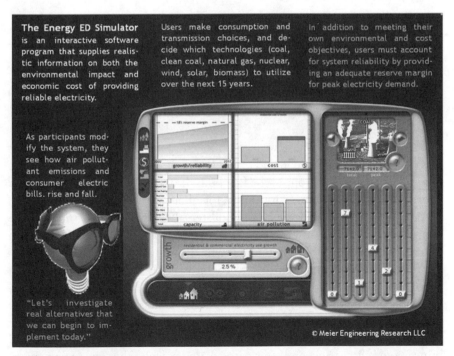

FIG. 12.1. Wisconsin's energy simulator game was developed by engineers at the University of Wisconsin.

money changed hands. We didn't make a dime off it. Paul did it mainly on his spare time. Now he's starting to think, if it's so successful, he should go to the utility companies to see if they would pay to improve it."

All in all it was a win–win situation. The public got information in a new way, the newspaper got a new entry point for citizens that advanced its earlier experiments with citizen input via town halls and conferences, the university got some good publicity and proffered some technical expertise to manage the challenges of explaining megawatts and tons. It also opened the door to thinking about new opportunities. Said Kulcinski, "What it forces us to do is put things in terms that are usable by the general public. We tend to talk a different language to each other, a kind of jargon. That's not the way most people converse. This forces us to step back and try to see things through the layperson's eyes. It's good for us and good for students. It helps the public understand us so they don't think we're black boxes" (personal communication, February 19, 2002).

POLLING AND SURVEY RESEARCH

Savannah Morning News and Georgia Southern University

Another win–win partnership has been in the works in Georgia since the early 1990s, when the *Savannah Morning News* reached out to Georgia Southern University in Statesboro to partner in a survey on race relations. That partnership has blossomed to include several more surveys. The surveys, by giving the newspaper critical community input, help to focus in-depth interviews in the field and follow-up civic mapping exercises. They also give market-research students hands-on field experience.

It all started when the newspaper hooked up in 1993 with two business school professors, Jim Randall and Don Thompson (who is now retired), for the race poll. The survey was one of the first polls the 65,000-circulation newspaper ever sponsored. The university did it for about $2,000 versus estimates of $6,000 to $10,000 from professional pollsters. "You can find attitudes in the community that might surprise you," said David Donald, the paper's precision journalism editor. "We need to find out why those attitudes are there, and polling is another way to get your ear to the ground" (personal communication, March 27, 2002).

Donald got involved in 1997. After learning some survey techniques at the university's graduate School of Sociology, he became an active partner with Randall, a professor of marketing. "He brings an academic viewpoint, and I bring a journalist's viewpoint, so we check up on each other for certain things outside our own line of sight," Donald said.

For Randall, the opportunity to engage students in a real project for credit is invaluable. Student teams brainstorm survey questions to get at the research objectives. They drive the 60 miles to Savannah, every evening for three weeks, to make the phone calls. They enter answers into a spreadsheet. Student teams analyze responses from different subgroups. "They really see the research process from start to finish, and learning these research skills is important," Randall said (personal communication, March, 2002). Moreover, the students get excited when they discover something. They also receive a small stipend to help offset their transportation costs.

The students tell prospective poll respondents they are also working on a class project. One benefit, noted Donald, is that "our response rates tend to be pretty high, especially considering the declining rates of participation in national surveys" (personal communication, March 27, 2002).

The newspaper–university partnership yields large-sample, community surveys—800 or more respondents and as many as 50 questions—for a fraction of what a professional pollster would charge. To date, the surveys have been the basis for projects examining Savannah's increasingly elderly community, the performance of its schools, and the future of the Savannah River.

The survey work, however, is just an early part of a process. Findings are creatively followed up with a tremendous amount of fieldwork, focus groups, advisory panels, and other citizen entry points. In the Aging Matter series, for instance, the survey research laid the groundwork for focus groups, reader advisory panels, and reporting to chronicle how the Savannah region was becoming older demographically and what that meant in terms of political, economic, social and infrastructure spending choices (M. D. Suwyn, R. Lester, M. Mayle, & J. R. Marino, personal communication, January 24, 2002).

In Vision 2010, A Learning Odyssey, the paper started with a citizens advisory group of 60 people who brainstormed how the public could take ownership of its schools. The group met more than 20 times and grew to 150 people over the course of a year. They also visited 21 model schools around the country and reported about their visits for the paper.

A survey fleshed out how the community viewed the public school system. Focus groups throughout the community followed. Businesspeople were asked to gauge how prepared high school graduates were for employment. Recent graduates talked about their K–12 experience. Focus groups of teachers, administrators, private-school students and faculty were also held.

In a follow-up survey in November 2002 of 1,500 people, 23% could accurately describe the Vision 2010 project and identify it with the newspaper.

For its project on the competing demands for Savannah River water, the paper conducted a survey on how much respondents knew about water resource issues. That was followed by tours of the river, interviews of port, city and environmental officials, and a town hall meeting. Later in 2003, the paper planned a follow-up survey to assess whether its reporting efforts had any impact on public knowledge of the issues.

POLLING AND TOURING

Hearst's San Francisco Examiner and San Francisco State University

When anecdotal evidence hinted at large demographic changes in the Bay Area at the end of the 1990s, the San Francisco *Examiner* tapped university expertise to chart the changes and get ahead of the Census. An early and valuable find was urban geographer Max Kirkeberg at San Francisco State. "I'm a geographer. Most of my information comes from research I do on three-hour walking tours of different neighborhoods, illustrating different themes," Kirkeberg said (personal communication, April, 2002). Reporter Annie Nakao first tapped Kirkeberg to take some reporters on a tour of changing neighborhoods. They talked about it with such enthusiasm that the paper asked him to do the same thing for editors. "We thought it was such an eye-opener that other people should see it. So we institutionalized it. We called it the New City Tour, and we tried to get as many of the staff as we could involved," said then-Managing Editor Sharon Rosenhause (personal communication, June 12, 2002).

Kirkeberg took the journalists to southeastern parts of the city unknown to tourists and known to journalists only by their images. For instance, they visited neighborhoods south of Mission Street, where warehouses were being converted to dot.com use and a lot of older businesses were being dislocated. "The biggest change was the replacement of the African-American majority with a rapidly growing Asian presence. I took them to neighborhood streets where they would be overwhelmed with shops with Chinese characters," Kirkeberg said. "To my surprise, or was it my naiveté, the reporters learned an awful lot," he said. "I thought reporters would know the city but many were new to San Francisco or lived elsewhere. Everything I showed them seemed to be new to them" (personal communication, April, 2002).

Rosenhause agreed that, once the reporters hit the neighborhoods, they saw astounding changes. "Even people who'd been in San Francisco a very long time went to places they'd never been before and learned things they didn't know because it had changed so much." As many as 60% of the staff took the tour, which became a way to engage the journalists and help with their education. Rosenhause said the paper got a lot of "buy-in" to a year-long series labeled "The New City." (See Fig. 12.2.)

FIG. 12.2.   San Francisco's "New City" project benefited from polling by San Francisco State.

The project also involved a multilanguage poll—in English, Spanish and Chinese—of 700 city residents, and again the paper turned to San Francisco State, with support from the Pew Center for Civic Journalism. Finding a pollster who was as excited about the work as the newsroom was key. The *Examiner* hired the Public Research Institute at San Francisco State to do the multilingual survey. Said Rosenhause, "I knew we had made the right choice when the director, Rufus Browning, told us: 'This is the project I've waited all of my career to do'" (1999).

BUILDING A NEIGHBORHOOD COLLEGE

Journal Star, Peoria, IL, Bradley University and Illinois Central College

Editor Jack Brimeyer knew that leadership was an issue in Peoria. There was a shortage of people running for office, a shortage of civic volunteers, a shortage of candidates to challenge incumbents. He wanted to do journalism on the problem but he wanted it to have impact. He did not want a series that would be another "dead dog" project that lies on the page, and nobody wants to deal with it (Ford, 1998).

From the start, he sought the involvement of civic groups and the local university and community college, putting representatives on a steering committee. He wanted to be able to "hand off" the project, once the reporting was done, to others in the community who could "run with it." Little did he expect that it would result in the formation of a "Neighborhood College" to give emerging community leaders training in key skills.

An early stop was Bradley University, where John C. Schweitzer, head of the Communications Department, used the school to do five mail surveys—of local companies, minorities, volunteer groups, retirees, and alums of the Chamber of Commerce's leadership training school.

Another general phone survey—of 500 Peorians—was conducted by Joe Pitlik, statistics professor at Illinois Central, who got so excited about the project he ended up donating his time and freeing up $6,000 in funding from the Pew Center for Civic Journalism, later used to launch the Neighborhood College.

Also on the steering committee was Barbara Hartnett, who directed ICC's Professional Development Institute and was helping with the creation of a Center for Nonprofit Excellence.

The surveys helped the paper report a multipart, civic journalism series in 1996 called "Leadership Challenge" that triggered a town hall meeting for more than 300 people and had a major impact on the city ("The James K. Batten

Award," 1997). "One of the things that struck all of us in the Leadership Challenge was this notion that leadership is everywhere, and we need to nurture leadership and nurture the skills that people in neighborhoods were lacking," Hartnett recalled. "Many people in the neighborhoods had this innate ability to lead but they didn't know how to put together a newsletter or who to talk to in city hall. So that's what the Neighborhood College would do" (personal communication, April 23, 2002).

The Neighborhood College was initially sponsored at ICC and funded with grants, but it soon took off on its own. Now it's run off-campus once a year by the Neighborhood Empowerment project. Many of the graduates now serve on city commissions and boards.

The college is a low-budget enterprise, involving 12 Wednesday evenings. The speakers—the mayor and city council members, government officials and nonprofit leaders—are free. The only expenses are sandwiches, sodas, and a final dinner.

The schools enjoyed the credit they got for the project and the opportunity to be good community citizens. Bradley University found a way to work civic journalism into its curriculum. The paper got to tap a wealth of community resources and institutions that had their arms open when the journalists were ready to hand off the project.

PROVOKING COMMUNITY DIALOGUE

The Sun News, Myrtle Beach, SC, and Coastal Carolina University

Myrtle Beach became a city only in the 1950s. Now, it's the nation's second fastest-growing housing market, behind Las Vegas. Coastal Carolina University was created only in the 1970s. In the year 2002, however, the newspaper's year-long series on the area's exploding growth gave a new boost of energy to the university's somewhat stale model of hosting an annual economic conference. About 200 people came to an April "Growth Summit 2002," and the participants got first crack at playing a new computer game the newspaper unveiled, challenging participants to "Chart the Strand's Future." "The great thing here is we have a means for making something happen as a result of the Sun News reporting," enthused Harold Stowe, executive in residence at the university. "By putting some extra energy into it and creating an opportunity for something to happen at the end of a reporting effort like that, it will be a much more substantive conference than it has been for the past couple of years" (personal communication, March 20, 2002).

Facilitated break-out sessions on five topics identified in a *Sun News* series on growth the previous year helped to crystallize questions and issues. Local government leaders were pressed for answers. Participants were asked to fill out cards, saying what they think should happen and what role they'd like to play. Follow-up questionnaires were planned.

A call from *Sun News* editor Trisha O'Connor to the university president's office initiated the partnership. The paper and university split the costs; the university provided the facilitators; and the paper did the journalism. "Our goal is to put information out there for the community to make wise decisions; we're not making the decisions," O'Connor said (personal communication, March 13, 2002). "We wrote about what was happening here, and we went to other places, such as Fort Lauderdale, and wrote about what was happening there, good and bad. It's fascinating to hear people quote our stories back to us. We feel we have something important. We look forward to continuing it."

In Stowe's view, Coastal Carolina University has good resources, which can provide extra insight into managing the area's growth. If the university can reach out to get more of a community dialogue started on some of the issues, "maybe we could force things to happen at a little faster pace." While the newspaper gets a discussion venue to give some legs to its reporting, the university gets to showcase its expertise and engender a broader appreciation of the school as a community resource. The students, Stowe said, also benefit from a high-level "examination of the issues, which enhances their education (personal communication, March 20, 2002).

BUILDING INTERNATIONAL NEWS MODELS

Earlham College, the Dayton [Ohio] Daily News, the Palladium-Item, Richmond, IN

Well before the terrorist attacks of September 11, 2001, some newsrooms were struggling with their coverage of national and international news. Most news organizations, squeezed by space cutbacks, had trimmed their reporting of world news or were reduced to running wire stories.

Just how meaningful was this wire copy to readers? If it was incremental coverage of developments, could readers keep up with the issues or the cast of characters? Did readers even know where some Third World countries were? What would give them the attachment to be interested in the stories?

Cheryl Gibbs, an assistant professor at Earlham College in Richmond, Indiana, who had a strong background in working with Dayton's Kettering

Foundation on civic engagement, began asking what meaningful coverage would look like (personal communication, October 1, 1999). Could she and her journalism students build some new templates and test them with citizen focus groups?

With support from the Pew Center, she signed on the hometown *Palladium-Item* and the *Dayton Daily News* to help build and test the coverage models. Her students researched how news coverage engages people, then they surveyed how citizens get involved in the world, and what readers thought of the wire stories in the two papers. They concluded that people learn about other countries by visiting, studying, or working there. They sell American products abroad or buy foreign products in the United States. Sports events and business deals also help learning.

The students then developed a template for more civic ways to use wire stories, called "The Big Picture," which helped unpack national and international news events in ways that readers could understand, better reported how these events affected readers, and gave readers entry points for reading more about the country and contact information if they wanted to help or do something. "The Big Picture" feature was published for several months by the *Palladium-Item*. The coverage was designed to respond to feedback from readers who said they feel poorly informed about national and world events, and that the usually brief newspaper wire stories don't provide enough context. The newspapers, with student input, sought to engage readers by helping them follow or participate in the political process, learn more, express their views, or join with others to help.

"The Big Picture" coverage used pull-out boxes to deliver the essence of the conflict, longer wire stories to provide more context, lists of organizations offering assistance to guide readers who wanted to help, highlights of congressional activity to help people follow the political process, contact information to make it easier for people to express their views, and lists of activist groups to help people join with others. "Our participants told us that international news stories contribute to the public's perception of the media as 'negative.' Disasters and wars usually put countries on journalists' radar screens. The stories tend to focus on scarcity in underdeveloped countries—poverty, inadequate health care, food shortages—without making any effort to convey the countries' assets," Gibbs said (2002).

Moreover, while the study showed that journalists tend to turn to official sources for background information, readers liked the kind of information they might have found in travel books or gotten in a humanities class. When the news reports included this kind of information, the focus groups responded extremely favorably.

BUILDING CONTENT

The Oakland Post and the University
of California–Berkeley

Former Los Angeles *Times* reporter Bill Drummond had been inspired by the whole idea of civic journalism, harkening back to early experiments with voter-driven election coverage in the early 1990s. It was something he wanted to expose his students to as a journalism professor at the University of California–Berkeley. He had a track record of involving advanced-reporting students in stories on Marin City for a paper called *Marin City Focus,* which the students themselves literally hung on doorknobs.

This time, he sought an outlet that already had the presses and the distribution system, the *Oakland Post,* a minority-owned weekly that had been around for 40 years but didn't have much of a reporting staff. Drummond had known publisher Tom Berkley for years. "I approached him and said I have something to offer and, in return, I get something back for my students and he saw the wisdom of it," Drummond recalled (personal communication, March 13, 2002).

Drummond proposed that his students report and edit stories and actually lay out pages for a newspaper insert called "Inside Oakland." (See Fig. 12.3.) At the heart of the efforts were regular focus group meetings every other week during the course of the semester (W. Drummond, personal communication, October 1, 1998). Said Drummond, in reporting on the project to the Pew Center for Civic Journalism, "It was more than just another exercise in writing and publishing newspaper stories…. Most important were the focus groups, which met regularly with students to offer their views and to give writers and editors feedback about what they were doing" (personal communication, October 1, 1998). The comments and insights from the community residents in the focus groups informed story assignments throughout the project.

At the time the project was launched, Oakland was getting a lot of attention. Former California Governor Jerry Brown was running for mayor. Economic development was a big issue. Drummond felt the community would benefit from more reporting and research.

For three years the Berkeley students edited "Inside Oakland" sections. Drummond's radio class also did a news magazine program on KALX-FM, the Berkeley station that reaches Oakland. The students cross-promoted, on radio, news that was going to be in the newspaper, and promoted, in the paper, stories that were going to be on the radio.

The project ended before December 2001, when Berkley, the paper's publisher, died. His passing raised questions about the future of the *Post* and what

SUNDAY

February 21, 1999

Special Issue

VOLUME 3, ISSUE NO. 1

Inside OAKLAND

Art teacher Keith Williams recently appeared in a movie about Oakland, but he prefers appearing in front of his students at Havenscourt Junior High School.

From film to 'prime time'

BY CHRIS JENKINS
Special to the Post

Seeing himself on the big screen at the prestigious Sundance Film Festival was an out-of-body experience for Keith Williams, an art teacher at East Oakland's Havenscourt Junior High School.

"It was wild, just to be up there ... and (having) people coming up to you saying, 'Great job' and 'really liked your presence,'" said Williams, 35, who delivered a handful of lines in the independent film "Drylongso (Ordinary)."

Williams also designed T-shirts worn by several of the main characters in the movie. He said he took some playful needling from those closest to him.

"My whole family's calling me Muhammad," said Williams, referring to his role in "Drylongso."

"Part of the film was shot in my loft, too. My family called me up, talking about how they saw (all their old stuff)," Williams, who stands well over 6

feet and has tawny dreadlocks down to the middle of his back, said he found the filmmaking experience compelling. But his real passion continues to be nurturing young people through the visual arts. One of the reasons why he enjoyed working on "Drylongso," he said, was that its director, Cauleen Smith, made a conscious effort to portray African-Americans in a positive light.

Using art to empower children of all cultures has been one of Williams' goals since he began working with adolescents in the late 1980s. He painted murals in Los Angeles County after graduating from California State University-Long Beach.

"The opportunity to put energy into a community was really important to me," said Williams. "I've worked with the most vicious gangsters from eastside Long Beach to west-side Long Beach. Crips, Bloods, all of them, and what took their mind out of all that stuff sometimes was doing something positive in the community."

After moving to Oakland four years ago, Williams continued to teach art, but became frustrated when he saw many of his young students only two or three times a week. Although he was painting murals with elementary school children in West Oakland as well as working at various community centers and museums, he said he could not get into children's lives enough to make a difference.

But now that he's been at Havenscourt for two years, Williams said he is getting the in-depth contact with young people that he's been looking for.

"I try to maintain a level of consistency by being here every day and by being early every day, just to be able to be in touch with the day-to-day things that kids do," he said. "I think this (junior high school) age here is where I really can to get them, because their minds are a little more open to new things than some of the high school kids."

To prepare his students for each

see ARTIST page 8

Jack London jazz: battling a bad rap

Despite stigma, waterfront club provides oasis for music-thirsty

BY DIANE D. URBANI
Special to the Post

After 25 years riding the ups and downs of the nightclub trade, Yoshi's Japanese Restaurant and World Class Jazz House seemed headed for rock bottom in late 1996. Claremont-area residents wanted Yoshi's gone, preferring a genteel neighborhood rid of club-bound traffic. Moving was inescapable. But where to? Downtown Oakland's rents were reasonable, but Yoshi's operators doubted they could persuade enough of their clientele to brave the unknown.

"I would have rather been in San Francisco — that's the center of everything," said co-owner Kaz Kajimura, "but we couldn't get any sort of deal over there."

Kajimura and his partners, chef Hiro Hori and maitre d'hotel Yoshi Akiba, considered closing down.

"Then the city of Oakland found out, and they said, 'You guys are a landmark,'" Kajimura recalled. "They helped us by giving a loan to the Port of Oakland" — and by spring 1997, Yoshi's was slated to open on Embarcadero West at the edge of Jack London Square.

Kajimura realized he might be going to a place where the club couldn't stay afloat. Many Bay Area residents were afraid to come to his city after dark, according to questionnaires they filled out at Yoshi's old Claremont Avenue location.

"I wouldn't go to a nightclub in Oakland," Concord resident Diana Llata said flatly. "When I hear Oakland, I think, 'No.'"

"I know guys who won't come down here, period," said Gary Maricich of Walnut Creek.

All over the Bay Area, people read about Oakland's crime statistics: 4,342 aggravated assaults; 3,482 robberies; 306 rapes in 1997. When Oakland Police officer James Williams Jr. was killed in the line of duty January 10 — just 11 weeks after he'd come here from the academy — outsiders' view of Oakland grew even dimmer.

"Oakland has had that stigma of not being safe for many years," said Marshall Lamm, the publicist at Yoshi's.

But Kajimura learned that Jack London Square was Oakland's oasis.

"I checked with the Police Department before we got here," Kajimura said. "I found out the crime rate (around Jack London Square) is amazingly low."

Construction went ahead for the nightclub, the price was right and the architect designed an acoustically idyllic space. Kajimura and company crossed their fingers.

But the club's overhead ran dangerously high when Yoshi's moved into its new building in May 1997. "We went heavily into the red," said Kajimura. "I didn't know it we'd be able to continue."

Then Yoshi's booking agent Akvia Olaine brought in a string of young musicians, mixing them with the keepers of the faith who'd been playing the club for decades: Diana Krall and Oscar Peterson; Tuck and Patti and Poncho Sanchez. Show after show sold out. The jazz-hungry came from San Francisco, Mill Valley, Davis, Chico, and down from the suburbs of Piedmont and Contra Costa. They even came from Los Angeles and San Diego via the nearby Amtrak station. The nightclub's Web site, www.yoshis.com, sustained thousands of visitors each month. By the start of last year, Yoshi's was in the middle of a rebirth, inside its walls and outside. Jack London Square had turned into what Kajimura calls "an entertainment destination."

1998 was Yoshi's best year ever, the co-owner added. Club business boomed and he employs nearly twice as many

see YOSHI'S page 8

Want a speed bump on your street? Get in line

BY MATTHAI CHAKKO KURUVILA
Special to the Post

When two children died after a "joyride" in an East Oakland neighborhood, it wasn't much of a surprise to local residents. Cars scream by on 105th Avenue day and night, heedless of traffic laws or even the children riding their dirt bikes. Yet as neighbors mobilize to have speed bumps or other traffic-control devices implemented on their streets, the city of Oakland seems to have run out of the necessary resources to tackle such problems.

The Public Works Department has either spent or committed its entire budget for traffic control devices, and the

Police Department has temporarily reassigned all of its traffic officers to patrol beats.

On Sunday, January 31, Charles King, 14, Kelvin Johnson, 14, and Eric Carral, 13, apparently bored during the half-time of the Super Bowl, decided to take a stolen car for a drive. The jaunt ended at 5:20 p.m. when King drove the late-model Oldsmobile Cutlass into a parked produce truck on the 400 block of 105th Avenue.

Carral was pronounced dead on arrival at Children's Hospital in Oakland, and Johnson died a day later at Highland Hospital. King was sent home on February 5, according to a Children's Hospital spokeswoman.

The avenue is used as a thoroughfare despite its location in a residential area close to Sobrante Park Elementary School. Soon after the accident, residents began calling for the installation of speed bumps.

To have a speed bump put in, residents of a neighborhood must submit a petition with signatures representing 67 percent of the addresses on that block, according to Jyackuddy Jeeva, a supervising transportation engineer with the Department of Public Works' Traffic Engineering Division (traffic

signals and stop signs require city council approval). As long as the concerned street is not a primary thoroughfare or a bus route, the department usually authorizes the requested number of speed bumps.

But this year's funding for speed bumps has already been used up, Jeeva said. In each of the last two years, Public Works has allocated $350,000 for traffic control devices, with $50,000 going to each of Oakland's seven council districts every year. Almost all of the money designated for districts 6 and 7, which encompass East Oakland, paid for speed bumps. And the City Council's decision last fall to spend an additional $107,000 on speed bumps throughout the city was spent almost entirely in East Oakland.

The police don't track accidents by neighborhood, so it's difficult to tell whether the speed bumps are working, said Sgt. Doug Wayne of the Police Department's traffic investigations unit. But drivers' tendency to speed through the area necessitates more traffic control devices. "Speeding is a way of life down there," he said.

Some 133 blocks are slated for

see JOYRIDE page 8

Only a few items remain of the extensive shrine built in remembrance of two East Oakland boys who died after their January 31 "joyride" on 105th Avenue.

FIG. 12.3.   "Inside Oakland" was reported and edited by Berkeley students.

Drummond called a "perfect collaboration." "The students would spend their shoe leather and bus tokens to find out what was going on," Drummond said, "and he would publish it" (personal communication, October 1, 1998).

CIVIC MAPPING

The News Star, Monroe, LA, Louisiana Tech University, Grambling State University

One third of the *News Star*'s community is African American. One-half of its new hires are straight out of college. So any partnerships that help diversify the newsroom and better prepare young journalists for connecting with the community are of particular interest to Editor Kathy Spurlock.

Reginald Owens has had a particular interest in making sure the whole community is covered. An African American and associate professor of journalism at Louisiana Tech, he said, "I saw civic journalism as a tool to make sure we look at every element of the community" (personal communication, April, 2002).

When Spurlock proposed that Owens' students team with her reporters to map education issues, it paid off for both partners. The students developed more enterprise reporting skills, and the newspaper got the manpower to do civic mapping, an exercise that probes the layers of stakeholders in a community and their framing of issues. The result was "Passing the Test," a series of stories in 2001 that started on the front page and continued in a 12-page special section. (See Fig. 12.4.) It focused on Louisiana's high-stakes LEAP test, administered to fourth and eighth graders. Fourth graders were failing in alarming numbers. The project involved students from both Louisiana Tech and Grambling State, a historically Black college. The students can take combined classes by university agreement.

It worked this way: A couple of students were paired with a reporter from the paper, and then five of these teams adopted five schools and the geographic areas around the schools to map. The teams visited "third places" in the communities where people gather. They talked to store owners and people on their front porches. They set up meetings and did focus groups with faculty and parents, funded with support from the Pew Center for Civic Journalism. Their assignment was to come back with five sources for a story.

Owens and the paper then contracted with Louisiana Tech's alumni soliciting staff to do a survey of people in those communities, asking them about a dozen questions on education. Using the information from the survey, the focus groups, and the mapping, the teams came up with story ideas, and the students were assigned stories.

FIG. 12.4. A newsroom-university city mapping project in Louisiana led to critical coverage of students failing high-stakes testing.

The week after the stories were published, the students handed out flyers, inviting community residents to a town hall meeting; 250 people attended. "This is the first time some of those students were ever in a newsroom. This was their first professional byline. Now, they have an idea of what reporters really do and the problems they run into," Owens said.

"Right below the surface is the issue of race," he said. Owens said he was able to pair White and Black students to go into the schools, most of which were predominantly Black. "Some of these kids had never been into some of these types of neighborhoods and they got a chance to look at some social dynamics. They saw it for real. They ran into people who were suspicious of them because they were White."

Although, at first, people in the community were suspicious, one of the biggest results was that the community and the schools had a positive experience with the newspaper. "As a result of those stories, people called these schools and asked, 'What can we do?' And now they have volunteers coming in," Owens said. "That's what the project was all about" (personal communication, April, 2002). Spurlock agreed, "We essentially introduced the community to the issue and allowed the community to be involved in proposing solutions" (personal communication, April, 2002).

COLLABORATING WITH CIVIC PARTNERS

New Hampshire Public Radio, University of New Hampshire Survey Center, the New Hampshire Center for Public Policy Studies, New England Center for Civic Life, The New Hampshire Historical Society, Leadership New Hampshire

A grand collaboration, the New Hampshire Civic Connection, is seeking to do what any one of the partners, individually, cannot do alone: deal with a public-policy issue from beginning to end. In this case the issue is the quality of education in the state (Greenberg, 2002).

In New Hampshire, the hot-button issue is how to fund education. But to the partners, who started meeting in 2001, the question that needed to precede the funding question was: What is the quality of education? What do we need to fund good schools?

The group, all nonprofit organizations, started with a poll done by the Survey Center. "They're great," said Jon Greenberg, senior producer at New Hampshire Public Radio. "Whenever possible, they slip questions we have into polls they are already doing, so we've gotten a free ride" (personal communication, March 8, 2002).

The first poll explored the oft-repeated finding that, despite public skepticism about education, people are satisfied with their local schools. The Civic Connection took responses from telephone interviews and compared them with the actual performance of the respondents' school districts. So, the polling data "is attached to some hard information about how schools are performing," said Andy Smith, director of the Survey Center, which, with the Center for Public Policy Studies, is part of the university's Institute for Policy and Social Science Research (personal communication, April 23, 2002). The poll showed that, most of the time, that satisfaction is based on inadequate information. For instance, in districts that ranked in the bottom third, half the respondents thought the schools were doing a good or excellent job, Greenberg reported (2002).

The poll results have laid the groundwork for a series of local forums, focus groups, and a discussion series over the next 2 years to bridge the gap between the public's language and educators' language. "It's very nice to get insights into your work from others and see it carried through to a bigger audience, a different audience," Smith said (personal communication, April 23, 2002). Moreover, Smith said, it is seen as contributing not just to the debate on the quality of education, but giving the legislature some good information to work from. The partners have identified another poll they would like to do, and the group is seeking to raise $10,000 to fund it.

Doug Hall says his Center for Public Policy Studies would not have much impact without partners. Hall is credited with being a key instigator of the collaboration. "We are a quantitative research operation but we don't have the ability to disseminate information across a wide audience" (personal communication, April 23, 2002). Public television and radio, he pointed out, have the ability to get the information out, but they have reporters who hop from one subject to another every day, without deep expertise in any one area.

The New England Center for Civic Life, which is affiliated with Franklin Pierce College, convened state residents to discuss the quality of education. "We see the key to a more robust democracy as giving more information to citizens" said director Doug Challenger, a sociology professor (personal communication, April 24, 2002). But the center prefers a "public learning" model vs. an expert information model. "We believe the public has a productive way to talk about issues. There are insights and wisdom in their experience and knowledge of issues that is often overlooked or never tapped into, even by organizations that want to serve the public." By involving students in convening the public, the center is helping students broaden skills and their knowledge of community life. In all, the partners expressed satisfaction, even enthusiasm, for their efforts. Said Hall: "After we test it out for another year or so, we will pick another topic, mostly likely health care, that we can all work on to-gether" (personal communication, April 23, 2002).

CONCLUSION

As we can see in all these partnerships, there are some common denominators. They advance qualitative knowledge about particular issues, and they offer something to benefit all the partners.

For the newsrooms, the partnerships offer ways to tap the public for input or feedback, information that improves the journalism and often helps it rise above limp anecdotes. It makes the journalism more interactive by offering more entry points than the news organization alone could provide.

The collaborations also give the journalism more "legs," more ability to run with some momentum off the printed page or a newscast. It gives the journalists a sense that they are doing more than just a data dump, after which they pat themselves on the back and say their job is done. Indeed, if citizens can't figure out what to do with the data, the job is not very useful and hardly finished. Where the newsrooms can add value is in also helping the citizens, as well as elected officials, do their jobs. Finally, the efforts create new attachments, for both the universities and the newsrooms, with people in the community, and, as with any attachment, there is the potential for a long-term relationship.

For the university partners, these ventures have showcased significant ex-pertise and, often, challenged academics to use their intellectual muscle in new ways for the benefit of the community. Inevitably, when students participated, they got hands-on experience with real-life issues.

The partnerships can start when one party cold-calls another, as Editor Trisha O'Connor did in Myrtle Beach. They also can build from past acquain-tances, such as those that led to the creation of the energy software in Madison, WI. The best way to initiate the collaborations is for one party to simply reach out to the other with a specific idea. If there's a win–win scenario for both par-ties, there's usually a way to make it work. Often it is easier for the news organi-zation to make the initial overture because journalists, in general, tend to be skittish when asked to do something by non-journalists.

Each partner must be permitted the freedom to adhere to individual core missions. Importantly, partners who engage in advocacy must realize that the news organizations cannot.

Funding is not always necessary. As these examples show, many of the ven-tures built on activities that the individual partners would have done anyway. But the individual efforts would have delivered much less than the sum of the whole enterprise.

While the Pew Center funded many of these initiatives, others took on a life of their own after early partnerships proved their worth. In some cases, as with the "We the People Wisconsin" partnership, the news organizations have formed a collective nonprofit entity, which seeks funding from community corporations and foundations interested in supporting civic-engagement efforts. Most news organizations, though, won't accept funding from non-journalism outfits.

Funding for small local initiatives is usually most easily obtained from local foundations. University development officials often have lists of local funders who can be approached. The fdncenter.org Web site, hosted by the Foundation Center in Washington, DC, also provides a national list of foundations and a key-word search function that can help identify prospective funders. It's always best if you can find someone to introduce you or offer an endorsement letter. If that is not possible, you can usually research a foundation's Web site, which will often tell you whether an initial query letter or a full-blown grant application is preferred. Either should be followed up with a telephone call and a request for a meeting.

If your application is denied, ask the funder to recommend other sources of support. In truth, foundations usually fund individuals more than ideas, so it's important to note your track record and background.

For most of the collaborations in this chapter, qualitative research was just the beginning of the process. Survey work was done, not so much to produce a final news story as it was to unearth clues that needed to be fleshed out with some qualitative input. This often went by many names, such as focus groups, reader advisory panels, brainstorming sessions.

Strong research designs usually build in multiple points for information to flow in, thereby ensuring that the feedback is cross-checked and that the researchers can unpack nuances in a way that sheds informative light on the topic. Since most issues have more gray areas than black and white ones, the best results often occur when focus groups are asked to consider trade-offs or choices for dealing with an issue rather than to render a thumbs-up or thumbs-down opinion.

Successful collaborations should produce something useful for both the newsroom and the classroom. It's important for researchers to share preliminary results early with the newsroom. Too often, researchers can fall into deducing a simplistic cause and effect when editors can actually cite another obvious cause that will significantly change the analysis. Exchanging information to refine the analysis breeds a sense of cross-ownership that can feed an appetite for ongoing relationships.

In all cases, partners know they have a successful initiative when the community starts to react. This presumes, of course, that the partners have built in multiple venues for readers or viewers to respond and participate further, if they wish.

It's important to measure the response. For one thing, it provides fodder for evaluation. Second, it supplies feedback for future funders. So, track the attendance at meetings, count e-mails and phone calls, collect letters and formal commentary, pay attention to the number of volunteers or participants, and note outcomes. As important, report those responses back to your audience, to the university, to the publisher or general manager. It helps chronicle the momentum in the community, and it helps to build appetites for future initiatives.

The ultimate success occurs when the level of qualitative insight enables a news organization to articulate, with considerable authority, a community's collective wisdom and aspirations, and that prompts the community to take ownership of the problem.

ACKNOWLEDGMENT

Pew Center staff writer Pat Ford assisted with research for this chapter.

REFERENCES[1]

Ford, P. (1998). Leadership challenge: Building a new generation of leaders. *Don't stop there! Five adventures in civic journalism.* Available at http://www.pewcenter.org/doingcj/pubs/stop/leader.html
Gibbs, C. (2002, Winter). New views on old wire stories. *Civic Catalyst,* 12.
Greenberg, J. (2002, Winter). Civics physics: Energy matters in NH effort. *Civic Catalyst,* 13.
The James K. Batten Award for Excellence in Civic Journalism: Leadership Challenge/Peoria (IL) Journal Star. (1997). *News breaks: Can journalists fix it?* (Available from the Pew Center for Civic Journalism, 7100 Baltimore Ave., Suite 101, College Park, MD 20740).
Rosenhause, S. (1999, Spring). The Examiner maps the remaking of The New City. *Civic Catalyst,* 1, 15.
Still, T. (2002, Winter). Interactive game totes energy costs. *Civic Catalyst,* 6.

ENDNOTES

[1]Volume numbers for Civic Catalyst do not exist; all numbers listed are pages.

Glossary

John L. "Jack" Morris with Sharon Hartin Iorio
and volume coauthors

Accuracy: To achieve accuracy in news reporting, facts should be verified by at least one independent source to overcome mistakes, lies, false memories, and misinterpreted documents (Brooks, Kennedy, Moen, & Ranly, 1999, p. 220). The traditional definition of accuracy in news is repeating or paraphrasing faithfully what an interview subject says. In public journalism, accuracy is related to recognizing and reporting the complexity of the community being covered (Sirianni & Friedland, 2001 p. 220).

Anonymity: A promise of anonymity is a guarantee that a given respondent or source cannot be linked to any particular statement he or she makes (Wimmer & Dominick, 2000, p. 73).

Attribution: Attribution is the clause that tells a reader of a news story, either directly or indirectly, who is speaking. For example, a clause such as "he said" is called an attribution (Brooks et al., 1999, p. 207). Attribution for the first instance in which a speaker is mentioned in a news report should include identification, for example, Director of Research John Jones said ....

Analysis: The act whereby something is separated into parts, and those parts are given rigorous, logical, and detailed scrutiny, resulting in a consistent and relatively complete account of the elements and the principles of their organization (Holman & Harmon, 1986, p. 20).

Analytic generalization–Analytical inference: This is the process of generalizing "a particular set of results to some broader theory" (Yin, 1994, p. 36). Analytic generalization and inference, in the social sciences, are based on the findings of a study or studies.

Anecdote: In qualitative methodology, an anecdote is a short narrative detailing the particulars of an interesting event (Holman & Harmon, 1986, p. 22).

Balance: One explanation of balance is the difference between two items (Bremner, 1980, p. 57). In newswriting, balance often is satisfied by presenting two sides of an issue.

Batten Award: From 1995 to 2002, the Pew Center for Civic Journalism (which came to a close in 2002) presented the awards, named for Knight Ridder executive James Batten, to encourage best practices and innovations in civic journalism (Ford, Summer 2002, p. 22).

Behaviorism: An approach to research that aims to explain and predict human communicative behavior, behaviorism is marked by quantitative methods. In the disciplines of psychology and sociology, the behavioral approach is a theory and accompanying methods that focus on externally observable human actions rather than mental processes (DeFleur & Ball-Rokeach, 1989, p. 39).

Bias: When a researcher allows her or his personal opinions to influence otherwise fact-based conclusions, the research or writing based thereon is biased (Brooks et al., 1999, pp. 153–154).

Case study: A case study is used to examine many characteristics of a single subject (Severin & Tankard, 1992, pp. 30–31). The term case study generally describes research that may use a variety of data collection methods to examine a single subject or a set of closely interrelated subjects.

Chaos theory: Often applied to crises in the communication field, chaos theory explains how events occur in terms of confluence. The theory is radical in that it challenges rationalistic theories of prediction and control and linearity of thought.

Charles F. Kettering Foundation: This operating foundation sponsors inventive research that focuses on this question: What does it take to make democracy work as it should? (www.kettering.org)

Civic catalyst: This term is used in civic mapping to denote the respected leaders whom people look to in their everyday lives for community expertise and wisdom and who encourage others to get involved in civic life (Harwood & McCrehan, 2000). *Civic Catalyst* was the Pew Center for Civic Journalism quarterly newsletter.

Civic connectors: A term used in civic mapping denoting individuals who move between groups spreading ideas, often without having any official capacity (Harwood & McCrehan, 2000).

Civic journalism: Civic journalism is a broad label put on efforts by journalists to do their jobs as journalists in ways that help to overcome people's sense of powerlessness and alienation. The goal is to produce news that citizens need to be educated about issues and current events, to make civic decisions, to engage in civic dialogue and action—and generally to exercise their responsibilities in a democracy (Schaffer, 1999). The terms civic journalism and public journalism have been used interchangeably.

Civic mapping: This activity or method is a systematic way for reporters to identify the various layers of civic life and the potential sources and news in them so they can report first and best what is happening in a community (Harwood & McCrehan, 2000).

Communitarian: Communitarian philosophy stresses the balance between social forces and the person, between community and autonomy, between the common good and liberty, between individual rights and social responsibilities (Etzioni, 1998, p. x.). The term also refers to a person who practices this philosophy.

Community conversation: When this term is used formally, it denotes a group of citizens discussing a public issue at a media-sponsored meeting. The group is moderated by a reporter or other discussion leader whose primarily role is to listen (Morris, 2002, pp. 68, 127, 210).

Conclusion: A conclusion is an inference drawn from facts (Rackham & Bertagnolli, 1999, pp. 133–134). Conclusions are usually associated with quantitative research while a discussion or summary of the findings without stating an assumption about their meaning is associated with qualitative research.

Confidentiality: A promise of confidentiality assures a source or respondent that, even though he or she can be associated with a specific statement or response by the researchers or reporters, his or her name will never be publicly associated with it (Wimmer & Dominick, 2000, p. 73).

Conflict: Conflict occurs when a text or situation presents two opposing factions (Morris, 2002, pp. 68, 127, 210).

Construct validity: The level of construct validity is the degree to which a test, survey, experiment, observation, etc. measures an intended hypothetical construct, deemed to explain behavior (Gay, 1987, p. 542).

Content analysis: This is a quantitative and qualitative research method wherein researchers conduct a sweeping, systematic examination of groups of discourse. The aim is to compare–contrast message form and content in order to assemble frequencies and establish patterns of messages over time. It is marked by objectivity (reliability of content categories), systematicity (a representative sample of discourse), and generality (findings that show theoretical relevance based on the comparisons produced). Quantitative content analysis uses de facto (nonjudgmental) categories such as observable demographic factors. Qualitative content analysis uses interpretive (judgmental) categories such as value appeals (Holsti, 1969).

Context/contextualizing: The researcher's construction of the phenomenon or the journalist's reporting of the experience under study in terms of individuals and the social worlds in which they live is contextualizing. Providing context is also recreating experience in terms of conduct, constituencies, and surroundings (Huberman & Miles, 2002, p. 359).

Deduction: The process whereby a researcher starts with a theory and then seeks to learn whether empirical (observable) data support it is deduction (Frey et al., 1992). A reasoning process that moves from general to specific ideas is deductive (Rackham & Bertagnolli, 1999, pp. 314–315).

Detachment: The dominance of scientific thought and methods in Western civilization sanctified the most distanced observer as being the most reliable (Merritt, 1995, p. 18). The distance of such a nonpartisan observer is marked by lack of involvement and separation from the context of the research.

Emic and Ettic: In qualitative research, the emic represents the insider's (or research subject's) perspective; whereas, the ettic is the outsider's (or objective) perspective. When the researcher or reporter writes from the emic perspective, the insights should be shown to the subjects to cross-check the accuracy of the description (Potter, 1996, p. 42).

Empirical research: The natural sciences are based on empiricism, the belief that the world is measurable and all objects and actions can be perceived (Wimmer & Dominick, 2000, p. 12). Empirical research is a systematic and critical investigation of natural and social phenomenon. It can be conducted by qualitative methods or quantitative methods or both via observation or collecting data or evidence.

Enterprise story: An enterprise story is a news story that focuses on a process, not a specific event (Gibbs & Warhover, 2002, p. 427). Coverage of a murder is not enterprise reporting; a story that addresses why the murder rate is higher in one particular area of the community over others is.

Entry points–portals: These are terms for opportunities in news coverage for citizen input, such as town hall meetings or focus groups, that move the journalism beyond simply providing information to engaging their audiences actively in analyzing and using information (Ford, Spring 2002, p. 1). The terms also apply to opportunities for individuals to use electronic technology for the purpose of interaction with each other and news organizations regarding events and issues in the news.

Ethics: Ethics is the study of philosophic principles from which can be derived actions that resolve moral problems (Lambeth, 1992, p. 80).

Ethnography: This is a qualitative research method wherein researchers enter the field. Through living in the community under study and participating in community life, ethnographers learn how people communicate with each other in certain settings in order to understand the tacit rules that govern their interactions. As an encompassing term, ethnography or ethnographic study can be used interchangeably with the terms field work and participant observation.

Epistemology: This is the study of knowledge sources. In communication, epistemic inquiries are based on how theories and research contribute to our knowledge of communication acts and processes.

Evaluation research: The study and assessment of program plans, their implementation and their impact (Wimmer & Dominick, 2000, p. 369).

Experiment: An artificial environment that is controlled to isolate variables and find evidence of causality is an experiment (Wimmer & Dominick, 2000, pp. 210–218). An experiment often consists of at least two groups—in one group an independent variable is manipulated and in the other group no manipulation takes place. The research observes any effects that result in the experimental and control groups and draws conclusions based on the observation.

Fact: A fact is an assertion that can be verified by other observers (Rackham & Bertagnolli, 1999, pp. 130–135).

Fairness: A news story often has more than two sides. Fairness involves finding all sides of the issue and including responses from anyone who is being attacked or whose integrity is being questioned (Brooks et al., 1999, p. 15).

Feature story: News stories developed without short deadline pressures are called feature stories or features. They often concern trends, personalities, and lifestyles (Brooks et al., 1999, p. 563).

Focus group: A discussion of approximately 6–12 people moderated by a leader trained to elicit comments from all members about a predetermined topic is a focus group. Focus groups are used to gather preliminary information for a research project, to develop questionnaires, to understand reasons behind phenomena, or to test preliminary ideas or plans (Wimmer & Dominick, 2000, p. 119). They can also be used to verify findings of previous research and to elicit comprehensive, subjective responses to specific questions.

Focused interview: Conducted one-on-one, the focused interview method is similar to both the in-depth or personal interview and focus group interviewing, but focused interviews can get at more complex topics than focus groups without risk that the individual responses will be influenced by others' comments. The purpose of focused interviews is to identify underlying commonalities that may be consistent among the responses. Focused interviews provide background for enterprise or political reporting or can stand alone as the subject of a news report.

Framing–News frame: Frames are conceptual tools, such as a conflict narrative or explanatory narrative, that media and individuals rely on to convey, interpret, and evaluate information (Denton, Summer 1998, p. 4). Frames call attention to some aspects of reality, while obscuring other elements (Entman, 1993, p. 55) in much the same way that the frame of a picture provides a boundary for and draws attention to the image that it surrounds. Traditionally, journalists have focused on conflict in framing news reports, but researchers have identified other news frames: moral values, economics, powerlessness, and human impact (Neuman, Just, & Crigler, 1992, pp. 60–77).

Generalization: An inference about a population is a generalization. In probability sampling, generalizations are statistically significant only when the sample has been selected randomly and contains enough subjects to minimize sampling error (Wimmer & Dominick, 2000, pp. 85–99). Being able to generalize the results of a research project to a larger population is an end result of quantitative research; qualitative research differs in that its results offer explanation rather than prediction and seldom are generalized (Huberman & Miles, 2002).

Hard news–News stories: Also known as spot news and deadline stories, hard news is a type of news written under pressure of short deadlines as information becomes available (Brooks et al., 1999, p. 558).

Hawthorne effect: This phenomenon was identified at Western Electric Company's Hawthorne Plant in Chicago in 1927. The Hawthorne effect occurs when the subjects in an experiment realize that something special is happening to them. The feeling of being special alters the subjects' behavior thus posing a threat to the validity of a research project (Meyer, 1991, p. 175). Studies that use control groups do not face this problem.

Hutchins Commission: The Hutchins Commission, was so called because its chair was University of Chicago President Robert Hutchins, but its official title was the Commission on Freedom of the Press. Created on the suggestion of Henry Luce, then publisher of *Time* magazine, to investigate increasing controls or management of the press, the commission concluded in 1947 that freedom of the press in the United States was in danger because of its monopolistic nature, adding that a free society depends on truthful, comprehensive, and intelligent reporting of events presented in a context that gives them meaning (Brooks et al., 1999, p. 17; Folkerts & Teeter, 1989, p. 464).

Impact: This refers to the number of people likely to be affected by a news story (Morris, 2002, pp. 68, 127, 210). Impact also can refer to the level or degree of effect produced by a situation.

Induction: The process whereby a researcher first gathers data and then develops a theory from them, often referred to as 'grounded theory,' is induction (Frey et. al., 1992). A reasoning process that moves from specific to general ideas is inductive (Rackham & Bertagnolli, 1999, pp. 314–315).

Interaction: Three types of interactional situations are face-to-face interaction, in which the participants in the exchange are immediately present to one another; mediated interaction, that involves the use of a technical medium such as paper and pen, a telephone, or a personal computer; and mediated quasi-interaction that involves relations established by mass media (books, television, etc.). Mediated quasi-interaction information is directed to an indefinite range of potential recipients.

Interactive journalism: Journalism that actively provides entry points for people to interact with the information, tell their own stories, and participate in public dialogue can be termed interactive (Schaffer, 2001). Use of Web sites, e-mail news discussion groups, and other technology that people may employ to interact with each other and news organizations also is called interactive journalism.

In-depth interview: Also known as an intensive interview, an in-depth interview provides detailed background to answers, permits observation of nonverbal responses, can last several hours, is tailored to the respondent, and can be influenced by the relationship established between interviewer and subject (Wimmer & Dominick, 2000, p. 122).

Life history: A research technique that focuses on one individual's life; life history is a form of biography or autobiography. Life histories may be essays about one's life or journal writing (Bertaux, 1981; Smith, 1988).

Marketing research: The goal of advertising is to sell a product to people who have the desire for the product and the ability to buy it. Marketing research attempts to identify audiences for particular products (Biagi, 2001, p. 235).

Natural Laws–Natural Science: This is a system of thought holding that all phenomena can be explained in terms of natural causes without attributing spiritual or metaphysical significance to them (Danesi, 2000, p. 158).

Neutrality: In newswriting, the concept of neutral reportage was advanced in a 1977 U.S. Court of Appeals ruling when the judge overturned a libel verdict because the *New York Times* had accurately reported a libelous statement without taking sides in the issue. This concept, however, has not attained the status of a reliable constitutional defense (Teeter, Le Duc, & Loving, 1998, pp. 259–263). A canon of reporting, neutrality requires the journalist to remain impartial and not express opinion in news coverage.

Null hypothesis: A term used in quantitative research, the null hypothesis is a statement that measurable differences are due to chance alone (Williams, 1992, p. 66).

Nut graph: When a news story opens with a scene, quotation, or anecdote, the paragraph that links the opening to the main idea of the story, or lede, is called the nut graph (Brooks et al., 1999, pp. 183–184).

Ontology: The study of essence or origin, in communication, ontological inquiries are based on those communication factors that make us human.

Opinion: An opinion is an inference or conclusion drawn from facts (Rackham & Bertagnolli, 1999, pp. 130–135). It is a belief held toward a specific object, such as a man, or an issue, or a belief held toward an event or activity. Individuals hold many opinions, some of which may conflict. Different situations may trigger one of many personal opinions to be prominent for an individual at a particular moment in time.

Operationalization: An operational definition of a variable specifies procedures that enable a researcher to experience or measure a concept (Wimmer & Dominick, 2000, p. 12).

Oral history: This research technique addresses the personal experiences of ordinary people involved in the historical process (Brennen, 1996, p. 571; Thompson, 1990).

Participant observation: A field observation that involves the researcher as participant in the behavior under study is called participant observation (Wimmer & Dominick, 2000, p. 47).

Personal concern(s): Personal concerns are the problems of individual citizens that are shared by or resonate with the general public and these concerns may be quite different from political issues. National Gallup polling has surveyed the important problems facing the U.S. population since 1975 (Iorio & Huxman, 1996, pp. 98–100).

Pew Center for Civic Journalism: The Pew Center, funded by the Pew Charitable Trusts from 1992 through 2002, was an incubator for civic journalism experiments that enabled news organizations to create and refine better ways of reporting the news to engage people in public life (www.pewcenter.org).

Phenomenology: This is an approach to research that aims to understand and appreciate the meaning of human messages. It is marked by qualitative methods. Phenomenology is also a specific social science theory based on the belief that consciousness is always directed at objects; as such, phenomenology is the study of the forms and manifestations of experience as they are perceived by the mind (Danesi, 2000, p. 172).

Political Issue(s): As problems common to the general public, political issues are those that are presented on politicians' and media agendas as having solutions in or being related to government action.

Population: Any class of object (including humans) or event defined on the basis of its unique and observable characteristics is a population (Williams, 1992, p. 11).

Postmodernism: Postmodernism in art and philosophy questions traditional assumptions about certainty, identity, and truth based on the belief that words are abstract symbols without fixed meanings (Danesi, 2000, pp. 180–181).

Pretest–Post-test: In a social scientific experiment, after two samples are randomly selected from a population, each is given the same pretest and post-test, but only one sample receives the experimental treatment between the tests (Wimmer & Dominick, 2000, p. 218).

Public journalism: Also known as civic journalism, public journalism is a practice of journalism that listens to citizens, considers alternative framing of news stories, stimulates public understanding of social and political issues, advances possible solutions, and continually evaluates its communication with the public (Lambeth, Meyer, & Thorson, 1998, p. 17).

Public opinion: There are at least four definitions of public opinion. First, modern polling assumes that public opinion is an aggregation of many individual opinions (results of a survey); second, that public opinion is the opinions of the majority; third, that they are what is communicated consensus—social norms; and fourth, that they are merely a fiction or reification and do not exist in reality (Herbst, 1993, p. 43–46).

Public sphere: This abstract concept refers to civil society where rational, critical debate, free from domination of the state, occurs (Thompson, 1995, p. 237). In common usage, the realm of media, politics, and opinion processes is often referenced as the public sphere.

Precision journalism: Newswriting based on intensive and systematic fact finding (Meyer, 1973, p. 13), precision journalism uses quantitative social science research methods to collect and interpret large amounts of informational data and report the findings in a way that can be easily understood.

Professional ethics: This is the study of philosophic, professional principles related to career or employment situations from which can be derived actions that resolve moral problems (Lambeth, 1992, pp. 80, 106–107).

Pulitzer prizes: Endowed by newspaper publisher Joseph Pulitzer, these annual awards from the trustees of Columbia University are given for outstanding work in journalism and the arts (Goldstein, 1997, p. 170).

Purposive sample: This is a nonrandom sample of a population where subjects are selected on the basis of specific characteristics or qualities (Wimmer & Dominick, 2000, p. 84).

Random sample: This is a type of sampling or subject selection in which a collection of objects or events is defined in a way so that each one in the population has an equal chance of being selected (Williams, 1992, p. 52).

Reliability: This standard for judging research quality is the consistency of measurement both internal and external to the study (Williams, 1992, pp. 29–30).

Replication: An independent verification of a research study (Wimmer & Dominick, 2000, p. 432), in general, replication entails repeating a research study in order to verify its findings.

Respondents: The subjects or participants in a research project are called respondents.

Rhetorical criticism: This is a qualitative research method wherein researchers perform a close, systematic inspection of discourse via a selected communication theory that serves as a lens. The aim is to describe, interpret, and evaluate message content in order to gain greater insight for how and why persuasion works. Rhetorical criticism can also be called communication analysis or media analysis.

Sample: A subgroup or subset of a population is called a sample (Wimmer & Dominick, 2000, p. 432).

Secondary sources: A secondary source is research performed by others to come to some conclusion about a topic or make some kind of an argument.

Secondary research: This is a form of editing, in which quotations (and sometimes summaries, phrases, and syntheses of the material read) from this scholar and that scholar are collected to produce an essay or article. Secondary researchers use the research that others have done. (Berger, 2000, p. 23).

Sensationalism: In a broad sense, most good writing is sensational because it appeals to the senses of touch, taste, smell, sound, and sight. Most media critics use the term when referring to news that attracts attention by appealing to prurient interest or shock value (Ward, 1997, p. 29).

Social capital: Those stocks of social trust, norms, and networks that people can draw on to solve common problems are social capital. Networks of civic engagement, such as neighborhood associations, sports clubs, and cooperatives, are essential forms of social capital (Friedland, Sotirovic, & Kaily, 1998, p. 195). Social capital is the value or power accrued when people know one another and, as a result, work together (Ford, Winter 2002).

Social responsibility: This is a philosophy that calls for self-regulation of freedom of the press for the betterment of society.

Source: A person or persons who provide information that is relevant, useful, and interesting to a news audience (Brooks et al., 1999, pp. 4–6).

Stakeholders: People or organizations who stand to be gainers and losers in a public course of action are often labeled stakeholders (Morris, 2002, pp. 68, 127, 210).

Statistical inference: This is the process of estimating a characteristic of a population from a characteristic of a sample of the population (Williams, 1992, p. 51).

Structural functionalism: This social scientific theory is based on the idea that the organization of a society provides the source of its stability (DeFleur & Ball-Rokeach, 1989, p. 31).

Subjectivity: Subjective writing presents personal impressions and experiences (Rackham & Bertagnolli, 1999, pp. 130–135).

Survey: Asking questions of a sample or all of a population constitutes a survey. The methodology includes selecting a subject, constructing the questions, writing instructions, presenting the questions, achieving a reasonable response rate, and interpreting the results (Wimmer & Dominick, 2000, pp. 160–190).

Textual analysis: Text, broadly speaking, is any work of art in any medium. Texts can be company contracts, newspapers, government documents, even street signs or tattoos. Through careful reading and analysis the researcher or reporter can uncover information on something else besides the words themselves (Watson, 1997, pp. 80–84). To the researcher this usually is something about the social world of the writer or the intended audience. To the reporter textual analysis may uncover buried facts or provide leads to other information.

Thick description: In qualitative research, description that is thick presents essential themes and strictures discovered in the context of the respondents' or subjects' setting, their language, their emotions, and their terms (Huberman & Miles, 2002, p. 359). Thick description is a shorthand term for the web of meanings that sustain a culture (Lindlof, 1995, p. 52).

Third places: The layer of civic conversations and spaces where people gather to talk and do things together, such as churches, diners, and barbershops are called third places where reporters can go for information (Harwood & McCrehan, 2000).

Type I error: In quantitative research, Type I error occurs when the researcher rejects a null hypothesis, or rejects the research premise that there is no difference between the groups under study, and claims there is a difference, when, unbeknown to the researcher, the findings are wrong and in reality there is no difference.

Type II error: In quantitative research, Type II error occurs when the researcher accepts a null hypothesis, or accepts the research premise that there is no difference between the groups under study, when, unbeknown to the researcher the findings are wrong and in reality there is a difference.

Validity: The standard for judging research quality is the degree to which a measurement technique, research procedure, or research finding is accurate (Frey, Botan, Friedman, & Kreps, 1992); that is, measures what it claims to measure.

Values: These are underlying principles of courses of action (Morris, 2002, pp. 68, 127, 210).

Variable: An observable characteristic of an object or event that can be described according to some well-defined classification or measurement scheme can be called a variable (Williams, 1992, p. 11).

REFERENCES

Berger, A. A. (2000). *Media and communication research methods*. Thousand Oaks, CA: Sage.

Bertaux, D. (Ed.). (1981). *Biography and society: The life history approach in the social sciences*. London: Sage.

Biagi, S. (2001). *Media/Impact: An introduction to mass media* (5th ed., instructor's ed.). Belmont, CA: Wadsworth –Thompson Learning.

Bremner, J. B. (1980). *Words on words: A dictionary for writers and others who care about words*. New York: Columbia University Press.

Brennen, B. (1996). Toward a history of labor and new work: The use of oral sources in journalism history. *The Journal of American History, 83*(2): 571–579.

Brooks, B. S., Kennedy, G., Moen, D. R., & Ranly, D. (1999). *News reporting and writing* (6th ed.). New York: Bedford–St. Martins.

Danesi, M. (2000). *Encyclopedic dictionary of semiotics, media, and communications*. Toronto: University of Toronto Press.

DeFleur, M. L., & Ball-Rokeach, S. (1989). *Theories of mass communication* (5th ed.). White Plains, NY: Longman.

Denton, F. (1998, Summer) Cracking the Spiral of Silence. *Civic Catalyst, 4.*

Entman, B. (1993). Framing: Toward a clarification of a fractured paradigm. *Journal of Communication, 43*(4), 51–58.

Etzioni, A. (1998). *The essential communitarian reader*. Lanham, MD: Rowman & Littlefield.

Folkerts, J., & Teeter, D. L. (1989). *Voices of a nation*. New York: Macmillan.

Ford, P. (2002, Winter). Lawrence, KS: Common ground on growth. *Civic Catalyst,*

Ford, P. (2002, Spring) Gaming the news—building new entry points. *Civic Catalyst,*

Ford, P. (2002, Summer). Batten award money takes many paths. *Civic Catalyst, 22.*

Frey, L., Botan, C., Friedman, P., & Kreps, G. (1992). *Interpreting communication*. Englewood Cliffs, NJ: Prentice-Hall.

Friedland, L., Sotirovic, M., & Kaily, K. (1998). Public journalism and social capital. In E. B. Lambeth, P. E. Meyer, & E. Thorson (Eds.), *Assessing public journalism.* (p. 195). Columbia, MO: University of Missouri Press.

Gay, L. R. (1987). *Competencies for analysis and application* (3rd ed.). Columbus, OH: Merrill.

Gibbs, S., & Warhover, T. (2002). *Getting the whole story*. New York: Guilford.

Goldstein, N. (Ed.). (1997). The Associated Press style book and libel manual (6th trade ed.). New York: The Associated Press

Harwood, R. C., & McCrehan, F. (2000). *Tapping civic life* (2nd ed.) [on-line]. Available at: http://www.pewcenter.org/doingcj/pubs/tcl/

Herbst, S. (1993). *Numbered voices: How opinion polling has shaped American politics*. Chicago: University of Chicago Press.

Holman, C. H., & Harmon, W. (1986). *A handbook to literature* (5th ed.). New York: Macmillan.

Holsti, O. R. (1969). *Content analysis for the social sciences and humanities*. Reading, MA: Addison-Wesley.

Huberman, A. M., & Miles, M. B. (2002). *The qualitative researcher's companion*. Thousand Oaks, CA: Sage.

Iorio, S. H., & Huxman, S. S. (1996). Media coverage of political issues and the framing of personal concerns. *Journal of Communication, 46*(4), 97–115.

Lambeth, E. B. (1992). *Committed journalism: An ethic for the profession* (2nd ed.). Bloomington, IN: Indiana University Press.

Lambeth, E. B., Meyer, P. E., & Thorson, E. (Eds.). (1998). *Assessing public journalism*. Columbia, MO: University of Missouri Press.

Lindlof, T. R. (1995). Qualitative communication research methods. Thousand Oaks, CA: Sage.

Merritt, D. (1995). *Public journalism: Why telling the news is not enough.* Hillsdale, NJ: Lawrence Erlbaum Associates.

Meyer, P. (1991). *The new precision journalism.* Bloomington, IN: Indiana University Press.

Morris, J. L. (2002). *A study of attitudes toward audience interaction in journalism: Citizen-based reporting.* Lewiston, NY: Edwin Mellen.

Neuman, W. R., Just, M. R., & Crigler, A. N. (1992). *Common knowledge: News and the construction of political meaning.* Chicago: The University of Chicago Press.

Potter, W. J. (1996). *An analysis of thinking and research about qualitative methods.* Mahwah, NJ: Lawrence Erlbaum Associates.

Rackham, J., & Bertagnolli, O. (1999). *From sight to insight: The writing process* (6th ed.). Fort Worth, TX: Harcourt Brace.

Schaffer, J. (1999). *Attack dog, watch dog, guide dog: The role of the media in building community* [on-line]. Available at: http://www.pewcenter.org/doingcj/speeches/s_batonrouge.html

Schaffer, J. (2001, Fall) Interactive journalism: clicking on the future. *APME News.*

Severin, J. W., & Tankard, Jr., J. W. (1992). *Communication theories: Origins, methods, and uses in the mass media* (3rd ed.). White Plains, NY: Longman.

Sirianni, C., & Friedland, L. (2001). *Civic innovation in America.* Berkeley, CA: University of California Press.

Smith, L. M. (1998). Biographical method. In N. K. Denzin & Y. S. Lincoln (Eds.), *Strategies of qualitative inquiry* (pp. 285–305). Thousand Oaks, CA: Sage Publications.

Teeter, D. L., Le Duc, D. R., & Loving, B. (1998). *Law of mass communications: Freedom and control of print and broadcast media* (9th ed.). New York: Foundation Press.

Thompson, J. B. (1995). *The media and modernity.* Stanford, CA: Stanford University Press.

Thompson, P. (1990). *The voice of the past: Oral history.* London: Oxford University Press.

Ward, H. H. (1997). *Mainstreams of American media history.* Boston: Allyn & Bacon.

Watson, R. (1997). Ethnomethodology and textual analysis. In D. Silverman (Ed.), *Qualitative research: Theory, method and practice* (pp. 80–98). Thousand Oaks, CA: Sage.

Williams, F. (1992). *Reasoning with statistics: How to read quantitative research* (4th ed.). Fort Worth, TX: Harcourt Brace Jovanovich.

Wimmer, R. D., & Dominick, J. R. (2000). *Mass media research: An introduction* (6th ed.). Belmont, CA: Wadsworth.

Yin, R. (1994). *Case study research: Design and methods.* Thousand Oaks, CA: Sage.

Author Index

Note: *f* indicates figure, *n* indicates endnote

Subject Index

Note: *f* indicates figure